The Early Finn Cycle

For Nancy Murray and Kathleen Hearn

The Early Finn Cycle

KEVIN MURRAY

FOUR COURTS PRESS

Typeset in 10.5 pt on 13.5 pt AGaramondPro by
Carrigboy Typesetting Services for
FOUR COURTS PRESS LTD
7 Malpas Street, Dublin 8, Ireland
www.fourcourtspress.ie
and in North America for
FOUR COURTS PRESS
c/o IPG, 814 N. Franklin Street, Chicage, IL, 60610.

© Kevin Murray and Four Courts Press 2017

First published 2017; reprinted 2023

A catalogue record for this title is available
from the British Library.

ISBN 978-1-84682-630-6

All rights reserved.
Without limiting the rights under copyright
reserved alone, no part of this publication may be
reproduced, stored in or introduced into a retrieval system,
or transmitted, in any form or by any means (electronic, mechanical,
photocopying, recording or otherwise), without the prior
written permission of both the copyright owner and
publisher of this book.

SPECIAL ACKNOWLEDGMENT

The author and publisher would like to gratefully acknowledge
the financial support received from the National University of Ireland
and the Research Publication Fund, College of Arts, Celtic Studies
and Social Sciences, University College Cork.

Printed in Ireland by SprintPrint, Dublin.

Contents

	ABBREVIATIONS	7
	PREFACE	9
	ACKNOWLEDGMENTS	11
	TEXT TITLES AND INITIAL LINES OF POEMS	13
	COMMON TERMINOLOGY	17
	INTRODUCTION	19
1	*Acallam na senórach*	21
2	The growth of the tradition	50
3	The nature of the *fian*	57
4	The conflict between Finn and Oisín	64
5	The early tales set around the river Suir	74
6	Further early *fianaigecht* sources	84
7	The background to *Tóraigheacht Dhiarmada agus Ghráinne*	95
8	*Tochmarc Ailbe*	106
9	Finn's boyhood deeds	117
10	The death of Finn	124
11	The early tradition of Fenian lays	130
12	The portrayal of Finn	140
13	Fothad Canainne	152
14	Later literary developments of the early *fianaigecht* corpus	160
	BIBLIOGRAPHY	164
	INDEX	188

Abbreviations

SOURCES*

AcS	*Acallam na senórach*
AFM	O'Donovan, *Annála ríoghachta Éireann: annals of the kingdom of Ireland by the Four Masters*
CGH	O'Brien, *Corpus genealogiarum Hiberniae*
CHA	Koch and Carey, *Celtic heroic age*
CIH	Binchy, *Corpus iuris Hibernici*
DF	MacNeill and Murphy, *Duanaire Finn*
DIL	Quin (general ed.), *Dictionary of the Irish language*
EIHM	O'Rahilly, *Early Irish history and mythology*
EIMS	Gantz, *Early Irish myths and sagas*
Fian.	Meyer, *Fianaigecht*
HDGP	Ó Riain et al., *Historical dictionary of Gaelic placenames*
LL	Best et al., *The Book of Leinster*
LL facs.	Atkinson, *The Book of Leinster … autotype facsimile*
LU	Best and Bergin, *Lebor na hUidre*
MD	Gwynn, *Metrical dindshenchas*
RC	*Revue celtique*
ZCP	*Zeitschrift für celtische Philologie*

OTHER COMMONLY USED ABBREVIATIONS

c.	*circa*
fl.	*floruit*
MS	manuscript
NLI	National Library of Ireland
NLS	National Library of Scotland
RIA	Royal Irish Academy, Dublin
s.n. / s.nn.	*sub nomine* / *sub nominibus*
s.v. / s.vv.	*sub verbo* / *sub verbis*
TCD	Trinity College Dublin
UCC	University College Cork
UCD	University College Dublin

* Full references are given in the Bibliography.

Preface

The last thirty years have witnessed significant activity in *fianaigecht* studies. Alongside numerous articles on various aspects of Fenian literature produced during this time, scholarship in the field has received a major impetus from the publication of two new translations of *Acallam na senórach*, the central text of the Cycle: *Tales of the elders of Ireland* by Ann Dooley and Harry Roe, and *The dialogue of the ancients of Ireland* by Maurice Harmon. This increased vitality in Finn Cycle studies is also evident from collections of essays such as *Fiannaíocht* (*The heroic process*), *An fhiannaíocht* (*Léachtaí Cholm Cille* 25), *Duanaire Finn: reassessments*, *The Gaelic Finn tradition*, *In dialogue with the Agallamh* and the *Proceedings of the Second International Finn Cycle Conference* (forthcoming). Over the same period, a number of theses concerned directly or indirectly with *fianaigecht* have been brought to fruition; many parts of these have made their way into print and have greatly enriched our field of study.[1] Particular mention must be made here of Natasha Sumner's catalogue of Fenian folklore which was prepared as a supplement to her doctoral dissertaton.[2] As a consequence of all of this endeavour, some parts of the Finn Cycle terrain have been well mapped out (such as the nature of the *fian*, the early materials for the Diarmaid and Gráinne story, the boyhood deeds, and the character of Finn mac Cumaill); nevertheless, other expanses of this scholarly territory have been traversed but infrequently.

Reliable general guides to this branch of study have been available as far back as Alfred Nutt's *Ossian and the Ossianic literature* (1899). The early witnesses to the Cycle were enumerated and delineated by Kuno Meyer in his 1910 volume *Fianaigecht* which also contains a number of important editions of materials from the corpus. A further brief introduction to the pre-modern body of literature focused on Finn mac Cumaill and his *fian* is Gerard Murphy's wonderful *Ossianic lore and romantic tales of medieval Ireland* (1955). Murphy, of course, was the pre-eminent Finn Cycle scholar of the first half of the twentieth century and there is no better guide to *fianaigecht* than his *Duanaire Finn*, volume III (1953), one of the most scholarly and learned books ever written on any aspect of medieval Gaelic literature. Dáithí Ó hÓgáin's wide-ranging study of the eponymous hero of the Cycle, *Fionn mac Cumhaill: images of the Gaelic hero* (1988), also serves as a useful access point to the material as a whole while the recent publication of

---

[1] The promised publication of 'Seanchas agus oileamhain Oisín mhic Fhinn', the doctoral dissertation of Máirtín Ó Briain, will be a fitting tribute to his memory.   [2] Available at https://scholar.harvard.edu/natasha sumner/

Joseph Flahive's *Fenian Cycle in Irish and Scots-Gaelic literature* (2017), the first volume in the new Cork Studies in Celtic Literatures series, has made available an excellent up-to-date handbook to the traditional Fenian literature of Ireland and Scotland from the earliest times to the modern era.

This book is envisioned as a complementary study to these aforementioned publications. It is intended as a guide to the early Finn Cycle and is written with the aim of steering readers through the broad range of relevant primary and secondary sources up to and including *Acallam na senórach*. Since 2003, I have occasionally taught a module entitled 'The Finn Cycle' to students in UCC; the idea for this volume grew out of this teaching. Thus, this work is aimed in the first place at third-level students though it is hoped that it will also be of material use to scholars of Gaelic literature generally and to anyone who would like to know more about the origins and development of the medieval *fianaigecht* corpus. As a consequence of these aims, the work may seem to be overly structured with its proliferation of headings and sub-headings, its abundance of footnotes and references, and its heavy indexing. But to borrow a quotation from a different scholarly context: 'the schematic nature of this book is deliberate, and is a feature of it that I am unable, after long reflection, to apologize for'.[3]

It was originally planned that a catalogue and discussion of the Cycle's early constituent texts – with a focus on their dates of composition and on the manuscripts in which they are found – would be printed as an appendix to this volume. However, this catalogue became too long and unwieldy for inclusion in the present work; it is anticipated that it will be published separately instead in the near future.

---

3 Frye, *Anatomy of criticism*, p. 29.

Acknowledgments

Many debts of gratitude were incurred over the past number of years while this book was being written; it is my pleasure to acknowledge these here. I have profited greatly over a long period from the advice, scholarly insights and camaraderie of my colleagues in the Department of Modern Irish, University College Cork; *míle buíochas*. I have likewise learned much from those who have taken 'The Finn Cycle' module, and from the postgraduate students in the Department of Early and Medieval Irish. Intermittently during the last few years, I have read *Acallam na senórach* from Laud MS 610 in the Departmental postgraduate seminar and am thankful to all involved for their input in helping to tease out the structure and makeup of the text. This volume has also benefitted materially from discussions with Seán Ó Coileáin and Joseph Flahive, both acknowledged experts in *fianaigecht* studies.

Grant funding was received from the National University of Ireland and from the Research Publication Fund of the College of Arts, Celtic Studies and Social Sciences, UCC, to help defray the costs of publication. These grants-in-aid are greatly appreciated. I wish to thank my friends, from within University College Cork and beyond, for their encouragement and support: Anne Connon, Clodagh Downey, Aidan Doyle, Hugh Fogarty, Jason Harris, Daragh O'Connell, Emer Purcell and David Woods. I want to express my gratitude to Martin Fanning and all at Four Courts Press in appreciation of their consummate professionalism in bringing this work to press. I gratefully acknowledge the support of my siblings, Catherine, Máire and Tomás; of the Hearn family; and especially that of my wife, Allie, and children, Tom, Anna, Alice and Lily, who have lived with the idea of this book for more years than I care to remember.

Many parts of this work were first presented at conferences: thank you to those who offered feedback and criticism on those occasions: 'Fothad Canainne in medieval Irish tradition', 13th International Congress of Celtic Studies, Bonn (July 2007); 'Early *fianaigecht* placenames', First International Conference on the Early Medieval Toponymy of Ireland and Scotland, Queen's University Belfast (September 2008); 'Finn mac Cumaill and his *fian* in west Cork', Cork Historical and Archaeological Society (February 2009); 'From the manuscript page to the printed page: editorial method and *Acallam na senórach*', Palaeography and Manuscript Seminar, University College Cork (September 2009); 'Re-analysing "The quarrel between Finn and Oisín"', Celtic Studies Association of North America, Annual Meeting, Ohio State University, Columbus (May 2011);

'Understanding the role of the author in the creation of the medieval Irish tale *Acallam na senórach*: lessons from the *Kalevala*', Public Lecture to the Finnish Literary Society, Helsinki (September 2011); 'The intertwining of *fíanaigecht* and *dinnshenchas* traditions', Society for Name Studies in Britain and Ireland: 21st Annual Conference (March 2012); 'Reading *Tochmarc Ailbe*: text and context', The 26th Irish Conference of Medievalists, University College, Dublin (June 2012); 'Editing *Acallam na senórach*: a test case', *Fíanaigecht*: The Second International Finn Cycle Conference, University of Glasgow (August 2014); and 'An fhilíocht luath sa bhfiannaíocht', Éigse Cholm Cille, Ollscoil Uladh, Doire (Mí na Márta 2017).

Above all else, I have reason to be particularly grateful to my colleagues – academic and administrative – in the Department of Early and Medieval Irish, University College Cork, for continuing to promote and nurture an atmosphere in which teaching and research have pride of place: to John Carey, Máire Herbert, Ciara Ní Churnáin, Siobhán Ní Dhonghaile, Emma Nic Cárthaigh, Caitríona Ó Dochartaigh, and Pádraig Ó Riain, I express my thanks for their continued friendship and support.

I incurred two major debts in the writing of this book: Mícheál Briody of the University of Helsinki read the entire work, made many suggestions for its improvement and clarified numerous issues for me with his incisive questions and comments; and my colleague and Head of Department, John Carey, also read the text in its entirety and his wise counsel and perceptive ideas greatly enriched the volume. I am deeply indebted to both for improving the final work so materially; for remaining errors and shortcomings, I alone am responsible.

Text titles and initial lines of poems[1]

A aencheard Bhérre 'O foremost artisan of Bear'
A bhen dén folcadh mo chinn 'O woman, bathe my head'
A chorr úd thall san léana 'O crane, yonder in the meadowland'
A lía Thulcha Tuaithe shuas 'O stone above on Tulach Thuaithe'
A Lorcáin mheic Luighdheach láin 'O Lorcán, son of Lughaidh Lán'
A Mór Maigne Moigi Siúil 'O Mór of Moyne of Mag Siúil'
A Rí Ríchid, réidig dam 'O King of Heaven, explain to me'
Acallam na senórach 'The colloquy of the ancients'
Aided Finn 'The death of Finn'
Aided óenfir Aífe 'The death of Aífe's only son'
Áirem muintire Finn 'The enumeration of Finn's people'
Aithed Gráinne la Diarmaid 'The elopement of Gráinne with Diarmaid'
Aithed mná Ailella maic Eógain la Fothad Canainne 'The elopement of Ailill mac Eógain's wife with Fothad Canainne'
Almu Lagen, les na fían 'Almu of Laigin, stronghold of the *fíana*'
Almu robo chæm dia cois 'Almu, she was fair on foot'
Amra Coluim Chille 'The eulogy of Colum Cille'
Annálad anall uile 'All the annal-writing heretofore'
Áonach so a Moigh Eala in rí 'This is a fair in Magh Eala of the king'
Apgitir chrábaid 'The alphabet of piety'
Áth Líac Find, cía lía diatá 'Áth Líac Finn, from what stone is it [named]?'
Áth Liac Find, cid diatá 'Áth Líac Finn: whence is it [named]?'
Baile binnbérlach mac Búain 'Sweet-voiced Baile son of Búan'
Banṡenchas 'Lore of women'
Bec innocht lúth mo da lua 'Small tonight the vigour of my heels'
Bretha crólige 'Judgements of blood-lying'
Bruiden Átha Í 'The contention of Áth Í'
Bruidhean chaorthainn 'The rowan-tree hostel'
Cath Cnucha 'The battle of Castleknock'
Ceisd agam ort a Cháoilte 'I have a question for you, o Caílte'
Ces Ulad 'The debility of the Ulstermen'
Codail begán begán beg 'Sleep a little, a little little'

---

[1] These have not been regularized but are generally given as in the standard published editions. I have modified some of the translations, however.

Cóir anmann	'The fitness of names'
Comthóth Lóegairi co cretim	'The conversion of Lóegaire to the faith'
Críth gablach	'The forked purchase'
Culhwch ac Olwen	'Culhwch and Olwen'
Dám thrír táncatar ille	'They came hither as a band of three'
Deargrúathar cloinne Morna	'The red rush of Morna's children'
Di chethairslicht athgabálae	'On the four sections of distraint'
Dinnsenchas Érenn	'Placename lore of Ireland'
Di suidigud tellaig Temra	'On the settling of the manor of Tara'
Do fallsigud Tána bó Cúalnge	'On the finding of *Táin bó Cúailnge*'
Domhnach lodmair tar Lúachair	'One Sunday we went over Luachair'
Duanaire Finn[2]	'The book of the lays of Fionn'
Duanaire Ghearóid Iarla	'The poem-book of Gearóid Iarla'
Échta Lagen for Leth Cuind	'The slaughters [inflicted] upon Leth Cuinn by Laigin'
Eirigh súas a Osgair	'Rise up, Osgar'
Eól dam i ndairib dréchta	'I am skilled in dense masses of compositions'
Eól damh senchus Feine Finn	'I know the lore of Finn's *fían*'
Esnada tige Buchet	'The songs of Buchet's house'
Éuchtach inghen Díarmatta	'Éuchtach, daughter of Diarmaid'
Feis tighe Chonáin	'The feast at Conán's house'
Fíanna bátar i nEmain	'The warriors who were in Emain'
Fíansruth	'The fían-stream'
Fil duine	'There is one'
Fochond loingse Fergusa meic Róig	'The cause of Fergus mac Róich's exile'
Fotha catha Cnucha	'The cause of the battle of Castleknock'
Fuar ar n-aghaidh a Loch Luig	'Cold our night in Loch Luig'
Fuaramar seilg iar samhain	'We had a hunt after Samain'
Historia Brittonum	'The history of the Britons'
Imacallam in dá thúarad	'The colloquy of the two sages'
Is maith do chuit, a Gráinne	'Good is your portion, o Gráinne'
Iss é súd colg in laoích láin	'This is the blade of the perfect warrior'
Lebor gabála Érenn	'The book of the taking of Ireland'
Ligi Guill i mMaig Raigni	'The grave of Goll in Mag Raigne'
Longes mac nUislenn	'The exile of the sons of Uisliu'
Macgnímrada (Macgnímartha) Con Culainn	'The boyhood deeds of Cú Chulainn'
Macgnímrada (Macgnímartha) Finn	'The boyhood deeds of Finn'

---

[2] Italicized this refers to the edition by MacNeill and Murphy; romanized, it is used for the manuscript of the same name.

Text titles and initial lines of poems

Maidhim in mhaidin fa ghlonn   'I boast the morning for the deed'
Marbad Cúlduib   'The slaying of Cúldub'[3]
Ochtur táncamar anuas   'As eight we came down'
Oenach indiu luid in rí   'Today the king went to a fair'
Reicne Fothaid Chanainne   'The poetic composition of Fothad Canainne'
Ro loiscit na lama sa   'Withered are these arms'
Sanas Chormaic   'Cormac's glossary'
Scél asa mberar combad hé Finn mac Cumaill Mongán   'A story from which it is inferred that Mongán was Finn mac Cumaill'
Scél Túáin meic Cairill   'The story of Túán son of Cairell'
Scéla Moṡauluim   'Tidings of Moṡaulum'
Senchas már   'The great tradition'
Senchas na relec   'Lore of the burial-grounds'
Serc Caillige Bérre do Ḟothud Chanainne   'The love of the Hag of Bear for Fothad Canainne'
Sermo ad reges   'A sermon to kings'
Sgríobh sin a Bhrógainn sgribhinn   'Write that, o Brógann, a writing'
Síaburcharpat Con Culainn   'The phantom chariot of Cú Chulainn'
Táin bó Cúailnge   'The cattle-raid of Cooley'
Tecosca Cormaic   'The instructions of Cormac'
Tesmolta Cormaic 7 aided Finn   'The eulogies of Cormac and the death of Finn'
Tochmarc Ailbe   'The wooing of Ailbe'
Togail bruidne Da Derga   'The destruction of Da Derga's hostel'
Tóraigheacht Dhiarmada agus Ghráinne   'The pursuit of Diarmaid and Gráinne'
Tromdháimh Ghuaire   'Guaire's burdensome company'
Úar in lathe do Lum Laine   'Cold the day for Lom Laine'
Úath Beinne Étair   'The cave of the hill of Howth'
Úathad mé a Temraig a-nocht   'Lonely am I in Tara tonight'
Uchán a sgíeth mo ríogh réil   'Alas, o shield of my bright king'
Uraicecht becc   'The small primer'
Vita tripartita Sancti Patricii   'The tripartite Life of Saint Patrick'

---

3 Its full title in the manuscript (RIA D iv 2) is 'Tuc*ait* faghb*ál*a in fesa do fin*n* inso 7 ma*rb*ad culduib' ('The cause of Finn's acquisition of knowledge here and the death of Cúldub').

Common terminology

áes dána: 'people of art'.

áes síde: 'Otherworld dwellers, supernatural beings'. Frequently equated with *Túatha Dé Danann*.

banfénnid: 'female *fían*-member, female *fían*-warrior' [plural *banfénnidi*].

coibche: 'bride-price'.

Cruithin: name used for distinct ethnic population groups found mainly in Ulster (Dál nAraide [Antrim] and Uí Echach Coba [Down]), and in various other places in Ireland; also used for the Picts of Scotland.[1]

dán díreach: a high-status form of poetry practised by professional poets utilizing strict metrical rules; it was composed in Ireland and Scotland from the twelfth to the seventeenth century.

díberg: 'robbery, plundering'; 'robber, brigand'.

díberg(ach): 'robber, brigand' [plural *díbergaig*].

díchetal di chennaib: 'extemporary chanting, poetical incantation'. One of the three attributes that privilege a *fili* and which Finn is said to possess.

dinnsenchas (dindsenchas): 'lore of places'.

dúnad: 'closure'. The technical word used for the repetition of the first word (or a variant thereof) of a poem at its end as a way of marking its conclusion.

Early Modern Irish: the form of the Irish language in common use from *c*.AD1200–1650.

Érainn: name used for distinct ethnic population groups found mainly in Munster. Like Laigin, perhaps they were in origin Celtic peoples who settled in Ireland before the Goídil. This view is much contested, however.

Fenian Cycle: an alternative name for *fíanaigecht*, used interchangeably with it; also known as the Finn Cycle.

fénnid: '*fían*-member, *fían*-warrior' [plural *fénnidi*].

fían: 'a band of roving men whose principal occupations were hunting and war, also a troop of professional fighting-men under a leader' (*DIL*) [plural *fíana*].

fíanaigecht: the material centred on the legendary character Finn mac Cumaill, his *fían* ('warrior-band'), his son Oisín and his grandson Oscar, though it also includes matter relating to other *fíana* and their leaders. Also commonly referred to as the Finn or Fenian Cycle.

---

[1] For convenient guides to the pronunciation of the commonest placenames and personal names cited throughout this work, see Dooley and Roes, *Tales*, pp xxxiv–xxxvii; Williams, *Ireland's immortals*, pp xxi–xxx.

fianas: 'the profession of a roving hunter and warrior; military service in a *fian*; warfare as a calling' (*DIL*).
fili: 'poet, man of learning' [plural *filid*].
fine: 'kin-group'.
Finn Cycle: an alternative name for *fianaigecht*, used interchangeably with it; also known as the Fenian Cycle.
geilt: 'a wild man; one who goes mad from terror' [plural *geilti*].
geis: 'taboo, injunction' [plural *gessa*].
gilla: 'a youth of age to bear arms'.
Goídil [singular Goídel]: the dominant Celtic settlers in Ireland, Scotland and the Isle of Man; generally anglicized as Gael.
imbas forosnai: 'knowledge which illuminates'. One of the three attributes that privilege a *fili* and which Finn is said to possess.
Laigin: population groups based in the east of Ireland who gave name to the later province of Leinster. Like the Érainn, perhaps they were in origin Celtic peoples who settled in Ireland before the Goídil.
laoithe fianaigheachta: 'Fenian lays'; also referred to as Fenian or Ossianic ballads.
Männerbund: a group of young male warriors.
Middle Irish: the form of the Irish language in use from *c*.AD900–1200.
Old Irish: the form of the Irish language in use from *c*.AD600–900.
rígfénnid: 'royal *fian*-member, royal *fian*-warrior'; a term frequently applied to Finn mac Cumaill.
roscad: 'rhetoric'. Used to describe stressed, highly alliterative language that is neither poetry nor prose [plural *roscada*].
Samain: the first of November, one of the 'quarter days', when the Otherworld was held to be accessible from this world.
senchas: 'learned lore, tradition, history'.
senchaid: 'a reciter of *senchas*, a historian' [plural *senchaide*].
teinm laído: 'chewing the pith?'. One of the three attributes that privilege a poet and which Finn is said to possess.
tinnscra: 'bride-price'.
túath: 'people, petty kingdom'.
Túatha Dé Danann: 'Peoples of the Goddess Dana'; Otherworld dwellers, supernatural beings.[2] Frequently equated with *áes síde*.

---

[2] As John Carey has pointed out ('The name "Tuatha Dé Danann"'), the evidence points to this appellation being no older than the late Middle Irish period.

Introduction*

The term *fianaigecht* ('The Fenian or Finn Cycle')[1] refers to the material centred on the legendary character Finn mac Cumaill and his *fian* ('warrior-band'), though it also includes matter relating to other *fiana* and their leaders, many of which are brought into Finn's ambit. It is classified by modern scholars as one of the four medieval Irish literary cycles along with the Ulster Cycle, the Cycle of Historical Tales (or Cycles of the Kings) and the Mythological Cycle.[2]

In a fashion recalling the expansion of Arthurian legend throughout Europe, the cult of Finn grew from localized beginnings to spread throughout the Gaelic-speaking world.[3] During this process, particularly under the influence of the synthetic historians in the tenth and eleventh centuries, a position was found for Finn and his *fian* in the historical and literary record. They were often portrayed as the standing army of king Cormac mac Airt, anachronistically defending Ireland in the third century against foreign invasion particularly by the Lochlannaig ('Norsemen'), often from a base at Almu (later Almha), the Hill of Allen in Laigin territory.[4]

Fenian lays and ballads began to be composed at least as early as the eleventh century and these became the dominant literary form of the tradition from the late medieval period onwards. The two most important extant ballad collections are those preserved in the sixteenth-century Scottish manuscript, the Book of the Dean of Lismore, and the seventeenth-century manuscript, Duanaire Finn (UCD Archives, Franciscan MS A 20[b]), compiled among Irish exiles in Ostend, Belgium. Prose material was also extensively cultivated, and includes the Middle Irish texts *Tochmarc Ailbe* and *Macgnímrada Finn*, the later *Feis tighe Chonáin*, the famous 'love-triangle' *Tóraigheacht Dhiarmada agus Ghráinne* and the central text of *fianaigecht* tradition, *Acallam na senórach*.

The fame of Fenian balladry had spread all over Europe by the nineteenth century, thanks to James Macpherson. He published three works in the 1760s

---

* This is partially based on my contribution on 'The Fenian Cycle' to *Medieval Ireland: an encyclopedia*.
1 In this work, these terms will be used interchangeably. **2** For discussion of these literary cycles, see for example Dillon, *Early Irish literature*; Poppe, *Of cycles and other critical matters*; Ní Bhrolcháin, *An introduction to early Irish literature*. **3** The early Fenian tradition does not seem to have attained the same prominence in the Isle of Man as in Ireland and Scotland, as the only piece of *fianaigecht* to survive in the Gaelic Manx song tradition is edited by Broderick, 'Fin as Oshin' and Ó Muircheartaigh, '*Fin as Ossian* revisited'. The later folk tradition is the subject of Broderick, 'Manx stories and reminiscences of Ned Beg Hom Ruy', i. introduction and texts; ii. translation and notes; and idem, 'Boddagh yn Cooat Laaghagh'. See now idem, 'Fíanaigecht in Manx tradition'. **4** For references and exact location, see *HDGP* 'A' s.n. Almha. On the question of standing armies, see Bruford, 'Oral and literary Fenian tales', pp 36–7;

that purported to be translations of poems written by Finn's son, Oisín (in Macpherson's spelling 'Ossian'). These 'translations' were, in the main, creations of Macpherson's own imagination, though based to a greater or lesser degree – depending on the work involved – on genuine ballad tradition. From Macpherson's 'Ossian' the term 'Ossianic' emerged, a word that is still occasionally used to refer to the cycle as a whole and to the ballad tradition in particular.

Throughout the literature and later folklore, Finn mac Cumaill is presented as a multi-faceted individual. The multiple engaging presentations of the complexity of his character and of other characters in the cycle, coupled with repeated evocations of the beauties of nature, the clever use of *dinnṡenchas* ('lore of places'), and the recurring presence of magic and the supernatural combined to place *fianaigecht* at the very heart of Gaelic culture, as is still the case in the modern folk tradition. This study is concerned primarily with the early Finn Cycle,[5] and with its emergence from fragmentarily documented beginnings to become the dominant Gaelic literary genre from *c.*1200 onwards.[6]

Ó Cróinín, *Early medieval Ireland*, p. 274. **5** The most important primary sources for the early Finn Cycle are noted in Murray, 'Interpreting the evidence', pp 48–9; this is an updating of the list discussed in greater detail in *Fian*. pp xvi–xxxi and is subjected to further scrutiny in Murray, *The early Fenian corpus*. Some of these materials do not have strong Fenian contexts – for example, some of the poems attributed to Finn, Caílte or Oisín – and such texts play only a marginal part in the following work. **6** The existence of *fianaigecht* as a literary genre is tacitly acknowledged by the medieval Irish themselves with the use of the term *fianṡruth* (literally '*fian*-stream') to refer to materials from this corpus. The significance of the term has been discussed by Flahive, '*A chloidhimh chléirchín in chluig* and the concept of the literary cycle'; cf. Stern, 'Fiannshruth'. See also *MD* iii, p. 20 (= *LL* iv, 25345), the metrical *dinnṡenchas* of Carmun, where Gwynn translates the phrase *Fian-ṡruth Find* as 'Tales of Find and the Fianna' (cf. O'Curry, *On the manners and customs*, ii, p. 45, who translates it as 'Finian tales').

CHAPTER ONE

Acallam na senórach

Acallam na senórach (*AcS*) 'The colloquy of the ancients' is the single-largest medieval Irish text.[1] The structure and content of the tale are predicated upon the premise that a small number of the *fían* of Ireland, under the leadership of Caílte mac Rónáin[2] and Oisín mac Finn,[3] have survived for centuries into the era of Saint Patrick; the extended narrative that is the *Acallam* details their intermittent wandering through the landscape with the saint, recounting stories about the heyday of the *fían* under Finn mac Cumaill. Although the *Acallam* stands at the end of this investigation chronologically, it can also serve as a departure point in any analysis of the early Finn Cycle.[4] It designates the conclusion of the cultivation of early *fíanaigecht* materials and represents a high-water mark of achievement within this tradition and within Gaelic culture generally. However, it also signals the beginning of this study because the themes, concerns and characters contained in the early fragmentary material also figure prominently in the *Acallam* where, conversely, they march to the sound of a different drum; this resonance will form an important part of the analysis of the whole.

[1] Editions are by Stokes, 'Acallamh na senórach' and O'Grady, 'Agallamh na seanórach' [vol. i]. Translations have been made by O'Grady, 'Agallamh na seanórach' [vol. ii] (supplemented by Stokes, 'Acallamh na senórach', pp 225–71); by Dooley and Roe, *Tales of the elders*; and by Harmon, *The dialogue of the ancients of Ireland*. Selected passages from *AcS* have been edited by Dillon, *Stories from the Acallam*, and certain brief sections translated by Dooley, 'From: Acallam na senórach (The colloquy of the ancients)'. Furthermore, pp 101–12 of O'Grady's translation have been reprinted in Cross and Slover, *Ancient Irish tales*, pp 457–68. Five Irish-language copies of the Book of Lismore version of the *Acallam*, along with three English translations of it by Seosamh Ó Longáin, are preserved in Ó Longáin manuscripts. Interestingly, a further six of their manuscripts contain abbreviated copies of the *Agallamh* not taken directly from the Book of Lismore; see Ní Úrdail, *The scribe in eighteenth- and nineteenth-century Ireland*, pp 190–1. [2] Also known as Caílte mac Crunnchon mic Rónáin: see Stokes, 'Acallamh', l. 5 (= O'Grady, 'Agallamh', i, p. 94; Dillon, *Stories from the Acallam*, l. 5). [3] Oisín's name is understood as meaning 'little deer' and in the Book of Leinster his mother, Blaí Derg, is said to have been in deer form when he was conceived: see Ó Briain, 'Oisín's biography: conception and birth', pp 460–7 esp. pp 465–6; *Fian*, p. xxvi §XXXII. [4] There is another shorter medieval version of the *Acallam* extant referred to as the *Agallamh bheag* (partially ed. Hyde, 'An Agallamh bheag'; trans. Pennington, 'The little colloquy'; full edition, as yet unpublished, by Kühns, 'An edition and translation of the *Agallamh bheag* from the Book of Lismore'); a narrative summary of the text is available in Kühns, 'Some observations on the *Acallam bec*', pp 125–30. An English translation of the text, made by Seosamh Ó Longáin and transcribed by John Windele in 1856, is available in RIA MS 12 I 2 (1109). There is also a later compilation, dated to c.1400 by its editor (Ní Shéaghdha, *Agallamh na seanórach*, i, p. xxxi), where Oisín, rather than Caílte, is the central character; for further details, see Hyde, 'The Reeves manuscript of the Agallamh na senórach'; Ó Muraíle, 'Agallamh', pp 103–5, pp 108–9; Dooley and Roe, *Tales*, pp xli–xliii. For the modern *Agallamh* tradition, see Ó Fiannachta, 'The development of the debate between Pádraig and Oisín'; Ní Mhurchú, '*Agallamh Oisín agus Phádraig*: the

INTRODUCTION

The *Acallam* is written in prose interspersed with poetry,[5] the 'prosimetrum' form so favoured in medieval Irish literary culture.[6] It is preserved incomplete in five manuscripts, the text breaking off abruptly in all witnesses.[7] It is a frame-tale (*Rahmenerzählung*)[8] that focuses, *inter alia*, on the accommodation reached between the native and Christian traditions in the encounters between Patrick, Caílte and Oisín.[9] In the journeying of saint and warriors around fifth-century Ireland, the different moral codes of the *fían* and the Church are compared and contrasted, with *fíanaigecht* ultimately accommodated within a Christian framework. The *Acallam* is a veritable treasure trove of Finn Cycle materials, cogently described as 'a reservoir into which a brilliant ... innovator had diverted several streams of tradition which previously had normally flowed in separate channels'.[10]

However, the *Acallam* must be deemed atypical within the medieval Fenian corpus. Though it is composed of traditional materials, the combination of its circular narrative, its pre-occupation with the politics (especially Church politics) of the day, and its juxtaposition and harmonization of the views and role of the Church, the *fían* and the Otherworld inhabitants (the Túatha Dé Danann), is unique to its author.[11] It is like using the stones of an Irish thatched cottage to construct a Swiss chalet: the materials may be the same and may be re-used with profit, but the construction methods and outlook of the builder are different.[12]

growth of an Ossianic lay'; eadem, '*Agallamh Oisín agus Phádraig*: composition and transmission'; eadem, 'An tAgallamh nua: athleagan déanach d'Agallamh na seanórach'. For a discussion of the entire *Agallamh* tradition, see Flahive, *The Fenian Cycle in Irish and Scots-Gaelic literature*, Chapter Three. **5** There is an alphabetic list of the poems in the text, with cross-references to the editions of O'Grady and Stokes, in Best, *Bibliography of Irish philology and of printed Irish literature to 1912*, pp 189–90. **6** For more on prosimetrum, see Mac Cana, 'Notes on the combination of prose and verse'; idem, 'Prosimetrum in insular Celtic literature'; Toner, 'Authority, verse and the transmission of *senchas*'; Parsons, '*Acallam na senórach* as prosimetrum'; Ní Mhaonaigh, 'Poetic authority in Middle Irish narrative: a case study'. **7** These are Oxford, Bodleian Library, MS Laud 610 (15th century); Oxford, Bodleian Library, Rawlinson MS B. 487 (15th century); Chatsworth, Derbyshire, Book of Lismore (late 15th century); UCD Archives, Franciscan MS A 4 (15th–16th century); UCD Archives, Franciscan MS A 20(a) (17th century). For further details, see Stokes, 'Acallamh', pp x–xiii; Ó Muraíle, 'Agallamh', pp 109–11; Dooley and Roe, *Tales*, pp xxxi–xxxii. Attention is drawn in Ó hUiginn, '*Fiannaigheacht*, family, faith and fatherland', p. 154 n. 24, to a further copy of the *Acallam* once extant, formerly in the possession of the Franciscans. **8** Defined by Stokes, 'Acallamh', p. ix, as 'a number of stories enclosed in the framework of a single narrative'. **9** For earlier accounts of the conversion of the *fían*, see the poems beginning *Ochtur táncamar anuas* (edited by Stern, 'Die Bekehrung der Fianna') and *Ro loiscit na lama sa* (edited by Meyer, 'Anecdota from the Stowe MS no 992', pp 185–6). **10** Murphy, *Ossianic lore*, p. 25. **11** Dooley, 'Pagan beliefs and Christian redress', p. 267, succinctly refers to this potent mix in terms of 'the laying down of a doubly sacralized sacred grid – the grid of the old gods at the base, the grid of the Christian order on top and, between them, the world of heroes and women that is acted upon by these two'. She sees its creation as a response to the 'new challenge felt in all the vernaculars, the common birth in the European twelfth century of the literary imagination – a freedom to invent with impunity and joy'. **12** As Dooley, 'The deployment of some hagiographical

THE MANUSCRIPTS AND THEIR TEXTS

There is an ongoing problem in treating the *Acallam* as a single unitary text as four of the five manuscripts attest to different versions of the narrative.[13] The Laud 610 text forms the basis of Whitley Stokes' 'best text' edition (with additional material from the Book of Lismore and Franciscan MS A 4) while Standish Hayes O'Grady edited and translated that contained in the Book of Lismore. As yet, no critical edition has been created that draws on all the manuscript witnesses and it remains unclear whether this can be a feasible goal for this long and detailed prosimetric narrative. Two of the manuscript texts, Rawlinson B. 487 and Franciscan A 4, have not yet even been transcribed *in extenso* so the degree to which they differ from those in Laud 610 and the Book of Lismore (which diverge quite a bit from each other) is still not understood fully.[14] Consequently, when we talk about the *Acallam*, we must be aware that we are in effect talking about the editions provided by Stokes and O'Grady over one hundred years ago – editions that bear only partial witness to the manuscript testimony.[15] Further editorial work may substantially change our viewpoint of this literary nexus.

ACALLAM NA SENÓRACH AS EPIC?

There are only two texts from medieval Ireland with genuine claims to be treated as epics – *Táin bó Cúailnge* and *Acallam na senórach*. An epic is generally understood to be a long narrative poem telling of a hero's deeds. It has been more rigorously defined as 'of or pertaining to a long poetic composition, usually centred upon a hero, in which a series of great achievements or events is narrated in elevated style'.[16] Can the term epic be meaningfully used with regard to the two longest medieval Irish narratives, the *Táin* and the *Acallam*? Since neither are poems, the term epic in its strictest sense cannot be applied to them though the definition of an epic as 'a long narrative poem' is based on its use with reference to famous Classical compositions such as the *Iliad* and the *Odyssey*.[17] Leaving the poetic argument to one side, we see that *Táin bó Cúailnge* can justifiably be

sources', p. 97, notes: 'The overwhelming impression left by this process of of literary transformation is that there are strong deviations from the general tenor of well-known *fianaigecht* scenarios when they appear in new guise' in *Acallam na senórach*. **13** The exception is the version in Franciscan MS A 20(a), which is a faithful copy of the text in Franciscan MS A 4, 'breaking off at the same point': Dillon, Mooney and de Brún, *Catalogue of Irish manuscripts*, p. 41. **14** This topic is discussed in detail in Murray, 'Editing *Acallam na senórach*: a test case'. **15** The often fractious nature of the relationship between the text's two principal editors is engagingly detailed in Parsons, 'Whitley Stokes, Standish Hayes O'Grady and *Acallam na senórach*'. **16** *New Webster's encyclopedic dictionary* s.v. 'epic'. **17** Dorson, 'Introduction', p. 4, believes that 'there is no good reason to exclude the prose of heroic saga from our conception of the folk epic, if we identify epic as a stirring traditional narrative of perilous adventure, daring and manhood honoring the

considered an epic,[18] whereas the *Acallam* fails on all but one count, that of length.[19] It uses no elevated style in its telling, is an assemblage of different anecdotes rather than a continuous heroic narrative, and the focal hero of the story – Finn mac Cumaill – has been pithily described as 'a revered and nostalgically remembered absence'.[20] Further, it has been observed by Seán Ó Coileáin that the differing geographies of the *Táin* and the *Acallam*, concrete in the former and largely imaginary in the latter, is in the main 'as useful a distinction as any between the milieu of the hero of epic and that of the adventurer of romance'.[21] As W.P. Ker has pertinently noted: 'Whatever Epic may mean, it implies some weight and solidity; Romance means nothing, if it does not convey some notion of mystery and fantasy'.[22]

DATE

Traditionally, most commentators on the *Acallam* have given its date of composition as '*c*.1200'. This represents the mid-way point between dating proposals advanced which have fluctuated between 1175 and 1225. More recently, a number of scholars have started to favour the later date as the more likely time of composition. The varying suggestions that have been made are here noted and examined chronologically.[23]

Whitley Stokes was very non-committal with regard to its dating. As Mellifont is mentioned in the text, he gave 1142 (the date of its founding) as the *terminus a quo* for its composition and thought that 'the mention of tithe points to the twelfth century or later'.[24] The second point cannot stand, however, as Kenneth Jackson has shown elsewhere that the claim to tithe payments was a vexed question in Ireland long before this time.[25] Based on linguistic criteria, Tomás Ó Máille inclined towards the 'first half or middle of the 12th century as the approximate date' of the *Acallam*,[26] while Alf Sommerfelt suggested a dating

---

heroes of a people'.   **18** See Ó hUiginn, 'The background and development', pp 35–41; Miles, *Heroic saga and classical epic*, pp 145–93.   **19** Ó Muraíle, 'Agallamh', p. 104, estimates that the *Acallam* contains about 70,000 words (*c*.55,000 prose/15,000 poetry) in comparison to the *Táin* (first recension *c*.44,000 words; second recension *c*.55,000 words). Recently however, Nagy, 'Keeping the *Acallam* together', p. 112, has argued that although it would be 'relatively unprecedented to label *AS* [*Acallam na senórach*] an epic ... that the designation fits, and not just because *AS* has to do with heroes and heroism, or because it established a trend ... *AS* is also epic in its nature and function in an etymological sense'.   **20** Nagy, '*Acallam na senórach*: a "tri-cycle"?', p. 75.   **21** Ó Coileáin, 'Irish literature', p. 531 (cf. Ó Coileáin, 'Place and placename', 45). For arguments that the geography of the *Acallam* may be more rooted in the reality of Ireland's topography than hitherto appreciated, see Ó Muraíle, 'Agallamh', pp 120–4.   **22** Ker, *Epic and romance*, p. 4.   **23** These arguments are outlined in Dooley, 'The date and purpose', 98, and discussed in some detail in Ó Muraíle, 'Agallamh', pp 105–8 and in Murray, 'Interpreting the evidence', pp 44–7.   **24** Stokes, 'Acallamh', pp 273 n. 53, 281 n. 919.   **25** Jackson, *Aislinge Meic Con Glinne*, pp xxv–xxvi; see also Ó Muraíle, 'Agallamh', pp 106–7.   **26** Ó Máille, 'Contributions', 1–2. He highlighted the following linguistic features in particular as pointing towards this date: the preservation of nasalization after singular

range in the mid- to late twelfth century.²⁷ Comparison of the *Acallam* with the Book of Leinster *Táin* and the Leabhar Breac passions and homilies led Myles Dillon to advance a date of *c*.1200 for its composition.²⁸ This remained his preferred dating as is evident from his editorial work on the *Acallam* where, without presenting supporting examples, he asserted that 'from the evidence of the language ... the *Acallam* is not to be dated earlier than *c*.1200'.²⁹ Twice more in the same publication, Dillon gives his opinion with regard to the date: 'written at about the end of the twelfth century' (p. ix) and '*Acallam na senórach* belongs to the end of the Middle Irish period, and the language is in a state of transition, not far removed from the Early Modern Irish of the Grammatical Tracts' (p. 23).

It was Gerard Murphy's opinion that 'the original *Acallam* ... seems to have existed about the year 1175, probably in a complete form'.³⁰ He placed *AcS* in the last quarter of the twelfth century because it is mentioned in the prose accompanying a *dinnṡenchas* poem on Tonn Chlidna that he would date to this period;³¹ here he was following Nessa Ní Shéaghdha who drew similar conclusions from this reference.³² Scholars have since wondered whether this reference to *AcS* necessarily predates the Book of Ballymote (late fourteenth century), the oldest vellum to contain it.³³ In his other published opinions concerning the date of the *Acallam*, Murphy was more circumspect. For example, in his essay in *Irish sagas*, he placed its composition 'towards the end of the twelfth century';³⁴ similarly in *Duanaire Finn* he opted for a date 'about the end of the 12th century',³⁵ a view also accepted by Jackson.³⁶

The three most substantial articles to deal in-depth with the date of the *Acallam* are those by Robert Nuner, Ann Dooley and Anne Connon.³⁷ Nuner has made the only thorough examination of the language of the *Acallam* to date and his conclusion is that 'the prose sections ... must date from a period at least as

---

accusatives; the occurrence of equatives in *–thir*; the forms of *indaas* 'than' present in the text; the preservation of s-perfect endings in *–sat*; the incidence of passive plural endings in *–it*. **27** Sommerfelt, 'Le système verbal dans Cath Catharda', §212 [*RC* 38, 36–7]. **28** Dillon, 'Nominal predicates in Irish' [*ZCP* 16, 319]. This was also Thurneysen's preference: *Die irische Helden- und Königsage*, p. 48. **29** Dillon, *Stories from the Acallam*, p. 25. **30** Murphy, *Ossianic lore*, p. 26. This is also Donald Meek's opinion ('Development and degeneration in Gaelic ballad texts', p. 141: '*c*.1175') but he does not give his reasons for assigning this date to the text. However, Murphy (p. 26) thought that the surviving versions of the *Acallam* and *Agallamh bheag* (as opposed to an 'original' *Acallam*) 'should be assigned to some date about the year 1200'. **31** Murphy, *Ossianic lore*, p. 24. **32** Ní Shéaghdha, *Agallamh na seanórach*, i, pp x–xii. **33** For the arguments and text, see Ó Muraíle, 'Agallamh', p. 107: *Et fós ar an dinnsenchus cétna amail ro can Cailti i n-aimsir Pátraig ar an Agallaim do-rónsat ar dindshenc[h]us Erenn*, 'Concerning yet the same *dinnṡenchas* as Caílte sang in the time of Patrick regarding the *Agallam* they made about the *dinnṡenchas* of Ireland' (from The Book of Ballymote, fo. 200va51–b2); cf. *Fian.*, p. xxx §LIV. See Nagy, 'Oral tradition in the *Acallam na senórach*', p. 78. **34** Murphy, 'Acallam na senórach', p. 122 (= Dillon, *Stories from the Acallam*, p. xv). **35** *DF* III, p. lxi. **36** Jackson, *Aislinge Meic Con Glinne*, p. xxvi. **37** Nuner, 'The verbal system'; Dooley, 'The date and purpose'; Connon, 'The Roscommon *locus* of *Acallam na senórach* and some thoughts as to *tempus* and *persona*', pp 53–6.

late as 1200–1225 ... the evidence seems to point to the later of the two dates mentioned, 1225, as the more likely date of compilation'.[38] As this quotation makes explicit, however, he only attempted to date the prose, arguing elsewhere (p. 236) that many of the verses may not have been composed contemporaneously with the prose, a view that is clearly correct.[39] Despite some criticisms of his methodological approach,[40] the later date of *c*.1225 which he proposed for the *Acallam* is now starting to win acceptance.[41]

In her indepth analysis of the narrative, Dooley argues that Cathal Croibderg (king of Connacht from *c*.1190 to 1200, and again from 1202 to his death in 1224) was 'the king almost certainly reigning at the time the *Acallam* was composed' and that its composition is to be placed in the west of Ireland.[42] She largely bases this view on her analysis of an incident in the *Acallam* where Patrick receives a chariot from a young man, Dub, to replace his own broken one.[43] Patrick renames Dub 'black' as Radub 'very black' and prophesies that his descendants, Uí Raduib, will receive prosperity and blessings; he then brings about the marriage of Radub to Aífe Derg, daughter of the king of Connacht. This scene must be read as containing a deliberate reference to Muinter Roduib of Clann Tomaltaig, a sept of Síl Muiredaig, whose lords 'were drawn from the Mac Airechtaig branch of the Úa Roduib line of Muinter Roduib'.[44] Their secular arm was based in central County Roscommon and their ecclesiastical arm controlled the Patrician foundation of Aghagower, County Mayo; they were closely associated with the Úa Conchobuir kings of Connacht. Dooley presents a closely reasoned analysis of this passage in *AcS* suggesting that it may reflect actual events in Connacht concerning Muinter Roduib in the opening decades of the thirteenth century before the decline in their fortunes under Áed Úa Conchobuir, king of Connacht after Cathal Croibderg. It is impossible to tie down exactly when these events might have happened, even assuming that the references are to Donn Óg, the later head of the Mac Airechtaig family who may have been married to a daughter of a Connacht king; however, Dooley favours a date towards the end of Cathal Croibderg's reign.

Connon has extended this analysis further to show that this later date is likely to be correct. Building on Dooley's identification of Muiredach mac Fínnachta in *AcS* with Cathal Croibderg, and by extension the identification of Muiredach's son Áed with Cathal's son of the same name, the fact that Áed mac Muiredaig is

---

38 Nuner, 'The verbal system', pp 308–9. **39** See Carney, 'Two poems from Acallam na senórach'; Ó Coileáin, 'The setting of *Géisid cúan*'; Parsons, '*Acallam na senórach* as prosimetrum'. **40** See, for example, Mac Eoin, Review of *Zeitschrift für celtische Philologie* 27. **41** For a more detailed summary of these arguments, see Murray, 'Interpreting the evidence', pp 45–6. **42** Dooley, 'The date and purpose', 103. **43** Stokes, 'Acallamh', ll 6632–90 (trans. pp 249–50). A fuller edition and translation of this material (with variants) is presented by Dooley, 'The date and purpose', pp 108–12. **44** Connon, 'The

king of Connacht at the end of the *Acallam* would point to a date of composition after the death of Cathal Croibderg (†1224) when he was succeeded by his son, Áed. If these identifications and analysis are accepted:

> then at least the final Connacht section of the *Acallam* likely dates to the years of Áed's rule: 1224 to 1228. It may be that the writing of the *Acallam* spanned the reigns of Cathal Crobderg and his son, or that the whole text was written after 1224.[45]

However, Connon notes as a caveat that Áed had been designated as Cathal Croibderg's heir at least fourteen years before his father died; thus, it is 'not impossible that the depiction of Áed as king was written before his actual succession to the throne'.[46]

One of the major internal dating points in the text is the mention at the outset of Mainistir Droichit Átha 'the monastery of Drogheda',[47] a reference to the Cistercian house of Mellifont that was founded in 1142. Since nobody, with the exception of Ó Máille (noted above), has suggested dating the *Acallam* to earlier than the mid-twelfth century, this diminishes its importance as a dating criterion. However, the deliberate citation of Mellifont is taken as important in another respect by Ann Dooley who sees in it 'the first indication … that the author intends to project a contemporary aspect and agenda on his compendium of tales'.[48] The three great saints of Ireland are grouped together in a gloss in the Laud version of *AcS* (*Patraic 7 Colum cill[e] 7 Brigit*),[49] and again in Rawlinson MS B. 487 with the fire on the rock of Cashel named as one of the three holy fires of Ireland along with 'the fire of Brigit … and the fire of Columcille' (*teine bríghde … 7 teine coluim chille*).[50] These references are seen as significant by Dooley in the context of the death of Tomaltach Úa Conchobuir (archbishop of Armagh) at Mellifont in 1201 as 'he was partial to the de Courcy ambition to establish a revitalized cult of Patrick, Brigid and Colm Cille at Downpatrick in the mid-1180s'.[51]

Even without invoking the person of Archbishop Tomaltach, if one reads these references as expressing overt support for de Courcy objectives, they assume great significance with regard to the date of the *Acallam*. However, although all versions mention *in tres teine béo ara mbia rath fa deired a nEirinn hi* ('the third lit fire

Roscommon *locus* of *Acallam na senórach*', p. 28.   **45** Ibid., p. 54.   **46** Ibid., p. 54 n. 132.   **47** Stokes, 'Acallamh', l. 53 (= O'Grady, 'Agallamh', i, p. 95; Dooley and Roe, *Tales*, pp 4, 225; Dillon, *Stories from the Acallam*, ll 52–3): *co hIndber mBic Loingsigh a mBregaibh, risi-ráidter Mainistir Droichit Átha isin tan so*, 'to Indber Bic Loingsigh in Brega, which is now called the monastery of Drogheda'. Dillon (p. 25) has tentatively suggested that *Mainistir Droichit Átha* may be a later additional gloss to the text.   **48** Dooley, 'The date and purpose', 99.   **49** Stokes, 'Acallamh', l. 5433.   **50** Rawlinson MS B. 487, fo. 45va26–7 (= Dooley and Roe, *Tales*, p. 151).   **51** Dooley, 'The date and purpose', 101 n. 11; Dooley and Roe, *Tales*,

which shall be blessed at the end in Ireland') and *triar álaind a n-aenbali* ('a beautiful triumvirate in one place'),[52] the explicit references by name to Patrick, Brigid and Colum Cille only occur in those manuscripts mentioned above and are not central to the whole *Acallam* tradition. Nevertheless, I would be inclined to agree with Dooley's assessment that they constitute 'a much more significant dating indicator than the foundation of Mellifont'.[53]

In summation, when we consider the detailed arguments advanced in the recent scholarship, we are left with outer limits of 1190 and 1228 for the composition of *AcS*, with modern opinion tending towards the latter date.[54] However, as we have seen, some of the constituent elements of this composite text date to different time periods; furthermore, we cannot be sure that the entire narrative has a unitary compilation date. Greater precision may not be achievable.

CONNACHT INFLUENCE IN THE *ACALLAM*

Along with an in-depth examination of the date of the text, Dooley's long article has served to highlight another aspect of the *Acallam*, i.e. the way in which the author has placed the province of Connacht at the very heart of the narrative, large sections of which are set in Roscommon, Sligo and south Donegal.[55] As will become clear in subsequent chapters, early *fíanaigecht* material tends to be localized in different areas around the countryside; however, Connacht does not feature heavily in the earliest written sources concerning Finn and his *fían*. For example, as we shall see later, the regular association of the death of Diarmaid ua Duibhne with Beann Ghulban, County Sligo, appears in the literature for the first time in *AcS* and this link, rather than representing pre-existing tradition, might have been created by its author.[56]

The king of Connacht, Áed mac Muiredaig meic Fínnachta, is singled out for special attention by Saint Patrick in the text. The advantage of naming Áed as king is that it linked his positive portrayal to the Síl Muiredaig, kings of Connacht at the time of the *Acallam*'s composition. In the narrative, we meet him both as man and boy.[57] We first encounter him as a dead boy brought back to life by the intercession of Patrick, the miracle also helping to convert the

---

p. 241 n. 151; Thanisch, 'What the Butlers saw', 43. See also Flanagan, 'John de Courcy', esp. pp 163–4, 175–6, and eadem, *The transformation of the Irish church*, p. 223. **52** Stokes, 'Acallamh', ll 5409–10, 5432. **53** Dooley, 'The date and purpose', 101 n. 11. **54** The later the date, the better we might understand what has been referred to as 'a process of chivalrization ... at work in this Irish compendium of lore': Nagy, 'Fenian female food', p. 310. **55** See the maps of the itineraries in Dooley and Roe, *Tales*, pp xliv–xlviii. **56** Chapter Seven, p. 97; Stokes, 'Acallamh', ll 1514–15 (= O'Grady, 'Agallamh', i, p. 127, ii, p. 138; Dooley and Roe, *Tales*, p. 47); Stokes, 'Acallamh', ll 6895–6 [trans. p. 257] (= Dooley and Roe, *Tales*, p. 194). **57** This presentation contributes to the distortion of time in the narrative; see below (pp 42–3) for more on this topic.

Acallam na senórach

multitudes.[58] Later in the tale, we see Áed rejecting the advances of the beautiful *síd* woman, Aillenn, daughter of Bodb Derg, because of Saint Patrick's insistence that he have only one wife.[59] Aillenn also grudgingly assents to Patrick's judgment on the matter.[60] However, after the death of Áed's wife, and Aillenn's acceptance of the Christian God, Patrick joins the two together in matrimony, this being declared to be the first marriage that he performs in Ireland.[61] As part of his blessing on the couple, he says:

> 'Do-bér immorro', ar Pátraic '.i. tri rig do gabail Eirenn uaithib, 7 rath Eirenn fo deired acco gan dibaid'. Ocus scribais Brogán na fácbala sin do choiced Connacht.
>
> 'I will give moreover', said Patrick, 'three kings of their descendants to rule Ireland and the prosperity of Ireland to the end without loss'. And Broccán recorded these injunctions concerning the province of Connacht.[62]

This scene is an expression of the author's understanding of what constitutes a proper relationship between bishop and king, between Church and state. This was an issue at the very heart of Church reform in twelfth-century Ireland.[63] Furthermore, these words, put into the mouth of Ireland's national apostle, also constitute unambiguous authorial support for the national ambitions of the Uí Chonchobuir kings of Connacht. Indeed, Dooley sees the *Acallam* as 'an expression of confidence in a bright new dawn of opportunity in Gaelic culture and polity in the west of Ireland'.[64]

Dooley has also argued for Aghagower, County Mayo (controlled by the ecclesiastical arm of Muinter Roduib), as a possible locus of composition of the

---

[58] Stokes, 'Acallamh', ll 1205–36 (= O'Grady, 'Agallamh', i, p. 120, ii, p. 130; Dooley and Roe, *Tales*, p. 38). [59] The importance of monogamous marriage is a major theme in the text and is discussed in detail below (pp 36–7). [60] Stokes, 'Acallamh', ll 6358–437 [trans. pp 245–7] (= O'Grady, 'Agallamh', i, pp 214–15, ii, p. 243; Dooley and Roe, *Tales*, pp 179–81). [61] Stokes, 'Acallamh', ll 7820–43 [trans. pp 269–70] (= Dooley and Roe, *Tales*, pp 217–18). For discussion, see Roe, '*Acallamh na senórach*: the confluence of lay and clerical oral traditions', p. 341; Dooley and Roe, *Tales*, pp xxviii–xxx; Dooley, 'The date and purpose', 104–5; Carey, '*Acallam na senórach*: a conversation between worlds', pp 86–7. [62] Stokes, 'Acallamh', ll 7837–40 [trans. p. 270] (= Dooley and Roe, *Tales*, p. 218). The mention of the taking of Ireland by three kings of Connacht (if taken to reflect contemporary concerns) would place the *Acallam*'s composition firmly after the reigns of Toirdelbach Úa Conchobuir (king of Connacht, 1106–†1156) and of his son Rúaidrí Úa Conchobuir (king of Connacht, 1156–86) who were both reckoned as *rig Érenn co fressabra* 'kings of Ireland with opposition'. It is unclear who the author has in mind as the third ruler. If not an eschatological statement about some future Connacht king, the most likely candidate would seem to be Rúaidrí's half-brother, Cathal Croibderg (king of Connacht c.1189–1200; 1202–†1224). For the dates, see Moody et al., *New history of Ireland*, ix, p. 223. [63] For a multi-dimensional approach to this topic, see Bracken and Ó Riain-Raedel (eds), *Ireland and Europe* (esp. Ní Mhaonaigh, 'Pagans and holy men'). The best recent general account is that by Flanagan, *The transformation of the Irish church*. [64] Dooley, 'The date and purpose', 123.

Acallam, because of the importance of Muinter Roduib in the Connacht portion of the text.⁶⁵ However, Connon has made a compelling case for seeing 'the Augustinian house of canons at Roscommon ... [as being] at the intersection of the *Acallam*'s physical and dynastic landscapes of Connacht' and that this 'argues strongly for the monastery as the text's *locus* of composition'.⁶⁶ A large part of Connon's argument is based on her acceptance of the significance of Muinter Roduib as put forward by Dooley; however, instead of seeing this as pointing to Aghagower as the place of composition, she would look to the Augustinian house of canons in Roscommon, located in the more powerful secular lordship of Muinter Roduib.⁶⁷ Roscommon, as a long-established centre of learning with a history of cultivation of *senchas*, is an ideal candidate for the place of composition of the *Acallam*, and this proposed location would help account for the text's emphasis on native lore, the importance it attaches to the reform ideology, and the significant interest it shows in many of the Connacht locations highlighted in the narrative.

Prior to the *Acallam*, the early *fían*-texts extant relating to Connacht are concerned with the character of Fothad Canainne,⁶⁸ not with Finn.⁶⁹ There seem to have been early and separate traditions about Fothad Canainne and his warrior-band that became bound up with the stories concerning Finn and his *fían*.⁷⁰ But, it is not until the composition of *AcS* that Finn's *féinnid* are so explicitly associated with Connacht in the literature. This most likely reflects authorial innovation, with a desire to connect the newly fashioned *Acallam* with its locus of composition, rather than with earlier traditions. Once established, these west of Ireland connections remain as part of *fíanaigecht* into the modern era.

THEMATIC APPROACHES

A text as long, varied and rich as the *Acallam* allows for a multitude of thematic approaches. Many scholars have mined the text with profit and their insights have helped facilitate our understanding of the narrative. Certain of the more prominent themes will be enumerated and briefly discussed here.

65 Ibid., pp 120–1. **66** Connon, 'The Roscommon *locus* of *Acallam na senórach*', p. 52. **67** Ibid., p. 30. See above p. 26. **68** However, as is evident in Chapter Thirteen below, the early genealogies do not connect Fothad with Connacht but with Loígis, Corcu Loígde and Dál nAraide. **69** Finn's uncle, Crimall, is living in Connacht in *Macgnímrada Finn*: Meyer, 'Macgnimartha Find', p. 201 §§16–17 (= Meyer, 'The boyish exploits', p. 185 §§16–17; Nagy, *The wisdom of the outlaw*, p. 213; *CHA* §93 pp 197–8) and Finn's first race is located in Connacht in the poem beginning *A Rí Ríchid, réidig dam: Fian.*, p. 46 §3 (= *LL* iii, ll 18023–6). Of course, Goll mac Morna is also consistently linked with Connacht: see Ní Uigín, 'Goll mac Morna', pp 240–1. This association of Goll with Connacht persists to the present day: see Ó hÓgáin, *Myth, legend and romance*, pp 246–7, s.n. 'Goll mac Morna'. **70** Ó Muirigh, 'Rangú litríocht mheánaoiseach na Gaeilge', pp 708–11 (cf. Chapter Thirteen, below, pp 157–8). See also Mac Cana, '*Fíanaigecht* in the pre-Norman period', p. 83, and McQuillan, 'Finn, Fothad, and *fían*', 1–4.

1 The role of the revenants

In several medieval Irish texts, such as *Scél Túáin meic Cairill* and *Do fallsigud Tána bó Cúalnge* to take just two of the more famous examples,[71] personages from an earlier age return to bear witness to events from the past.[72] A crucial aspect of some of these stories, including the *Acallam*, is the interaction between the revenant and a representative of a literate Christian Ireland, generally a saint, which functions as an explanation for the readership and listenership of how these tales moved into the literary sphere as well as containing an 'expression of saintly support for the project of maintaining the vernacular literary tradition'.[73] This device is also present in *AcS* where Caílte, Oisín and the surviving *fénnidi* are brought from their traditional third-century ambit into the time of Patrick, i.e., fifth-century Ireland.[74] The reason for their survival is explicitly mentioned in the text – to allow for the recording in written format of the stories concerned with Finn and his *fían* in order to provide 'entertainment for companies and lords to the end of time' (*gairdiugudh do dronguibh 7 do degdáinibh deridh aimsire*).[75]

For the creator of the *Acallam*, the employment of this literary device is also useful in 'authorizing' a particular version of the past. By naming Caílte and Oisín, the necessary authorities have been invoked: the story he tells is not just his version but is the 'true' one as related to Patrick by eye-witnesses. Of course, for a writer working in the period around 1200, naming Patrick as the receptor of native narrative tradition constitutes another appeal to authority. If Ireland's national apostle was guided by his angels to record these stories for posterity,[76] then later generations should take it that their preservation and cultivation is suitable work for clerics. Similar to the use made of the Pseudo-historical prologue to the *Senchas már*,[77] composed most likely *c.*AD800, in part to frustrate the efforts of reforming clergy, Patrick is invoked as the spirit of that 'old time religion': to paraphrase the hymn, 'if it's good enough for Patrick, then it's good enough for us'.

2 Harmonization of different viewpoints

The varying outlooks of Caílte, Oisín and Saint Patrick are harmonized in *AcS*, pointing towards the reconciliation possible between native culture and the

---

71 Editions by Carey, 'Scél Túáin'; Murray, 'The finding of the *Táin*'.   **72** This theme is discussed in detail by Nic Cárthaigh, 'Surviving the flood' (with specific reference to the most famous of all Irish revenants, Túán mac Cairill and Fintan mac Bóchra). The similar use of the 'proof of occurence' motif has been outlined in Murray, 'The role of the *cuilebad*'.   **73** See Nagy, *Conversing with angels and ancients*, pp 317–23 at p. 321.   **74** Caílte also functions as a revenant informant in an earlier *fianaigecht* tale, *Scél asa mberar combad hé Finn mac Cumaill Mongán*: see below, Chapter Six, pp 86–8.   **75** Stokes, 'Acallamh', l. 301 (= O'Grady, 'Agallamh', i, p. 101, ii, p. 108; Dooley and Roe, *Tales*, p. 12).   **76** Stokes, 'Acallamh', ll 293–303 (= O'Grady, 'Agallamh', i, pp 100–1, ii, p. 108; Dooley and Roe, *Tales*, p. 12).   **77** For this text, see McCone, 'Dubthach maccu Lugair'; Carey, 'The two laws'; idem, 'An edition'.

reforming Christian ethos; this is symbolized at the outset of the narrative with Patrick's baptism of Caílte and his companions.[78] One of the ways in which this reconciliation is facilitated is by presenting the *fían* as proto-Christians, possessing foreknowledge of the one true God and of the coming of Christianity:

> 'Maith a anam, a Cháilti', ar Pátraic, 'ar' chreideabairse do ríg nime 7 talman, nó an fetubair a beith ann etir?' Frecraidh Caílte sin: 'rofitir in flaithféinnid', ar Caílte, 'ór ba drai 7 ba fáidh 7 ba flaith é, 7 do thuicemarne uili cu raibhi Dia ann tré urchra aenoidche adconncamar'.

> 'Dear Caílte, did all of the *Fían* believe in the King of Heaven and Earth, or did you know of His existence at all?' Caílte answered, 'The chief and warrior knew, for he was a wizard, a seer and a prince. And we all understood from the destruction that we saw one night that there was a God'.[79]

The promised accommodation between native and Christian is further extended to include some of the Otherworld population, the *áes síde* or Túatha Dé Danann, 'now clearly the aristocrats of a supernatural race, divested of divinity but supercharged with magic'.[80] For example, the Otherworld musician, Cas Corach, seeks Heaven as a reward from Patrick for his music, a prize that the saint is only too happy to bestow.[81] Similarly, the Otherworld woman Aillenn, daughter of Bodb Derg, is permitted by Patrick to marry Áed, king of Connacht, after she accepts Christianity.[82] Nevertheless, the treatment of Cas Corach and Aillenn is exceptional; elsewhere we read that the Túatha Dé Danann are to be banished from the surface of the earth and that Patrick will put them 'into the steep slopes of hills and rocks' (*ind-étnaib cnocc 7 carracc*).[83]

While an accommodation between native and Christian had long been reached, this *modus vivendi* was under some pressure from the Church reform movement. Furthermore, the addition of the Otherworld to the narrative mix ensures that 'the *Acallam* is constructed in terms of three "times", or worlds, and not simply of two'.[84] For the author, however, it was a powerful combination, allowing him to address contemporary issues in a sophisticated way by manipulating traditional narratives.

---

78 Stokes, 'Acallamh', ll 314–24 (= O'Grady, 'Agallamh', i, p. 101, ii, p. 108; Dooley and Roe, *Tales*, p. 12). **79** Stokes, 'Acallamh', ll 1453–8 (= O'Grady, 'Agallamh', i, p. 125, ii, p. 136; Dooley and Roe, *Tales*, p. 45). **80** Williams, *Ireland's immortals*, p. 196. **81** Stokes, 'Acallamh', ll 3469–80 (= O'Grady, 'Agallamh', i, pp 170–1, ii, p. 191; Dooley and Roe, *Tales*, pp 105–6). **82** Stokes, 'Acallamh', ll 7826–33 [trans. pp 269–70] (= Dooley and Roe, *Tales*, pp 217–18). **83** Stokes, 'Acallamh', l. 7535 (= O'Grady, 'Agallamh', i, p. 229, ii, p. 260; Dooley and Roe, *Tales*, p. 210). **84** Carey, '*Acallam na senórach*: a conversation between worlds', p. 83.

3 Importance of writing and remembering

Literacy as a potent force in cultivating and preserving traditional lore, particularly tradition elicited in response to questions posed by Patrick,[85] is repeatedly stressed in the *Acallam*. Patrick keeps his scribe, Broccán, by his side and typical of his repeated remarks to him, on hearing another of Caílte's wondrous stories, is '*Scríbtar lat gachar' chan Cáilte*', '"Let everything that Caílte has recited be written down by you"'.[86] This is similar to the scene in the roughly contemporary *Buile Śuibne* in which Saint Moling addresses the *geilt* ('wild man'), Suibne, in the following words:

> 'gidh mor śire gach láoi d'Érinn techt gacha hespurtan chugum-sa go rosgriobhthar do sgéla lium'.
>
> 'however much of Ireland you may travel each day, you will come to me each evening so that I may write your history'.[87]

This injunction would be right at home in our text, as one of the central conceits of the *Acallam* is that it 'supposedly contains a series of oral performances rendered into a literary form'.[88]

The importance of writing in order to remember is contrasted with the faultiness of memory. So the opening injunction of the angels to take down the stories of the *fénnidi* is predicated on the need to record material that is in danger of being lost 'on account of forgetfulness and faulty memory' (*ar dáigh dermait 7 dichuimhne*).[89] Later in the narrative, before Caílte is due to recite Fenian lore to the men of Ireland at Tara, the *áes síde* offer him a drink of remembrance (*deoch cuimnigthi céille*)[90] so that he might tap into the wealth of lore lying dormant in his memory. Even on this occasion, the point of remembering is 'for the preservation by the authorities and the experts of the stories we recite until the end of time' (*do lesugud údar 7 olloman dona scelaib indesmait-ne ann co dered aimsire*).[91] In this way, native lore offers the prospect of some measure of immortality.

4 Position of the arts

The importance of the *áes dána* 'people of art' and their various professions is repeatedly mentioned in *AcS*; it was obviously an issue of great significance for its

---

85 On this structure, see Mac Cana, 'Narrative openers and progress markers in Irish', pp 107–12. On the function of questions in the *Acallam*, see Ó Cadhla, 'God and heroes'. **86** Stokes, 'Acallamh', l. 871 (= O'Grady, 'Agallamh', i, p. 113, ii, p. 122; Dooley and Roe, *Tales*, p. 28; Dillon, *Stories from the Acallam*, l. 514). **87** O'Keeffe, *Buile Suibhne*, pp 142–3 §76. **88** Nagy, 'Oral tradition in the *Acallam na senórach*', p. 84. **89** Stokes, 'Acallamh', ll 298–9 (= O'Grady, 'Agallamh', i, p. 101, ii, p. 108; Dooley and Roe, *Tales*, p. 12). **90** Stokes, 'Acallamh', l. 7259 (= O'Grady, 'Agallamh', i, p. 224, ii, p. 254; Dooley and Roe, *Tales*, p. 203). **91** Stokes, 'Acallamh', ll 7256–8 (= O'Grady, 'Agallamh', i, p. 224, ii, p. 254; Dooley

author. For example, we have already seen Patrick happy to reward the Otherworld musician, Cas Corach, with a guarantee of Heaven for his musical ability;[92] 'the close connection between music and the *síde* in general is stressed throughout the *Acallam*'.[93] In another incident, Cormac mac Airt addresses those who have been financially and socially disadvantaged by the death of Finn and the subsequent loss of his patronage. To the musicians he promises: '… *leth dligid uaimsi daib, 7 cobeis in tuarustail doberad Find daib dobérsa*' ('I have half entitlement for you and I will give equal of the stipend that Finn used to give you'), while to the poets he pledges: '*Prim[ṡ]ordan Eirenn acumsa daib*' ('I have the primary maintenance of Ireland for you').[94] This benevolent treatment of the *áes dána* is reflected once again later in the story when the giant woman, Bé Binn, bestows her arm-rings on them before her death.[95]

The consistent message throughout is that the *áes dána* deserve rewards both in this world and the next for the enhancement of joy and of understanding they bring to society. The author of the *Acallam* is making two clear points: as a member of the learned classes himself, he is permitted to share in these entitlements and, in contradistinction to the reform movement in the Church, he believes in reminding his audience of the role of the native learned orders and of the significance of the material which they cultivate.[96] He is emphasizing a point he has already made in another way: if native narrative material is deserving of the interest and time of Saint Patrick, then it is a worthy concern for all clerics.[97] However, the great anomaly is not the promotion of these concerns but that the author of the *Acallam* wishes to highlight 'not the departed heroes, whose tales have now been confided to the manuscripts of the Church; nor for that matter the elite *fílid*, who appear indeed not to figure in the *Acallam* at all; but the pupils of the last of the old gods'.[98] How this might be best interpreted is a matter as yet unresolved.

and Roe, *Tales*, p. 203). **92** See above p. 32. Williams, *Ireland's immortals*, p. 217 sees music here 'as a metaphor for the totality of Irish culture'. **93** Carey, '*Acallam na senórach*: a conversation between worlds', p. 87. **94** Stokes, 'Acallamh', ll 5300–1, 5304 (= O'Grady, 'Agallamh', i, p. 203, ii, p. 230; Dooley and Roe, *Tales*, p. 147). For the importance of music in the *Acallam*, see Nagy, 'Oral tradition in the *Acallam na senórach*', pp 91–3; idem, 'Oral tradition and performance in medieval Ireland', pp 283–6, 290–1; Dooley, 'The European context', pp 67–70. This importance is stressed in other broadly contemporary writings. For example, in the Book of Leinster we read of *Pípai, fidli, fir cengail, / cnámfir ocus cuslennaig, … conérne in rí rán fri mess / ar cach dán a míad díles*, 'Pipes, fiddles, gleemen, / bones-players and bag-pipers … the king, noble and honoured, pays / for each art its proper honour': *MD* iii, pp 20–1 (= *LL* iv, ll 25365–72). **95** Stokes, 'Acallamh', ll 6079–80 (= O'Grady, 'Agallamh', i, p. 214, ii, p. 242; Dooley and Roe, *Tales*, p. 170). **96** Nagy, 'Life in the fast lane', p. 118, has suggested that 'the *Acallam* may also reflect the resettling of that literary establishment outside the church and in the courts of kings and nobles'. **97** Ironically, as John Carey reminds me, though the *Acallam*'s ideology aligns it with the older monasteries and the later learned families, the research of Anne Connon links the text with new religious foundations such as Roscommon and Assaroe. **98** Carey, '*Acallam na senórach*: a conversation between worlds', p. 89.

5 Patrician elements in the Acallam

We must be careful not to analyse *AcS* solely as a compendium of Fenian lore; it is also important to give due weight to the Patrician elements in the text. Though the harmonization of the different moral codes of the *fían* and the Church – through the encounters between Patrick, Caílte and Oisín – is mainly achieved against a *fíanaigecht* backdrop,[99] the presence and reworking of earlier materials concerning Patrick comes as no surprise considering the pivotal role he plays in the narrative.[100] Similarly, if we follow Ann Dooley in seeing Muinter Roduib influence as central to the creation of the *Acallam*, the position of their ecclesiastical arm as controllers of the Patrician foundation of Aghagower would also lead us to expect to find cultivation of traditions associated with Patrick therein.[101]

It has been suggested that the famous episode in Tírechán's *Collectanea*,[102] in which Patrick raises an enormous swineherd from the dead, may have provided the inspiration for certain incidents in the *Acallam*.[103] Patrick strikes on a huge gravestone in Dichuil with his staff; a giant emerges, gives thanks to his liberator and then sheds bitter tears. He informs his listeners that he was killed by a *fían* a hundred years earlier; he wishes to walk with the saint who refuses his request because of the dread he would inspire. Patrick baptizes him and restores him to his grave. The sections in *AcS* that may be indebted to this narrative include the first meeting of the clerics with the *fénnidi*;[104] the episode concerning the excavation of the grave and grave goods of the giant, Garb Daire;[105] the rather lachrymose nature of the *fénnidi* throughout the *Acallam*;[106] and the opening of a grave by Caílte with his spear shaft.[107]

It seems clear that other elements of the Patrician dossier also influenced the composition of *AcS*; this accords with Máirtín Ó Briain's suggestion that much of the *Acallam* 'can be regarded as an extension of the expanding Patrician legend into secular literature'.[108] Ann Dooley and Anne Connon have also shown that materials drawn from the earliest Irish-language Life of Saint Patrick, the *Vita*

---

[99] See Roe, '*Acallamh na senórach*: the confluence of lay and clerical oral traditions'; idem, 'The *Acallam*: the Church's eventual acceptance of the cultural inheritance of pagan Ireland'. [100] See Murray, 'The reworking of Old Irish narrative texts in the Middle Irish period' for a discussion of some of the methodologies and aims involved in the creation of such multi-faceted texts. [101] Dooley, 'The date and purpose', 112–14, 120–2. [102] Bieler, *The Patrician texts*, pp 154–5 §40 (= *CHA* §99 pp 211–12). [103] Roe, '*Acallamh na senórach*: the confluence of lay and clerical oral traditions', pp 333–7; see Nagy, *Conversing with angels and ancients*, pp 131–3. [104] Text and further details given below, Chapter Twelve, p. 147. [105] Stokes, 'Acallamh', ll 2072–84 (= O'Grady, 'Agallamh', i, p. 140, ii, pp 153–4; Dooley and Roe, *Tales*, p. 64). [106] For example, weeping is first mentioned at the beginning of the story when Caílte, Oisín and Cáma shed tears for all their dead companions. Thus, the tone of regret in the tale is set right at the outset: Stokes, 'Acallamh', ll 24–5, 39–41 (= O'Grady, 'Agallamh', i, pp 94–5, ii, p. 102; Dooley and Roe, *Tales*, pp 3–4). For more on this topic, see below, pp 40–1, §10. [107] Stokes, 'Acallamh', ll 2749–56 (= O'Grady, 'Agallamh', i, p. 155, ii, p. 172; Dooley and Roe, *Tales*, p. 84). [108] Ó Briain,

tripartita, are regularly reflected in the *Acallam* while Patrician churches and sites historically associated with Patrick stand at the centre of many of the pivotal episodes in the narrative.[109] However, as this material is frequently recast and reworked, perhaps drawing on differing versions of Patrician traditions, Dooley has been led to query 'the range of source-material which the author/compiler ... had at his disposal'.[110] Furthermore, contemporary with the creation of *AcS*, we find efforts – such as the Life of Patrick by Jocelyn of Furness and the growth of Saint Patrick's Purgatory in County Donegal – to extend and strengthen the cult of the saint. Thus, the composition of the *Acallam* might also be better understood within this context.

6 The sanctity of marriage

One of the major focal points in the *Acallam* is the way in which the author repeatedly emphasizes the significance of monogamy and fidelity within marriage;[111] he also stresses again and again the importance of a woman receiving her correct bride-price (*coibche*).[112] As we have already seen, Áed mac Muiredaig is lauded for spurning the advances of Aillenn from the *síd*, because he is already married and has promised God and Patrick that he will be bound to a single wife (*a beith ar aenmnái chengailti*).[113] It is Patrick who later joins Áed and Aillenn together in wedlock after the death of Áed's wife.[114]

There are further incidents in the *Acallam* that point towards the author's fixation with marriage, and particularly with monogamous aristocratic marriage.[115] For example, Caílte gives magic herbs to the wives of the two sons of the king of Fir Maige, Lochán and Eógan, which cause their husbands to love them and forsake other women.[116] Similarly, when Áengus son of Eochaid Fáebarderg, king of Ulster, marries Úaine, daughter of Fíal, she is said to be his sole wife until death (*do bói d'aenmnái aici nóco ndechaid éc*).[117] And again, when Échna daughter of Muiredach mac Fínnachta, king of Connacht, is to marry Cas Corach of the *áes síde*, Caílte tells her that she will be legally bound to him as his only spouse (*naidmecar tusa a coraidecht aenmná dó*).[118] Even the sole example of

---

'Some material', p. 185. **109** Dooley, 'The deployment of some hagiographical sources', pp 98–104; Connon, 'Plotting *Acallam na senórach*'; eadem, 'The Roscommon *locus* of *Acallam na senórach*'. **110** Dooley, 'The deployment of some hagiographical sources', p. 100. **111** For discussion, see Dooley and Roe, *Tales*, pp xxviii–xxx. **112** For example, see Stokes, 'Acallamh', ll 2771–6, 4066–77, 5792–9 [final two not in O'Grady] (= O'Grady, 'Agallamh', i, p. 155, ii, pp 172–3; Dooley and Roe, *Tales*, pp 84–5, 120, 162). However, *coibche* can also be advocated outside of marriage as with Caílte and Scothníam: see Stokes, 'Acallamh', ll 3893–918 (= O'Grady, 'Agallamh', i, p. 180, ii, pp 202–3; Dooley and Roe, *Tales*, pp 117–18). **113** Stokes, 'Acallamh', ll 6406–7 (= O'Grady, 'Agallamh', i, p. 214, ii, p. 243; Dooley and Roe, *Tales*, p. 180). **114** See above, p. 29. **115** See Donahue, 'The *Acallam na senórach*: a medieval instruction manual'. **116** Stokes, 'Acallamh', ll 954–88 (= O'Grady, 'Agallamh', i, pp 115–16, ii, pp 125–6; Dooley and Roe, *Tales*, pp 31–2). **117** Stokes, 'Acallamh', l. 3333 (= O'Grady, 'Agallamh', i, 168, ii, 187; Dooley and Roe, *Tales*, p. 101). **118** Stokes, 'Acallamh', l. 7544 [trans. p. 261] (= Dooley and

Acallam na senórach

the seduction of a married woman is muted in the story by having the characters involved (Manannán and his wife Uchtdelb, Aillén and his sister Áine), all of the *áes síde*, form unions with each other.[119]

The reforming of marriage law was a topic of major concern in Ireland at the time of the composition of *AcS* with the matrimonial issues raised not just confined to this text. For example, Ruairí Ó hUiginn has shown that in the Middle Irish version of *Tochmarc Emire* earlier traditions concerning Cú Chulainn's relationships with Emer, Scáthach, Úathach and Aífe were reworked to highlight the immorality of multiple unions. The narrative stresses the high price that Cú Chulainn paid for his actions: the slaying of his only son, Connlae, and his being left without issue.[120] Thus, the emphasis placed on the sanctity of marriage by the author of the *Acallam* was part of a wider Church agenda which surfaced elsewhere in the literature of the time.[121]

7 The importance of baptism

The reform agenda which percolates the *Acallam* is nowhere more explicit than in the significance that the author attaches to the sacrament of baptism. As already noted, one of the first major events which occurs when the central characters are brought together is Patrick's baptism of Caílte and his fellow *fénnidi*.[122] This is prefigured shortly before in the narrative when Patrick initially meets these warriors:

> gabhus in t-esríat do chrothad uisci choisricatha ar na feraibh móra uair ro bhúi míle léighionn do dheamhnaibh uas a ceannaibh conuic in lá sin.[123]

> he took the sprinkler and shook holy water on the big men because a thousand legions of demons had been over their heads until that day.

This exorcism of the demons is then followed by the actual baptism of the warriors.[124] Similarly, in the body of the text, the king of Ireland, Díarmait mac Cerbaill takes Patrick with him to Tara 'to baptize and to bless and to instruct the men of Ireland in his own law and rule' (*do baisted 7 do bennachad 7 d'ordugud fer nEirenn ina cirt 7 ina riagail fein*).[125]

Roe, *Tales*, p. 210). **119** Stokes, 'Acallamh', ll 3649–84 (= O'Grady, 'Agallamh', i, 175, ii, 196–7; Dooley and Roe, *Tales*, pp 111–12). **120** Ó hUiginn, 'Rúraíocht agus rómánsaíocht', 85–7. He has developed these arguments further in his Quiggin lecture: *Marriage, law and Tochmarc Emire*, esp. pp 39–46. **121** See above, n. 61 for references to the secondary literature on the issue of marriage in *AcS*. **122** See above, pp 31–2, §2. **123** Stokes, 'Acallamh', ll 66–8 (= O'Grady, 'Agallamh', i, p. 95, ii, p. 103; Dooley and Roe, *Tales*, p. 5). The symbolism of this scene is elucidated by Nagy, 'Some strands and strains', pp 95–6. **124** Stokes, 'Acallamh', ll 314–24 (= O'Grady, 'Agallamh', i, p. 101, ii, p. 108; Dooley and Roe, *Tales*, p. 12). **125** Stokes, 'Acallamh', ll 2698–9 (= O'Grady, 'Agallamh', i, p. 154, ii, p. 170; Dooley and Roe, *Tales*, p. 82).

The emphasis on this theme in the work has prompted Máire Ní Mhaonaigh to advance the hypothesis that 'the author of the *Acallam* may well have been affected by theological discussion focusing on the necessity and ultimate efficacy of baptism'. She is referring here to writings such as those by Honorius Augustodunensis that popularized ideas such as the Devil being subordinate to God, and the belief that clean-living pagans might be saved; such ideas led to a renewed emphasis being placed on baptism and 'permeate much of twelfth-century European religious writing and surface in secular narrative as well'.[126] If this is true, it shows the composer of *AcS* to the forefront in engaging with the Church reform movement in Ireland on both an intellectual and theological level.[127]

8 *The payment of clerics*

A topic intimately bound up with the baptismal and matrimonial issues raised above is that of the proper payment of clergy for the performance of their duties: it is a theme that is repeatedly mentioned in the narrative.[128] Thus, for example, after the baptism of the *fénnidi*, Caílte bestows a one-hundred-and-fifty-ounce 'ridged block of red gold' (*lia druimnech dergóir*) upon Patrick as payment.[129] Similarly, Áed mac Muiredaig, king of Connacht, gives as a fee for his marriage to the Otherworld woman, Aillenn, 'the choice of a homestead in every territory from Leac Lomenaig – also called Limerick – to Leac Essa Ruaid [Assaroe, County Donegal]' (*ragha baile cacha tuaithe o Leic Lomenaig – rissa raiter Luimnech –, co Leic Essa Ruaid*).[130] Furthermore, the proper remuneration for preaching and for spreading the Gospel is also highlighted.[131]

The repeated insistence on clerical fees parallels the payments to the *áes dána*, noted above, which also occupies the author's attentions. As someone who may have been reckoned as a member of both cadres, and whose family members may likely have belonged to the same social groupings, his interest in both these issues is understandable. However, he does not prefer one function above the other: for him, both exist in harmony. One can simultaneously promote a reform agenda while defending and cultivating native traditions, and get paid for both roles besides.

---

126 Ní Mhaonaigh, 'Pagans and holy men', pp 152–3. **127** See the discussion of baptism in the *Agallamh bheag* in Kühns, 'Some observations on the *Acallam bec*', pp 130–6. **128** For brief discussion, see Nagy, 'Some strands and strains', pp 96–7. **129** Stokes, 'Acallamh', l. 320 (= O'Grady, 'Agallamh', i, p. 101, ii, p. 108; Dooley and Roe, *Tales*, p. 12). **130** Stokes, 'Acallamh', ll 7835–6 [trans. p. 270] (= Dooley and Roe, *Tales*, p. 218). **131** Stokes, 'Acallamh', ll 4823–8 (= O'Grady, 'Agallamh', i, p. 192, ii, p. 218; Dooley and Roe, *Tales*, p. 135); Stokes, 'Acallamh', ll 5393–401 (= O'Grady, 'Agallamh', i, p. 205, ii, p. 232; Dooley and Roe, *Tales*, p. 151).

9 Mythological elements in the Acallam

Gerard Murphy, following Alfred Nutt,[132] believed that *fíanaigecht* 'should be classified neither with semi-historic heroic lore nor with history ... rather to the classes of mythology and folklore, which have normally no relation to history'.[133] This was also the conclusion of O'Rahilly who saw in Finn another reflex of the divine hero.[134] A central support underpinning these positions is that from earliest times Finn's foes are often from the Otherworld and that Finn himself can be compared and associated in many ways with the divine Lug.[135] As Joseph Nagy has noted, these mythological resonances 'extend from the Old Irish Fenian corpus through Middle and Early Modern Irish Fenian literature down to the Fenian folktales collected by folklorists in the twentieth century'.[136]

Following on from this, it would be reasonable to expect the *Acallam* to be a repository of mythological motifs, allusions and personages; this is only partly the case, however. Notwithstanding the large portion of the narrative devoted to the immortal Túatha Dé Danann and to the long-lived *fénnidi*, their presentation tends to be more muted than one might expect. Their magical attributes, while recounted, tend to be underplayed and their powers are seen as no match for what can be achieved by the Christian God and his followers. Patrick and his retinue are shown to take a very matter-of-fact approach in dealing with the *fían*-warriors and *áes síde* and, furthermore, the many extraordinary aspects of Finn's character are not unduly emphasized within the tale.

However, one section in the *Acallam* that does resonate very fully with mythological aspects of Finn's make-up attested elsewhere is his confrontation with Aillén mac Midna.[137] This Otherworld dweller comes every Samain to burn Tara and its treasures with fire from his mouth. No one can defeat him as he plays magical music to send his opponents to sleep. Ten-year old Finn arrives at the court of Conn Cétchathach, king of Tara, and volunteers to defend Tara. He receives a magical poisonous spear from the *fénnid*, Fíacha mac Conga. Upon Aillén's arrival, Finn is able to resist slumber by keeping its point to his forehead. He then uses a magical cloak to smother the fire started by Aillén, pursues him from Tara and kills him with the spear as he is re-entering the *síd* of Carn Finnachaid. As a reward for his actions, Finn is appointed leader of the *fían* of Ireland in place of Goll mac Morna, the warrior responsible for killing his father, Cumall:[138]

---

132 Nutt, *Ossian and the Ossianic literature*, esp. pp 9–18.   **133** *DF* III, p. 212.   **134** *EIHM* pp 271–81 at p. 277.   **135** These arguments are discussed in detail in Chapter Twelve, pp 149–50.   **136** Nagy, *The wisdom of the outlaw*, p. 2.   **137** The parallels with earlier traditions are explored in Chapter Five, pp 77–8.   **138** Stokes, 'Acallamh', ll 1662–761 (= O'Grady, 'Agallamh', i, pp 130–2, ii, pp 142–5; Dooley and Roe, *Tales*, pp 51–4). Later folk versions of this story have been printed in *DF* III, pp l–lii. Murphy also draws attention to an Early Modern Irish lay on the same topic: *DF* II, p. lii n. 2.

'Maith, a anam, a Ghuill mheic Morna', ar Conn Cétchathach, '(do ro)gha duit, Eire d'facbáil nó do lámh do thabhairt i láim Find'. '(Dar mu b)réithir', ar Goll, 'as í mu lámh dobér i láim Find'.

'Well, Goll, son of Morna', said Conn Cétchathach, 'make your choice. Leave Ireland or give your hand to Finn'. 'By my word', said Goll, 'I shall give Finn my hand'.[139]

This short narrative concerning Aillén is replete with mythological motifs: the Otherworld resident who breathes fire from his mouth; the entrancing music (*ceol sírrechtach*) that puts to sleep everyone who hears it; the magical spear that can counteract the effect of this music; the wonderful fire-engulfing cloak; the slaying of Aillén with the magical spear and his subsequent beheading. Nevertheless, one gets the impression that the full mythological possibilities of this passage have not been entirely realized,[140] a passage which serves an important narrative function in restoring the leadership of the *fían* to Clann Baíscne under Cumall's son. Although this ties the result of these actions very much to this world rather than to the Otherworld, Finn's besting of Goll in the process also seems to contain strong mythological resonances.

It is probable that the author of *AcS* was re-using and re-fashioning earlier narratives, and that 'some of the personages, some of the story-patterns, and some incidental details ... reflect the Celtic, and even the Indo-European heritage of Ireland';[141] as we have seen, however, he often did this in innovative ways, and by departing to some extent from his traditional sources. Modern commentators often find themselves at a loss in trying to understand the rich mythological significance of some medieval Irish texts because the contexts within which the mythologies first emerged are not fully delineated or understood. Indeed, some of the usages in the *Acallam* would suggest that medieval authors were also separated by some distance from the cultures in which these mythologies originated and developed. Nevertheless, 'in the manner of providing a frame of reference a twelfth-century editor must also continue to have a considerable advantage over a twentieth-century critic'.[142]

10 *Tears in the tale*

The lachrymose nature of the *fían*-warriors in the *Acallam* has already been alluded to; they are ready 'to break into tears at the slightest excuse'.[143] Many of

139 Stokes, 'Acallamh', ll 1758–61 (= O'Grady, 'Agallamh', i, p. 132, ii, p. 145; Dooley and Roe, *Tales*, p. 54). **140** These are detailed more fully below in Chapter Twelve, pp 149–50. **141** This quote pertains to *Táin bó Cúailnge* but, to my mind, can also be appropriately applied to the *Acallam*: see Ó Cathasaigh, 'Mythology in *Táin bó Cúailnge*', p. 131. **142** The citation is from Ó Coileáin, 'The setting of *Géisid cúan*', p. 235, but is of immediate relevance to the matter under discussion here. **143** Roe, 'Acallamh na

Acallam na senórach

the frequent examples of weeping in the narrative are associated with Caílte: we may instance his sobbing on the grave of Diarmaid ua Duibhne,[144] his keening for his fallen companions,[145] and his bemoaning the loss of Finn.[146] Patrick tries to console Caílte by reminding him that although nearly all his friends are dead, his acceptance of the one true God is a great compensation;[147] it may be 'that Caílte's tears represent a shift from terrible, deadly despair to a grief which is mediated and overcome by knowledge of Christian salvation'.[148] Many of the stories Caílte relates are grief-laden and demonstrate that 'it is extremely dangerous for a youth to excel too quickly or conspicuously in life; and ... that women spell trouble for *fénnidi*'.[149]

This continued recourse to tears sets the tone of sorrow that suffuses the tale:[150] 'everything is tinged with the gentle regret aroused by the remembrance of things past, the cherished memory of a happy life in which one has shared'.[151] There is a profound sense in the *Acallam* that the age of the heroes is not only gone but that it will never be seen again, that it now forms part of a distant and dimly-remembered past.[152] In one of many such incidents to focus on the tears of Caílte, we find it said:

> ro chaiestar déra fírthruaga falcmara annsin os chind na cloiche ic cuimniugud na muintire moire ro bói os chind na cloiche sin co minic reime.

> Standing there on top of the rock he wept flowing tears of great sadness, remembering the great people that often stood on that rock with him in earlier times.[153]

One of the central conceits of the narrative is that when the final band of *fénnidi* departs from this world, it is only their fame that will live on in the stories which have been written down by Patrick's scribe, Broccán, based on their imperfect retelling of events.[154] Thus, it is literacy, spreading with Christianity, which will preserve the memory of this age for future generations.

senórach: the confluence of lay and clerical oral traditions', p. 337. Examples cited in Mills, 'Sorrow and conversion in *Acallam na senórach*', 2–7. **144** Stokes, 'Acallamh', ll 1520–1 (= O'Grady, 'Agallamh', p. i, 127, ii, p. 138; Dooley and Roe, *Tales*, p. 47). **145** Stokes, 'Acallamh', ll 3378–9 (= O'Grady, 'Agallamh', i, p. 169, ii, p. 185; Dooley and Roe, *Tales*, p. 102). **146** Stokes, 'Acallamh', ll 6533–4 (= O'Grady, 'Agallamh', i, p. 216, ii, p. 244; Dooley and Roe, *Tales*, p. 183). **147** Stokes, 'Acallamh', ll 4595–9 (= O'Grady, 'Agallamh', i, pp 187–8, ii, p. 212; Dooley and Roe, *Tales*, p. 129). **148** Mills, 'Sorrow and conversion in *Acallam na senórach*', 13. **149** Nagy, 'Compositional concerns', p. 153. **150** See Nagy, 'Life in the fast lane', p. 118. **151** Rees and Rees, *Celtic heritage*, p. 69. **152** In some ways, this is similar to the position concerning *Beowulf* adopted by Tolkien, 'Beowulf: the monsters and the critics', p. 33: 'its maker was telling of things already old and weighted with regret, and he expended his art in making keen that touch upon the heart that sorrows have that are both poignant and remote'. **153** Stokes, 'Acallamh', ll 4198–201 (= O'Grady, 'Agallamh', i, p. 184, ii, p. 207; Dooley and Roe, *Tales*, p. 124). **154** And yet, ironically, there is one curious gesture in the opposite direction. When the main characters of the narrative

11 Flexibility of time

One of the devices used in *AcS* to further create a sense of distance between the internal time of the narrative, the remembered past of Finn and the *fían*, and the 'real time' of the audience is the author's method of deliberately manipulating time to create a sense of disjointedness.[155] As noted above (pp 28–9), for example, Áed mac Muiredaig appears in the text both as boy and man. Similarly, Caílte, Oisín and their companions are given extra-long lives so that they may survive from the era of Finn, traditionally placed by medieval scholars in the third century AD, until the coming of Patrick in the fifth century.[156]

These attempts by the author to manipulate time, and to create a sense of distance between the events narrated and the audience of the work, are further in evidence in the interactions he constructs between the various categories of characters in the text. The *Acallam* 'unequivocally presents the gulf which divides ordinary mortals from the dwellers in the *síde* in the same terms as that which divides pagans from Christians'.[157] And yet, the gulf between this world and the *síd*, for example, may be bridged with certain characters moving quite freely between both domains. And, typical of other medieval Irish texts, time in the Otherworld does not run parallel to time in this world.[158]

However, the situation is even more complex than is suggested by the episodes described above. As John Carey has argued:

> While we might have a half-unconscious predisposition to associate the text's 'pagan past' and 'Christian present' respectively with myth (to whatever extent modified by transmission and reinterpretation) and with history (to whatever extent idealized and reconstructed), in fact the latter is at least as fabulous as the former.[159]

This final point is readily illustrated as the elastic nature of time in the text is emphasized further by the creative manipulation of historical tradition. Thus, for any audience familiar with Irish history, the naming of Díarmait mac Cerbaill

---

assemble together at Uisnech in the presence of Díarmait mac Cerbaill, king of Ireland, he re-establishes the *fían* (with the agreement of Oisín and Caílte) under the leadership of Donn mac Áeda of Clann Morna: Stokes, 'Acallamh', ll 2277–97 (= O'Grady, 'Agallamh', i, pp 144–5, ii, pp 159–60; Dooley and Roe, *Tales*, pp 70–1). **155** See Nagy, *Conversing with angels and ancients*, p. 321. **156** Discussed in Ó Briain, 'Some material', pp 184–7. **157** Carey, '*Acallam na senórach*: a conversation between worlds', p. 83. **158** For discussion, see Carey, 'Time, space, and the Otherworld'. However, Williams, *Ireland's immortals*, p. 211, would see the Otherworld of the *Acallam* as lacking 'the unsettling dimension common to otherworld(s) elsewhere in medieval Irish literature', including what he refers to as 'uncanny timeslips'. Furthermore, he would see (pp 218–23) the emphasis placed on Bodb Derg and his offspring in the text as troping 'the gradual evanescence of the Túatha Dé Danann' (p. 213). **159** Carey, '*Acallam na senórach*: a conversation between worlds', p. 76.

(†565) instead of Lóegaire mac Néill as the king of Tara to meet with Patrick must have added to the disconnection and sense of dislocation.[160]

Thus, disjointed time that allows for the assembling of protagonists from different eras stands at the heart of the narrative's construction. The Patrician 'past' resonates with the 'present' of the audience to anticipate a bright Christian future, a future which can even accommodate some of the Otherworld denizens, notably Cas Corach. However, for the *fían*, their past is past, even though they receive retrospective Christianization and have the tales of their deeds recorded for the entertainment of future generations.[161] That the text breaks off incomplete in all the manuscript witnesses complements this preoccupation with time; it adds to the sensation of dislocation, as if the text 'could begin, resume, or be put on hold at any point'.[162] Taken together, these various strategies employed by the author all serve to place the audience at some remove from the narrative.

What these various thematic approaches to the *Acallam* illustrate is that a text of this length, complexity and sophistication is amenable to myriad different interpretations and analyses. The themes briefly enumerated and discussed above reflect those that have attracted a body of critical commentary to date. As the text attracts more and more scholarly attention, new areas of study will be identified and developed. As our knowledge of the intellectual climate in Ireland at the time of the composition of the *Acallam* increases, and as our understanding of the date and context of the narrative becomes more nuanced, new research questions and approaches will continue to emerge.[163]

The arrangement of the *Acallam* is also an important issue, as theme and structure in the text are interdependent. It is configured as a frame-tale, which contains within it approximately two hundred briefer narrative sequences, frequently referred to as 'sub-tales' or 'in-tales'.[164] Geraldine Parsons has analysed two of these in detail to illustrate how 'the *Acallam*'s frame-tale contains the information necessary to decode a theme's treatments in the sub-tales'.[165] Consequently, as with the handling of time in the text, the structure facilitates the presentation of various discrete, though interlocking, chronological layers in the narrative. Nevertheless, the text is not just self-referential:

---

160 Ó Briain, 'Some material', p. 185, has suggested that this substitution was effected because Díarmait mac Cerbaill is regularly presented in other sources as 'a preserver of traditional lore'. The place of Díarmait within the *Acallam* and within *fíanaigecht* more generally has been discussed by Ó Macháin, 'Aonghus Ó Callanáin, Leabhar Leasa Móir agus an *Agallamh bheag*', pp 157–60; cf. Dooley and Roe, *Tales*, pp xx–xxi. 161 See Carey, '*Acallam na senórach*: a conversation between worlds', pp 86–9; Schlüter, '"For the entertainment of lords and commons of later times"'. 162 Nagy, 'Compositional concerns', p. 150. 163 The central role of Joseph Falaky Nagy in keeping scholarly interest focused on *Acallam na senórach* over many years is justly recognized; the extent of his contribution is evident from the bibliography to this volume. 164 See Parsons, 'The narrative voice in *Acallam na senórach*', pp 109–10. 165 Parsons, 'The

in the *Acallam*, there is frequently an implied narrative that remains to some degree beyond the text compelling one to draw from other sources for its completion. Whether these sources are traditionally supplied, or even whether there may have been a tradition to supply them in every instance, is a secondary question: the result is a random series of what we may call 'out-tales' in whose creation we imaginatively participate, following out, as we must, the textual allusion which can sometimes amount to what reads as a brief summary supplied by way of etiological explanation. These 'out-tales' function as loosely attached satellites of the larger narrative, itself the aggregate of a fixed series of self-sufficient in-tales.[166]

Thus, the narrative continually reaches out beyond itself; in this, it is similar to earlier examples of *fianaigecht* with 'cross-references to other materials as well as … espousal of themes attested elsewhere in Fenian literature'.[167]

THE ROLE OF THE AUTHOR: LESSONS FROM THE *KALEVALA*?[168]

It is not easy to evaluate the role of the *Acallam*'s author in moulding and fitting together the traditional materials at his disposal, in composing new sections as required, and in shaping the whole to create a fresh and engaging narrative.[169] We are aware of some of the written literature that he may have used,[170] and the forms that it took, but we obviously cannot delineate the rich oral tradition that he had access to. As has been noted with regard to medieval Irish literature in general, it 'had two modes of transmission, the oral and the written, and it is the interaction of these two modes which constitutes the great problem – and in some ways the peculiar interest – of Irish literary history'.[171] To circumvent this difficulty, I believe that a comparative analysis of the achievement of the author of the nineteenth-century Finnish epic, the *Kalevala*,[172] though separated in date from *AcS* by over six hundred years, has much to tell us about how a literate Irishman may have created the *Acallam* so many centuries earlier.

The author of the *Kalevala*, Elias Lönnrot (1802–84), collected most of its constituent elements from traditional rune singers, primarily in Karelia on the

---

structure of *Acallam na senórach*', 13. **166** Ó Coileáin, 'Place and placename', 57. **167** Murray, 'Genre construction: the creation of the *dinnshenchas*', 17. **168** This section benefitted enormously from the close attention of Dr Mícheál Briody. **169** Alter's comment about the role of the author of Genesis 38 could equally be applied to the author of the *Acallam*: 'But even if the text is really composite in origin, I think we have seen ample evidence of how brilliantly it has been woven into a complex artistic whole' (Alter, *The art of Biblical narrative*, p. 20). **170** However, as Nagy, 'Observations on the Ossianesque', 438, has noted, 'about certain important stories within the Fenian canon, as we know them from other sources, the *Acallam* is silent'. **171** Mac Cana, 'Irish literary tradition', p. 35; see Slotkin, 'Medieval Irish scribes', 442. **172** The two most authoritative English translations are those of Magoun and Bosley.

borders of Finland and Russia,[173] in the second quarter of the nineteenth century.[174] As his field notes still survive, it is possible to compare the materials he gathered with the first edition of the epic, which ran to 12,078 lines, and which was published in 1835. Investigation of this publication, now designated the 'Old *Kalevala*', shows us that the bulk of its contents derives from native oral culture. Traditionally, it was understood that Lönnrot's crucial and creative authorial contribution consisted of welding these materials into a narrative whole, providing the links between different sections and modifying the oral materials as necessary in the interests of internal harmony and literary aesthetics. Ever since the late nineteenth century, however, scholars of the *Kalevala* have become more and more aware of the extent of Lönnrot's reworking of the traditional material he collected. Väinö Kaukonen, who from the 1940s has been arguing that the *Kalevala* deserves attention primarily as a literary work, believes that the title of the original volume itself, *The Kalevala, or old Karelian poems about the ancient times of the Finnish people*, is misleading as 'the Kalevala is the continuous poetic work written by Lönnrot and not a collection of old, prehistoric poems'.[175]

Of even more interest in contemplating how long literary pieces are fashioned from a predominantly oral tradition, we may instance the second edition of the *Kalevala*, published in 1849.[176] Lönnrot had collected and received much additional traditional oral poetry in the intervening years, some of which he published in a companion volume called the *Kanteletar* in 1840–1.[177] Working with this new material, Lönnrot expanded and adapted the narrative with the later work now known as the 'New *Kalevala*' which, with its 22,795 lines, is nearly twice as long as the first edition. This has led to it being described as 'Lönnrot's epic'.[178] To illustrate the extent of Lönnrot's role in its construction, one may instance the treatment of the poem *Kilpalaulanta* 'The singing match', recently analysed by David Gay. The two versions recorded in 1825 and 1833 from the epic singer Ontrei Malinen survive as do the texts of the versions created

---

173 The various regions where *Kalevala* poetry was preserved have been enumerated by Kuusi, 'Epic cycles', pp 144–5.   **174** These materials were collected by Lönnrot from among non-literate keepers of the tradition. As a committed Christian, who often preached in his local Lutheran Church and who was chairman of the Finnish Hymnal Committee for the last twenty years of his life (see Pentikäinen, *Kalevala mythology*, pp 72–4), Lönnrot's role and outlook may be compared with that of the author of *AcS*. A central difference, however, is that though thoroughly versed in the folk poetry tradition, Lönnrot came to it from the outside; in contrast, the learned and educated Christian author of the *Acallam* most likely emerged from within the tradition, perhaps even a member of one of the learned families who were keepers and cultivators of native *senchas*.   **175** Kaukonen, 'The Kalevala as epic', p. 161.   **176** Honko, 'The Kalevala as performance', p. 13, has pointed out that in total there are five versions of the *Kalevala*. Alongside the 'New' and the 'Old', there is also an earlier 1833 'Proto-*Kalevala*' of 5,052 lines (not published until 1929), which itself was an expanded form of three independent poems cycles known as the 'Cycle *Kalevala*'. Later, an abridged version of 9,732 lines known as the 'School *Kalevala*' was issued by Lönnrot in 1862.   **177** English translation available in Bosley, *The Kanteletar*.   **178** Honko, 'The Kalevala: the processual

by Lönnrot for the 1833, 1835 and 1849 versions of the *Kalevala*. Gay argues that in the first two versions the poem is modified and lengthened but remains faithful to the original in spirit and in style; however, he believes that the final version of 1849 'moves so far from the traditional sources that they are recognizable only as the inspiration for the poem'; 'what Malinen recited in 30 lines becomes almost 150 lines in the 1849 *Kalevala*'.[179]

The scholarly work done on this corpus of traditional oral poems is not confined to the *Kalevala* and the *Kanteletar* as the Finnish collections of native folk materials are the most comprehensive in the world. Thus, scholars are able to situate the publications of Lönnrot fully within the tradition from which they sprang.[180] Material continued to be collected orally into the twentieth century and some of it shows the influence of earlier written sources; the interplay of the oral and the written is not confined to medieval Ireland but is a universal at different levels in all societies.[181]

The differences between the *Kalevala* and the *Acallam* need to be stressed at the outset. The *Kalevala* is recognized as an epic while, as noted above, the *Acallam* is not; the *Acallam* has epic length but does not qualify on any other grounds. However, what the author of *AcS* did create – a long iterative text, tedious and beguiling in turn, repetitive and inconsistent but with sustained passages of brilliance – has a status as one of the most important narratives from medieval Ireland. Another important difference is that it is the 'New *Kalevala*', the longer and later version, which is taken as the ultimate realization of the epic nature of the traditional materials, so much so that it has almost entirely displaced the earlier versions in both public and scholarly discourse. The opposite is the case with *AcS* with the later versions seen as less culturally significant. Even the preservation in the Franciscan A 4 manuscript of the earlier *Acallam* of many additional readings not found in the other witnesses has been seen as a negative, with Stokes referring to it as 'inferior to the older versions, the scribe or redactor indulging overmuch in those strings of alliterating adjectives which debase the later compositions in Gaelic prose'.[182] Such attitudes have a lot to do with medievalists' attraction to earlier sources rather than later ones, even though

---

view', p. 182. **179** Gay, 'The creation of the *Kalevala*', pp 71, 73. **180** See Bosley, *The Kalevala*, p. xxv: 'Of the material collected, about a million and a quarter lines were eventually published ... There is half as much again unpublished material in the archives of the Finnish Literature Society, and large collections in Russian Karelia and Estonia'. **181** As Mícheál Briody points out to me, though the bulk of Finnish rune poetry was collected in the nineteenth century, some of it has very ancient roots in terms of its metre and aspects of its mythological and cosmological content. Thus, in utilizing the *Kalevala* to elucidate the *Acallam*, we may be rubbing shoulders with a tradition as old, if not older, than *fianaigecht*. For more on these matters, see Kuusi, Bosley and Branch, *Finnish folk poetry epic*, pp 21–77; Siikala, 'Transformations in the Kalevala epic'. **182** Stokes, 'Acallamh', p. xii. Cf. the comments of Dooley and Roe, *Tales*, p. xxxi.

frequently these later sources may be fuller, more coherent and better developed, and may contain additional materials every bit as traditional as the older contents.

As discussed above, the importance of Christianity in the *Acallam* is constantly stressed; in contradistinction, Felix Oinas has argued that Lönnrot's 'editorial practices betray his tendency to reduce the Christian and legendary features, while strengthening both the heathen and the historical-realistic elements'.[183] This is not to say that Lönnrot was not staunchly Christian in his outlook;[184] however, there is no distinct religious viewpoint being advanced in the *Kalevala* in contradistinction to *AcS* where the Church reform agenda colours the treatment of the constituent traditional elements throughout. This lends a contemporary edge to the work produced by the *Acallam*'s author that distinguishes it from the *oeuvre* of Elias Lönnrot. The *Kalevala*'s author's great statement was the actual creation of the epic itself, its existence fanning the flames of nationalism in nineteenth-century Finland – a national epic for a people aspiring to nationhood. The author of the *Acallam*, however, combined native narrative materials with astute social commentary on the ongoing ecclesiastical reform; he was intent on demonstrating that an accommodation between supposedly opposing viewpoints was feasible and beneficial to both.

The integrity of the *Kalevala* has been questioned on the grounds of Lönnrot's qualifications as a rune singer and on whether the transformation he wrought on the oral material at his disposal was allowed for in the tradition. In his defence, Lauri Honko has argued that 'we will understand the different Kalevalas much better if we see in Elias Lönnrot a singer who has a great narrative in mind and performs it when asked to do so'.[185] Though the *Acallam* also represents something new within its cycle of tales, its authenticity has not been questioned because its author was writing from within the culture at a high-water mark in the tradition. Though it would seem less likely, it is possible that our literate Christian author may not have been a member of the caste traditionally charged with the preservation and cultivation of this material and thus felt free to fashion it to its own ends. In this way, he may have been similar to Lönnrot who was steeped in native oral culture, but was not of the culture, and thus may have felt at liberty to innovate in ways in which the traditional culture bearers were reluctant to do.

183 Oinas, *Studies in Finnic folklore*, p. 37. **184** See above n. 174. **185** Honko, 'The Kalevala as performance', p. 14. What Honko is invoking here is the idea of the 'immanent epic' (see Poppe, *Of cycles and other critical matters*, p. 13, following Clover, 'The long prose form', p. 24): 'there can exist a "whole" epic in the minds of performers and audiences alike even though it never be performed as such'. In this reading, therefore, one of Lönnrot's great achievements is the actual performance of the epic.

This short comparative detour to the *Kalevala* and its author is suggestive for those interested in how the author of the *Acallam* may have gone about his work: a literate Christian, most probably a cleric, who valued his native tradition as highly as he did his faith, cultivating material that must have been preserved orally for the most part, fashioning a long narrative that could be added to and supplemented (as happened with the later medieval version);[186] a *literatus* who understood the importance of preserving in written format aspects of a society's oral culture; an artist who shaped and created a literary monument largely out of traditional materials.

In a way, the great difference between the two works is that Lönnrot's *modus operandi* in creating the *Kalevala* can be assessed by modern scholarship while no such avenue is open to scholars interrogating *AcS*. We have only partial insights into its author's methodology, we have only limited information concerning his sources, and we do not have his working materials. Perhaps by examining what Lönnrot accomplished with the *Kalevala*, we might also attain a better understanding of the nature of our author's endeavours and achievements.

CONCLUSIONS

There are as many different interpretations of the *Acallam* possible as there are scholars willing to take up the challenge of engaging with this long and detailed text. It can facilitate numerous approaches to give us a window on particular medieval attitudes towards topics such as the role of the Church, the nature of kingship, the interaction between literacy and orality, and the importance of the Otherworld – to name just a few of the more obvious concerns that have been detailed more fully above. It is undoubtedly a watershed text in Irish: it utilizes older traditional materials but adds much that is new, and it is laced throughout with astute social commentary, 'an untraditional text fashioned in traditional prosimetrum form out of what we generally assume to have been more-or-less traditional sources'.[187]

On the cusp of the Medieval and Early Modern Irish linguistic boundary and the longest text from the period, by breaking off incomplete in all manuscript copies there is a sense in which the narrative appears to be continuous and cyclical, never destined to reach a concluding point.[188] Yet, for all this, *AcS* has a strong internal coherence based on its central conceit: the mutual

---

186 See above, p. 21 n. 4 for details. **187** Ó Coileáin, 'Place and placename', 54. **188** This has prompted Nagy, 'Finn and the Fenian tradition', p. 35, to suggest that perhaps the *Acallam* 'was never supplied with an ending – the ambition to fuse together such disparate elements of medieval Irish culture having defeated any satisfactory attempt on the part of the author to achieve textual closure or thematic resolution'.

accommodation possible between the viewpoint of the Church and the native traditions of secular society. Of course, this accommodation privileges the position of the Church. The literary world presented at the end of the text is one of almost unqualified Patrician hegemony: the old *fénnidi* dead (with only two exceptions); the Túatha Dé Danann about to be banished underground (again with only two exceptions); and the kings subservient and in awe of Saint Patrick's powers. Though the *fían* and the Otherworld do not in any way stand in for native society in the text, they represent that which the Church found hardest to accept in the indigenous culture. The *Acallam* makes a sustained attempt 'to reconcile the irreconcilable',[189] so much so, that one is left with the distinct impression that its author believed he had succeeded in squaring the circle.

---

[189] Nagy, 'Compositional concerns', p. 157.

CHAPTER TWO

The growth of the tradition

From the foregoing analysis of *Acallam na senórach*, and its importance to Irish literary culture, one would be forgiven for assuming that *fianaigecht* was one of the dominant genres of written narrative materials from early medieval Ireland. Nothing could be further from the truth. Aside from eleventh- and twelfth-century texts of reasonable length such as *Tochmarc Ailbe*, *Macgnímrada Finn* and *Fotha catha Cnucha*, and some substantial poems of a similar date preserved in sources such as Duanaire Finn, the early written tradition is fragmentary, disjointed and marginal. As Gerard Murphy states:

> the evidence of ... early references to Fionn goes to show that in the eighth, ninth and tenth centuries, when tales of the Mythological, Heroic, and King cycles were flourishing, Fionn, though well known to men of learning, was confined in their learned lore to short anecdotes connecting him with fighting, hunting, wooing, and otherworld incidents all over Ireland.[1]

Proinsias Mac Cana held a similar view noting that 'the written record of what must have been a vital and prolific literature about Fionn and his *fian* remains quite sparse and sketchy until the eleventh century'.[2]

Furthermore, Fenian tales are noticeable by their absence from the medieval Irish tale-lists, with only five titles that can be definitely connected to the Finn Cycle, two of which were in the original list with a further three added later.[3] This prompted its editor to remark with regard to *fianaigecht* that 'there is little here to suggest a dramatic surge of recognition within the period from *c.*1000 to the first half of the twelfth century'.[4] This situation may be contrasted with the comment in the poem beginning *A Rí Ríchid, réidig dam*, attributed to Gilla in Choimded

---

1 Murphy, *Ossianic lore*, p. 11. **2** Mac Cana, '*Fianaigecht* in the pre-Norman period', p. 83. This is also evident from the appraisal of the early *fianaigecht* corpus presented in Murray, 'Interpreting the evidence'. See also the early survey by Curteis, 'Age and origin of the Fenian tales'. **3** The medieval Irish tale-lists are thought to derive from an earlier list which is no longer extant, the compilation of which is generally dated to the tenth century: see Thurneysen, *Die irische Helden- und Königsage*, p. 24; Mac Cana, *The learned tales*, p. 66; Toner, 'Reconstructing the earliest Irish tale lists', p. 114. For further discussion, see Ní Chonghaile and Tristram, 'Die mittelirischen Sagenlisten'. **4** Mac Cana, *The learned tales*, p. 106. However, if some *fianaigecht* lays were already in existence in the period about AD1000 as has been suggested by Carey ('Remarks on dating', p. 18), this would modify the picture presented here.

úa Cormaic (*fl.* twelfth century?), that there were no less than 120 stories relating to the *fiana* that every genuine *fili* could recite (*sē fichit findscél na fiann foclas cech fili fírían*).⁵ How *fianaigecht* moved from the wings to centre stage by the end of the Middle Irish period remains one of the thorny questions of Irish literary culture. A number of scholars have addressed this issue and I present here, in chronological order of publication, the suggestions advanced to date.⁶

MACNEILL'S RACIAL ORIGIN THEORY

Eoin MacNeill thought the material associated with Finn mac Cumaill to be unique, considering it to be 'the hero-lore of a subject, not of a ruling race' and argued that we only have written fragments from the Old Irish period because it 'was not maintained by the literati of the dominant race'.⁷ The later adoption of the genre by the ruling class he ascribed to the decline in racial distinction between free and unfree over time and to the need of the synthetic historians of the tenth and eleventh centuries to 'associate the conquering people with the traditions of the conquered' in their writing of history; 'the Fenian cycle thus became the property of the whole nation without any burden of learned prestige'.⁸

Many aspects of this scenario command our attention.⁹ That the Finn Cycle never had the prestige of the Ulster Cycle in early medieval Ireland is now accepted doctrine; the extant manuscripts bear ample witness to this state of affairs. However, to move from this uncontested position to asserting that *fianaigecht* was the preserve of subject peoples is more problematic. Marie-Louise Sjoestedt thought it '*a priori* probable … that the dispossessed classes played a part in the elaboration and diffusion of these myths';¹⁰ unfortunately, such opinion must remain in the realm of informed speculation as we have no evidence to support such a view for the early period.¹¹ However, the fact that what seems to be the oldest extant Fenian reference connects Finn with the Laigin,¹² in poetry that closely associates them with the kingship of Tara, would tend to undermine important aspects of MacNeill's arguments.

---

5 *Fian.* p. xxix (= *LL* 18161-2). **6** See the succinct discussion and analysis in Ó Coileáin, 'Place and placename', 48–51. **7** *DF* I, pp xxxii, xxxiv. This situation, if true, would point to the early oral tradition of *fianaigecht* as more the preserve of the common people than of the learned classes; on this question, see Ó Coileáin, 'Place and placename', 47–9. Interesting parallels with the later Ossianic controversy have been drawn by Nagy, 'Observations on the Ossianesque', 439. **8** *DF* I, p. xxxix. **9** An early critical response to MacNeill's theory was published by Nutt, *Ossian and the Ossianic literature*, pp 53–60. **10** Sjoestedt, *Gods and heroes of the Celts*, p. 88. **11** For the later period, however, the fact that original vassal peoples such as 'the Osraige are politically prominent in the tenth century' (see Dooley and Roe, *Tales*, p. xvi) – as are the ecclesiastical families of the Laígis and the Fothairt at a subsequent period – may add some weight to these arguments. It is possible that the rise in prominence of such groups may have had a bearing on the Middle Irish cultivation and dissemination of Fenian compositions. **12** See below, Chapter Six, p. 84.

MURPHY'S THEORY OF CHANGING STYLES

According to Gerard Murphy, *fianaigecht* was marginal to literary endeavours in medieval Ireland because it was not cultivated at the king's court by the *áes dána* but by 'simple folk, seated by their firesides'.[13] He believed that the arrival of the Anglo-Normans after the invasion of 1169 brought about a change in literary taste throughout the country. It is his opinion that the 'new' Ireland which emerged was:

> closer in many ways to contemporary medieval Europe than to ancient Ireland [and that] it is hardly to be wondered at if its stories tend to manifest the same love of marvellous and romantic themes which we find in the contemporary *romans* of France and 'lying sagas' of Iceland.[14]

According to this theory, the emerging taste for the fabulous gave impetus to native stories that also contained these elements; thus, because of the nature of their construction, materials concerning Finn assumed a more central position within the literary canon. Part of Murphy's analysis, which helped confirm him in this opinion, is how these changing tastes can also be traced in the type of foreign material that the Irish *literati* sought to translate into their native language. Before the arrival of the Anglo-Normans, Irish interests ran to translations of quasi-historical texts such as the Alexander story, the destruction of Troy and the civil war of the Romans; later adaptations focused more on adventure stories: typical examples include the labours of Hercules, the quest for the Holy Grail and the travels of Marco Polo.[15] These later adaptations are taken as evidence of a major change in literary taste that had occurred centuries before and which Murphy believed was partly responsible for the rise to prominence of romantic tales and *fianaigecht* lore.[16]

While this theory has much to recommend it, particularly with regard to the cultivation of Finn material in the later medieval period, it has one major drawback: it does not help us to understand the position of *AcS* within the written culture of medieval Ireland. We must assume, unless we believe the composition of the *Acallam* to be completely exceptional, that its existence points to the important cultural position won for *fianaigecht* by the early thirteenth century at the latest; the earlier existence of *Macgnímrada Finn* and *Tochmarc Ailbe* also points in the same direction. Therefore, changing literary tastes in post-Norman Ireland can have had little or nothing to do with the early exponential

---

13 Murphy, *Ossianic lore*, p. 5. **14** Ibid., p. 30. **15** For a succint overview, see Ní Mhaonaigh, 'Classical compositions in medieval Ireland'. **16** See Murphy, 'Irish storytelling after the coming of the Normans', pp 71–4.

growth of the Finn Cycle. We must look elsewhere for the relevant catalysts at this period.

MCCONE'S THEORY: THE CONFLICT WITH THE CHURCH

It is Kim McCone's belief that the major reason the Finn Cycle material was marginalized in the early medieval period was because the Church violently opposed a literature that glamorized *fianas* ('*fían* membership'):

> The evidence points ... to a marked clerical aversion to the *fían* in the early period because it embodied values that were perceived as a threat to the hierarchical, settled society of the *túath* in which the Church had a vested interest. In time this aversion seems to have diminished as the threat of the *fían* receded.[17]

As we shall see in the next chapter, there is a lot of evidence to back up this assertion, particularly the way in which the Church deliberately associated *fianas* with robbery and plundering (*díberg*).[18]

There is a further reason to suppose general antipathy by the Church towards the *fían*: geographical location. Many churches were located along boundaries.[19] It was also in these liminal areas that the *fíana* seem to have been based:[20] thus, it is likely that certain ecclesiastical foundations were living cheek-by-jowl with *fénnidi*.[21] Contention among neighbours with such different outlooks concerning issues such as law and order, hunting and the provision of food must have arisen: literary censorship was one of the potent ways in which the Church could express its disapproval.

BAUMGARTEN'S THEORY OF SOCIETAL RELEVANCE

Attention has been drawn to the paucity of genealogical references to Finn and members of his *fían*.[22] Notwithstanding the fact that the earliest Fenian reference is most likely that preserved in a genealogical poem,[23] Rolf Baumgarten expands on this observation arguing:

> The Fenian tales (though otherwise equal to other Old Irish learned tales) were not of societal relevance, i.e., they had no tribal, historical, genealogical,

---

17 McCone, 'Werewolves, cyclopes, *díberga*, and *fíanna*', 2. **18** For discussion, see Sharpe, 'Hiberno-Latin *laicus*'. **19** The importance of boundaries to the Celtic peoples is demonstrated in Ó Riain, 'Boundary association'. **20** For discussion of the evidence, see FitzPatrick, '*Formaoil na fíann*'. **21** See Dooley and Roe, *Tales*, p. xiii. **22** *EIHM* p. 274. **23** Corthals, 'The rhymeless "Leinster poems"', 121–2. See below, Chapter Six, p. 84.

or religious function. This, possibly, explains their absence ... from the extant type of pre-Norman codices and from the tale-lists. They were treated as equal in other learned functions, e.g. as illustrations in legal ... or lexicographical contexts.[24]

Many peoples claimed association with Finn and his *fían* but – unlike certain characters from the Ulster Cycle, historical tales, and saints' Lives who were treated as nodal figures in genealogies – population groups did not claim descent from these *fénnidi*. This fundamental distinction underpins Baumgarten's idea of lack of societal relevance and bolsters his argument that this may have contributed to the early lack of cultivation of Fenian literature.

FURTHER ARGUMENTS

There is unity of opinion that the Finn Cycle remained peripheral to Irish written culture until ownership of it was assumed by the dominant classes and their *literati* in the later Middle Irish period. Underlying the various viewpoints advanced by previous scholars, is, as Seán Ó Coileáin has observed, the idea that there were

> two parallel traditions in the early period: higher and lower, literary and non-literary; and although the precise motives supplied for the submergence and later emergence of *Fianaigheacht* in literary tradition vary with regard to emphasis they are all clearly related to social status of one kind or another.[25]

This reading encapsulates the overarching concerns of the various opinions advanced thus far. While agreeing to a greater or lesser degree with all of these theories, I feel that there are further reasons for the rapid growth of *fianaigecht* during the eleventh and twelfth centuries, some of which have been alluded to in previous scholarship.

First, from the late Old Irish period onwards, the genre of literature known as *dinnsenchas* 'lore of places' came to the fore and began to be extensively cultivated.[26] As Ann Dooley and Harry Roe have argued: 'it is undeniable that the largest growth [in Fenian tradition] seems to occur in the *Dinnshenchas* ... genre which is rapidly achieving outstanding literary popularity and elaboration in the period between the tenth and the twelfth centuries'.[27] Many of these *dinnsenchas* compositions, both prose and poetry, contain references to Finn and his *fían* and the increase in literary cultivation of *fianaigecht* seems to be expressly bound up with this growth in popularity of *dinnsenchas*.[28]

24 Baumgarten, 'Placenames', p. 16. **25** Ó Coileáin, 'Place and placename', 50. **26** See Herbert, 'Múineadh na fiannaíochta', pp 45–6. **27** Dooley and Roe, *Tales*, p. xv. **28** For discussion, see Murray,

The growth of the tradition

Second, the work of the synthetic historians in the Middle Irish period (mentioned above by MacNeill), and the concomitant growth in an ideology of national identity,[29] seem to have led to further cultivation of *fianaigecht*. Under this new dispensation, the *fían* was reinterpreted as a national standing army under the leadership of Finn mac Cumaill and under the control of king Cormac mac Airt; a societal position was thus found for Finn and his *fían* in this new synthetic history.[30] Proinsias Mac Cana would see the influence going in the other direction, however. Though crediting the synthetic historians with drawing 'the *fiana* in from their characteristic habitat on the margins of society', he believes that this was done in recognition of 'the popularity and widening acceptance of *fianaigecht*'.[31] The disadvantage of Mac Cana's position is that one must then attempt to explain its rising popularity in other ways; crediting the synthetic historians with initiating this development removes this need.

Third, the impact of the Viking invasions and settlements should not be underestimated.[32] These events were to prove of major interest to generations of Irish *senchaide* and tales concerning these invaders found a literary home within the Finn Cycle. Zimmer even believed, mistakenly, that the names Oisín and Oscar had Norse origins, and thought the character of Finn to be modelled on a Norse warrior Kvetil Hvíte, known in Irish as Caittil Finn, defeated in battle in Munster in 857.[33] Christiansen argues that the dominant cycle at the time, the Ulster Cycle, had attained 'full development' before the arrival of the Vikings and that as a consequence by the early medieval period it had an 'inability to develop new stories'.[34] What is clear is that literary tradition concerning the Vikings 'has been almost completely absorbed into … that vast store of song and story centred around Fionn and his men'.[35] This gave further impetus to the expansion of *fianaigecht* literature.

Fourth, it may be argued that part of the reason for the growth of the Finn Cycle was because it became integrated into mainstream learned literary culture by *filid* in the Middle Irish period. Donncha Ó hAodha has shown with regard to the societal interactions between high-status *filid* and lower-status *baird* in the early Middle Irish period that *filid* took over the more popular poetic metres of the *baird* by 'incorporating all the rhyming syllabic metres of the *bard* into the

'The treatment of placenames in the early *fianaigecht* corpus'. Some of the relevant early texts are listed in Murray, 'Interpreting the evidence', pp 48–9 (§§IX, XIV–XVII, XXVIII, XXXIX, XLI–XLII, XLIX, LIV, LXII–LXIV). Most of these are discussed in more detail in *Fian*. pp xxii–xxx. **29** On this topic, see Ó Corráin, 'Nationality and kingship'. **30** See comments of Bruford, 'Oral and literary Fenian tales', pp 32–4. **31** Mac Cana, '*Fianaigecht* in the pre-Norman period', p. 99. **32** See, for example, Byrne, 'The Viking age'. **33** Zimmer, 'Keltische Beiträge III'; 'Ossin und Oskar'. See discussion in Flahive, *The Fenian Cycle in Irish and Scots-Gaelic literature*, p. 66. **34** Christiansen, *The Vikings and the Viking wars*, p. 7. The composition of new Ulster Cycle tales in later periods gives lie to this assertion: see Ó hUiginn, 'Growth and development in the late Ulster Cycle', esp. pp 143–51. **35** Christiansen, *The Vikings and the*

curriculum of the *fili*'.³⁶ Consequently, if we accept the arguments advanced by John Carey, which would push back the dating of some of the Duanaire Finn lays to the same time period,³⁷ assumption of the literary control of this material by *filid*, material which originally belonged to the domain of the *baird*, would help account for the explosion of literary cultivation of *fianaigecht*.

Finally, the very widespread (though fragmentarily attested) nature of the early tradition probably contributed to its expansion. As Finn Cycle material was being cultivated at numerous diverse places throughout Ireland, it was in a position to develop in more than one location in the country. Furthermore, for this rapid expansion to occur, *fianaigecht* must also have been an important and well-cultivated part of the 'oral literature' (*litríocht bhéil*) of medieval Ireland.³⁸ Because modern scholarship finds it difficult to quantify the material created, preserved and transmitted orally, some commentators prefer to dismiss the importance of orality; this position is inherently counter-intuitive and illogical, however, when dealing with a society that was predominantly non-literate.³⁹

CONCLUSIONS

The additional arguments advanced above do not contradict the opinions offered by previous scholars. Indeed, it is my belief that the expanding literary cultivation of *fianaigecht* materials in the Middle Irish period is best explained by a combination of all of these different theories: they are not mutually exclusive, nor can they presume to supply the full picture. The increase and growing importance of Fenian literature from the seventh to the twelfth centuries reflects the emergence of a previously marginalized genre into the literary mainstream.⁴⁰ Though we might debate the precise methods by which such growth came about, it is evident that by the start of the thirteenth century the Finn Cycle was sufficiently vital and productive to sustain the creation of a rich and ambitious narrative such as *Acallam na senórach*.

Viking wars, pp 5–6. Within *fianaigecht* from the late Middle Irish period onwards, Norse warriors (Lochlannaig) most often resemble Otherworld dwellers in their presentation, and are portrayed as inveterate invaders of the land of Ireland, defended by Finn and his *fian*. **36** Ó hAodha, 'The first Middle Irish metrical tract', p. 212. **37** These arguments are summarized in Chapter Eleven, p. 131. **38** For discussion of the term, see Ó Coileáin, 'Place and placename', 54. As Mac Cana, '*Fianaigecht* in the pre-Norman period', p. 82, has observed: 'there was a prolific tradition of *fianaigecht* during the pre-Norman period which was recorded only casually and sparsely – and often belatedly – in the surviving texts'. **39** The various viewpoints are delineated in Ó Coileáin, 'Oral or literary?'. For a recent book-length treatment of the topic, see Johnston, *Literacy and identity in early medieval Ireland*. For specific reference to the Finn Cycle, see Nagy, 'The sign of the outlaw'; idem, 'Oral tradition in the *Acallam na senórach*'; idem, 'Oral tradition and performance in medieval Ireland'. **40** A different interpretation is advanced by Bruford, 'Oral and literary Fenian tales', p. 34: 'Older traditions there certainly were, but it is hard to believe that much of the setting and atmosphere of literary or indeed any *fiannaíocht* as we know it goes back far beyond the *Agallamh*'.

CHAPTER THREE

The nature of the *fían*

Among the theories concerning the paucity of *fíanaigecht* in the early sources just discussed is Kim McCone's argument that Finn Cycle material was kept marginalized in early medieval Ireland because the warrior-bands that this material extolled were still perceived by the Church as a threat to society. It will become clear from a survey of the investigations carried out by Richard Sharpe, McCone and others that the early Church focused more on the *fénnid* '*fían*-member' as a plunderer and marauder rather than as a warrior and hunter.¹

FÉNNID AND DÍBERG(ACH)

The *fénnid* was a member of a *fían*, defined in *DIL* (s.v.) as 'a band of roving men whose principal occupations were hunting and war, also a troop of professional fighting-men under a leader'.² The *díberg(ach)* also operated in groups: as Sharpe makes clear from his study of early hagiographical texts, bands of *díbergaig* are consistently presented as publicly accepting a 'vow of evil' (*votum mali*), as wearing 'devilish signs' (*signa diabolica*) and as being engaged in brigandage, robbery and plundering.³ The author of *O'Mulconry's glossary* makes clear the distinction between the two:

> Dibergg .i. di-bi-arg .i. ni la laochacht adrīmt[h]er ut arg fiann, ar nī bī i cōir laochachtae diultad Dē 7 giallnæ Demuin.⁴
>
> *díbergg*, i.e. di·bi·arg 'non-be-warrior', i.e. it is not with warrior-like behaviour he is enumerated like a *fíana* warrior, for rejection of God and submission to the Devil is not proper to warrior-like behaviour.

---

1 See, for example, Sharpe, 'Hiberno-Latin *laicus*'; McCone, 'Werewolves, cyclopes, *díberga*, and *fíanna*'; idem, 'Hund, Wolf, und Krieger bei den Indogermanen'; idem, *Pagan past*, pp 203–32; idem, 'Cúlra Ind-Eorpach na féinne'; idem, 'The Celtic and Indo-European origins of the *fían*'; Etchingham, *Church organization in Ireland*, pp 302–4; Enright, 'Fires of knowledge'.   **2** McCone, 'The Celtic and Indo-European origins of the *fían*', p. 21, offers the following derivation: '*Fían(n)*, then, was derived, in all likelihood, from *wēd– "wild" by means of a collective suffix *–*nā* and, as such, will have meant something like "wild bunch"'. For earlier suggestions regarding the word's etymology, see *Fían*. pp v–vi; Hamp, 'Goídil, Féni, Gẃynedd', idem, '*Fían*¹³.   **3** Sharpe, 'Hiberno-Latin laicus', 82–6; cf. Nagy, *Conversing with angels and ancients*, pp 295–9. John Carey, however, brings a counter-example to my attention, attested in both *Compert Con Culainn* §7 and *Tochmarc Emire* §22 [here cited] (van Hamel, *Compert Con Culainn and other stories*, pp 7, 29): *Fossuidiur a ndánu 7 a ndíberga*, 'I support their professions and their *díbergaig*'. This would seem to point towards *díberg(ach)* being understood as 'warrior of the tribe' here.   **4** Stokes,

This distinction is not drawn, however, in the very early genealogical poem beginning *Find Taulcha* 'Finn [and] Taulcha' where Finn's *fían* is referred to as a *tuath-cuire* 'an evil band'.[5] To circumvent these issues of terminology and interpretation, Mac Cana has pithily remarked that 'when the *fíana* were good, they were very, very good, but when they were bad, they were *díbergaig* – more or less'; furthermore, he has suggested that

> in the wake of the regularization of the Fian's position as Cormac's army in the learned doctrine of the tenth and subsequent centuries, *fiannas* was identified with the *féinnid*'s activity in the service of the king, *díberg* with his activity as a freelance without the constraints and responsibilities attaching to the king's patronage.[6]

Attractive and all as this suggestion may be, its focus on the period from the tenth century onwards leaves unaddressed the situation regarding the fluctuation in terminology in the Old Irish period.

In the earliest written religious sources, writers tended to conflate the nature of the *féinnid* and the *díberg(ach)*. Thus, in *Apgitir chrábaid*, a text which may be as old as the seventh century,[7] we read:

> Cetharda fo-[f]era fiannas do duiniu .i. to-imairc crícha; to-formaig écraiti; etar-díben sǣgul; ar-cuirethar píana.[8]

> The four things that '*fían*-membership' causes to mankind, i.e., it contracts territories, it increases enmity, it destroys life, it prolongs torments.

This is similar to the treatment of *díberg* 'brigandage' in the Old Irish penitentials where it is enumerated as a sin for which no remission of penance is allowable; homicide, druidism, satire, incest and heresy are also cited in the same category.[9] This unity of presentation of *féinnid* and *díberg(ach)* also features outside of religious sources; in *Togail bruidne Da Derga*, for example, these terms are used interchangeably.[10] We can interpret such unity in two different ways: as reflecting

---

'O'Mulconry's glossary', §309. Though McCone ('Werewolves, cyclopes, *díberga*, and *fíanna*', 4) seems to implicitly regard this entry as a relatively late one (contrasting it with 'older sources') – and despite the absence of a Latin, Greek or Hebrew etymology – nevertheless this entry belongs to MacNeill's first stratum which he thinks 'was compiled not later than the middle of the eighth century, and ... probably as early as the middle of the seventh century': MacNeill, 'De origine Scoticae linguae', 113. **5** Corthals, 'The rhymeless "Leinster poems"', 121–2. Alternatively, but less likely to my mind, *tuath-cuire* might be translated as 'troop of the *túath*'. **6** Mac Cana, '*Fianaigecht* in the pre-Norman period', p. 97. **7** For the most recent discussion of the dating of the text, see Ó Néill, 'The date and authorship of *Apgitir chrábaid*'. **8** Hull, '*Apgitir chrábaid*', 72 §25; cf. McCone, 'Werewolves, cyclopes, *díberga*, and *fíanna*', 5. **9** Binchy, 'The Old-Irish table of penitential commutations', 58–9 §5; cf. Sharpe, 'Hiberno-Latin *laicus*', 82 and McCone, 'Werewolves, cyclopes, *díberga*, and *fíanna*', 3. **10** See, for example, Knott, *Togail bruidne Da*

the original position in earlier texts before a (notional) distinction was introduced, or else as a deliberate manipulation by the Christian scholars who redacted and transmitted these materials and who were concerned to equate *fénnidi* with *díbergaig* in their desire to highlight the evils of *fían*-membership.[11]

THE EVIDENCE OF THE BREHON LAWS

It is in medieval Irish legal sources, however, that we become aware of the social functions that were such an important part of the make-up of the *fían*. For example, in *Di chethairslicht athgabálae* there is mention of *fían*-warriors who are allowed to commit lawful depredations (*fogla dílsi*) and who are entitled to their honour-price.[12] In *Comthóth Lóegairi co cretim*, we read of *fénnidi* involved in the legal process known as distraint (*athgabál*).[13] In the same vein, Kim McCone draws attention to the role in *Críth gablach* of the *fergniae* who seems to have been 'a relatively senior *féindid* who served the king and, under certain circumstances, other members of the *túath* as an enforcer of law and order'.[14] He is described as being *i fochlu fénnid, fergniae fri forngaire ndoirseo*, 'in the *fían*-warrior's seat, a *fergniae* to guard the door'.[15] In the Heptads, one of the *fergniae*'s duties is given as the collection of a woman's bride-price;[16] this was obviously seen as work suitable for *fénnidi* as it is mentioned repeatedly in connection with the *fían* in *Acallam na senórach*.[17]

One of the more interesting ways in which *fían*-warriors are portrayed in the legal sources as having an important societal role is with regard to the prosecution of bloodfeud (*dígal*), which occurred when the payments for unlawful killing were not forthcoming. The best description of this practice is preserved in a section in *Críth gablach*,[18] described by its editor as 'perhaps the most obscure passage in the whole of CG' and by McCone as 'notoriously obscure'.[19] Its exact interpretation is much disputed with differing analyses and translations offered

Derga, Index s.nn. *díberg, dbergach, féindid, fían, fíanlag*; cf. McCone, 'Werewolves, cyclopes, *díberga*, and *fíanna*', 4. For a discussion of the significance of *díberg* in the text, see O'Connor, *The destruction of Da Derga's hostel*, pp 82–103. **11** See above, Chapter Two, p. 53. **12** *CIH* v, p. 1699.19–21 (= Hancock et al., *Ancient laws of Ireland*, i, pp 206–7); cf. *Fían*. p. ix. **13** *LU* l. 9787: *Aithgabáil do fennethaíb*, 'distraint for *fían*-members'. **14** McCone, 'Werewolves, cyclopes, *díberga*, and *fíanna*', 7 (cf. idem, *Pagan past*, p. 212). **15** Binchy, *Críth gablach*, p. 23 §43 (ll 591–2) [incoporating the emendation proposed in McCone, 'Werewolves, cyclopes, *díberga*, and *fíanna*', 7]. See discussion in Nagy, *The wisdom of the outlaw*, pp 256–7. **16** *CIH* iii, p. 795.30 (cf. Hancock et al., *Ancient laws of Ireland*, v, pp 366–7 §LXXVI). See Thurneysen, *Die Bürgschaft*, p. 58 and *DIL* s.v. *fergnia*. **17** For references, see Chapter One, p. 36 n. 112. **18** Binchy, *Críth gablach*, pp 14–15 §25 (ll 358–67): 'Aire échta, cid ara n-eperr? Arindí as n-aire cóicir fácabar fri dénum n-échta i cairddiu co cenn mís do dígail enechruccai túaithe dia ndéntar dédenguin duini. Mani dernat co cenn mís dotíagat for cairdes ná[d] lenat a lepthai cucai anall. Cia rogonat doíni din chairddiu in cóicer cétna[e] ascomren aire échta tara cenn, ná[d] té(i)t tír ná humachaire ind acht lestra[i] lóge bó. Beirthius dano dia n-airitiu(th) sechtair co cenn cairdi [í]ar lín a chomairce 7 a charat. A dám 7 a folog amal airig ndésa dligthir'. **19** Binchy, *Críth gablach*, p. 71; McCone, 'Werewolves, cyclopes, *díberga*,

by MacNeill, Binchy, McCone and McLeod.[20] However, one thing remains clear: the subject of the paragraph, the *aire échta* 'freeman of slaughter', derives his status and payments from his legally sanctioned position as an avenger. In this role, he has command of a 'group of five', a group that is elsewhere mentioned with regard to the prosecution of bloodfeud.[21] McCone has drawn attention to other legal references which make it clear that the *aire échta* was reckoned as a *féinnid*.[22] For example, in *Di chethairslicht athgabálae*, we find the phrase IM CERT CACH FENNEDA 'CONCERNING THE RIGHT OF EVERY FÍAN-MEMBER', which is glossed *.i. cach set dlegar don fennid, uair is amal fer tar crich .i. int airig echta*, 'i.e. every *sét* which is legally due the *fían*-member, because he is like a man beyond the border, i.e. the *aire échta*'.[23] Similarly, in *Bretha crólige*, the word *dibergad* (recte *díbergach*) is glossed *.i. int aire echta*.[24]

Taken together, the legal sources reflect the established role for *fíanas* in medieval Ireland and provide sufficient evidence to show that the *fían* and its members occupied a marginal, though legally regularized, position within society.

COMPOSITION AND HISTORICAL BACKGROUND OF THE *FÍAN*

Though the sources do not make explicit who exactly were enumerated as *féinnidi*, scholarship has focused on two main categories in society from which *fían*-warriors seem to have been drawn.[25] First, many tended to be free-born youths between the ages of fourteen and twenty who had not yet come into their inheritances; these young men became *féinnidi* for a short time until they rejoined regular society as fully-fledged members.[26] In theory, *fían*-membership allowed them to sow their wild oats in a formalized though liminal setting; it removed their potentially disruptive influence from the home; it honed their skills as hunters and fighters; and it also allowed them to forge bonds of loyalty and alliances with people outside of their own kin-group (*fine*). Second, we know that there were *féinnidi* who were more-or-less permanent members of the *fían*. Some of these may have been men, like Finn, who were the sons of *féinnidi*; some may have had unfree or semi-free status from birth; while others simply may have

and *fíanna*', 7. **20** MacNeill, 'Ancient Irish law: the law of status or franchise', 297–8; Binchy, *Críth gablach*, pp 70–1; McCone, 'The Celtic and Indo-European origins of the *fían*', p. 17 (cf. McCone, *Pagan past*, pp 211–12); McLeod, 'The lord of slaughter', pp 107–11 esp. p. 110. **21** See Murray, 'A Middle Irish tract', p. 255 §9: *Trían do c[h]rú c[h]óiccir ind*, 'a third of the *cró* for five there'. The 'third' is a reference to 'the third of enforcement' (*trían tobaig*); cf. Kelly, *A guide to early Irish law*, p. 126. Mention is also made of this 'group of five' in *Tecocsa Cormaic* §8.5 (Meyer, *The instructions*, p. 18). **22** McCone, 'Werewolves, cyclopes, *díberga*, and *fíanna*', 7–8; cf. idem, *Pagan past*, pp 211–12. **23** *CIH* ii, p. 95.24–9. **24** Binchy, 'Bretha crólige', 40 §51. **25** See discussion in Nagy, *The wisdom of the outlaw*, pp 20–1. **26** The well-known comment from *Tecocsa Cormaic* §31 expresses this succinctly: *fénnid cách co trebad* 'everyone is a *fénnid* until acquisition of land' (Meyer, *The instructions*, p. 46). However, as Seán Ó Coileáin has pointed out to me, this maxim could also be translated as 'Everyone is a champion until put to the test'.

The nature of the fían

preferred this way of life. In the general run of things, these men were not expected to inherit and re-join regular society;[27] however, it is probable that formal societal warrior positions, such as the *fergniae* discussed above, would have been drawn from this group.

The type of young man just mentioned who had not yet come into his inheritance was categorized in Irish law as a *macc beoathar* 'son of a living father', a category further subdivided in three: (i) *macc té* 'warm son' who depends on his father and cannot make independent contract; (ii) *macc úar* 'cold son' who fails in his filial duty and thus loses the legal support and backing of his father and kin; (iii) *macc ailte* 'reared son' who is granted a large measure of independence by his father and who may farm land and marry. Thus, either the *macc té* (with the permission of his father) or the *macc úar* (outside of his father's control) would have been suitable candidates for *fíanas*.

The *macc úar*, however, would have had no expectation of receiving any inheritance if he had been proclaimed by his father and would have belonged among those who were more-or-less permanent members of the *fían*. Kuno Meyer believed that:

> They were often men expelled from their clan (*éclaind*), or landless men (*díthir*), sons of kings who had quarrelled with their fathers, men proclaimed, or men who seized this means to avenge some private wrong by taking the law into their own hands.[28]

However, a different interpretation of the terms *éclann* and *díthir* has been proposed by Marie-Louise Sjoestedt, and in this she has been followed by Kim McCone. She argues that when a candidate is accepted as a *fénnid*:

> he breaks all connections with his own clan ... He is *écland* ('clanless'), and has no other kindred, no social group save the *fían* ... The depredations that he does ... are in fact necessary to his subsistence, for as an *écland* he is also *díthir* ('landless').[29]

In this scheme of things, the youth is only temporarily clanless and landless until such time as he receives his inheritance and re-joins his kin-group. McCone finds support for this interpretation in his analysis of the term *óenchiniud*, traditionally

---

27 A convenient discussion of the structure of medieval Irish society is to be found in Kelly, *A guide to early Irish law*, esp. pp 1–16. For what follow, see ibid., p. 81.   **28** *Fian.* p. ix. He cites a reference from *Fochond loingse Fergusa meic Róig* in support (*LL* v, ll 33429–30): *Tanaic dias oac fene do Emain Macha. Da écland da threnfer*, 'Two *fían*-warriors came to Emain Macha. Two kinless ones, two champions'.   **29** Sjoestedt, *Gods and heroes of the Celts*, pp 83–4.

translated as 'sole offspring'. He would rather see the *óenchiniud* as 'a junior member of the *fían* legally cut off from his kin only until such time as he inherited sufficient wealth to become a full member of the *túath*',[30] and has elsewhere pointed to the depiction of the *óenchiniud* as a warrior which would tend to back up this reading of the evidence.[31]

McCone has also argued convincingly in a number of publications that the make-up and structure of the *fían* reflect the survival in Ireland of the *Männerbund*, the organization of young male warriors into groups, a phenomenon that is attested in various cultures throughout the world, and which was obviously an important part of the structure of Indo-European society.[32] Ann Dooley and Harry Roe have further speculated that:

> it is possible that Celtic warbands formed the basis of the expanding military profile of La Tène Celts in Europe from the fifth century on, and that their experience as mercenaries ... provided a powerful incentive to the continuance of such institutions.[33]

Such continuance of practice into medieval Ireland might be suggested by the evidence. McCone has seen the *fían* as superseding the earlier term *cuire*, which he traces back to Proto-Indo-European **koṛios*, defined as 'a vagabond sodality, mostly consisting of wolfish youths';[34] interestingly, as previously noted, the earliest mention of Finn refers to his *tuath-cuire* 'evil band'.[35] Furthermore, as Peter McQuillan has pointed out, in early Irish dynastic poetry, genealogies and annals, the references to *fíana* and *fénnidi* are to their overseas raiding expeditions.[36]

There are also female *fían*-members, *banfénnidi*, attested in the literature. The most famous of them all is Scáthach Búanann (also known as Búanann), the warrior responsible for completing the martial training of Cú Chulainn.[37] Similarly, Finn is reared and trained as a warrior by two *banfénnidi*.[38] Other female *fían*-warriors include Creidne,[39] Findabair,[40] and, most famously, Ness

---

30 McCone, 'Werewolves, cyclopes, *díberga*, and *fíanna*', 11.   **31** McCone, *Pagan past*, p. 205.   **32** For references, see above, p. 57 n. 1.   **33** Dooley and Roe, *Tales*, p. xi.   **34** McCone, 'The Celtic and Indo-European origins of the *fían*', pp 21–2.   **35** Corthals, 'The rhymeless "Leinster poems"', 121–2.   **36** McQuillan, 'Finn, Fothad, and *fían*', 5–7. Examples include the genealogical poem beginning *Find Taulcha* (Corthals, 'The rhymeless "Leinster poems"', 121–2), and *Scél asa mberar combad hé Finn mac Cumaill Mongán* (White, *Compert Mongáin*, pp 73–4, 79–81).   **37** See Meyer, 'The oldest version' and Miller, 'The role of the female warrior in Early Irish literature', pp 155–237, for the earliest telling of this tale. In *Sanas Chormaic*, she is called *mumi na fían* 'the foster mother of the *fíana*' and further described as *daghmáthair ac foircetal gaiscid do fíanuib*, 'a good mother for teaching weaponry to *fíana*': Meyer, 'Sanas Cormaic', p. 11 §104 (= O'Donovan, *Sanas Chormaic*, p. 17). See *DIL* s.v. *Búanann*. Some texts treat Scáthach and Búanann as one character; others as two. Perhaps they were in origin two separate characters who were sometimes merged.   **38** See Nagy, *Wisdom of the outlaw*, pp 101–4.   **39** *Fían.* pp xi–xii (trans. Ní Dhonnchadha, 'Creidne the she-warrior').   **40** *LL* i, ll 2119–20: *Findabair ... sech ba femen ba fennid*,

mother of Conchobur mac Nessa.[41] However, mentions of *banfénnidi* seem to be confined to literary sources and, as noted by Máirín Ní Dhonnchadha, 'women's active role in warfare was in reality extremely limited'.[42]

CONCLUSIONS

Alwyn and Brinley Rees point to 'the intense pleasure found in a life shared with members of one's own special group' as a distinguishing feature of *fían*-warriors, contrasting this with 'the harsh individualism and clamorous rivalry which characterizes so many of the Ulster stories'.[43] Furthermore, there is additional information in the literary sources concerning the attributes of a good *fénnid*, with a particularly appealing account given in *Áirem muintire Finn*.[44] The author of this humorous narrative, which probably dates to *c.*1200, expected prospective *fénnidi* to be prime poets, amazing athletes and wondrous warriors before actually joining the *fían*. Outside of this romanticized telling, however, it is clear from the sources examined that *fíanas* was a regulated institution in medieval Ireland, one which conferred benefits both on the warriors involved and on society that could call on the martial abilities of the *fían* in times of need. Though aspects of this institution may be traced through evidence concerning the Continental Celts back to an Indo-European past, it was the Church's role in depicting this warrior-band that primarily shaped its presentation in early medieval literary sources in Ireland. An understanding of the historical *fían*, and its conceptualization in the literature, forms an essential backdrop to the study of *fíanaigecht*.

'Findabair … though she was a woman was a *fénnid*' or 'Findabair … who was both a woman and a *fénnid*'. **41** Meyer, 'Anecdota from the Stowe MS. no 992', pp 174, 179 (= *CHA* §73 p. 60). **42** Ní Dhonnchadha, 'The semantics of *banscál*', 31. **43** Rees and Rees, *Celtic heritage*, p. 63. **44** O'Grady, 'Airem muintiri Finn'; for analysis of such initiation practices, see Nagy, 'Fenian heroes and their rites of passage'. In a recent thesis, as yet unpublished, Josephine O'Connell has made a strong case that this tale's constituent elements (titled respectively *Airem muinntari Finn* 'The enumeration of the household of Finn' and *Anmonna oesa fedma Find* 'The names of the retinue of Finn') should be considered as distinct narratives focused on a similar subject matter.

CHAPTER FOUR

The conflict between Finn and Oisín

'The quarrel between Finn and Oisín', provisionally dated to the second half of the eighth century, is one of the earliest *fianaigecht* texts extant.[1] It consists of a poem of sixteen quatrains in the form of a riddling dialogue between Finn and Oisín with a short prose preface setting out the context of the poem. The introduction informs us that Finn had spent a year searching Ireland for his son but Oisín had been avoiding his father because of some unspecified quarrel between the two.[2] When Finn finally finds him they nearly come to blows and it is said that Oisín does not immediately recognize his father. During the contention of words between the two, however, recognition dawns on Oisín, combat is avoided and father and son are reconciled with words of mutual respect:

> Oisín: A ṡenláich, dígnais etir ócbadu,
> ní bu accobar do chrád manip ág ar óclachu.
>
> Find: Inna hule immalle ní bu messa doïb de,
> dia mbem inar comardus ó ascomartmar ar nglé.

Oisín: 'Oh ancient hero, you are not wont to be among youths; I had no desire to harm you if you had not been boastful against warriors'.

Finn: 'Taking all these things together, none is any the worse for it, if we are on the same level, since we have settled our dispute'.

THE 'FATHER-AND-SON COMBAT'

Attention has been drawn in previous scholarship to the international theme, known as the 'father-and-son combat', which it has been suggested may underlie this text.[3] This theme, also known as 'Sohrab and Rustam' after the famous Persian legend concerning the conflict between Rustam and his son, Sohrab, is

---

[1] Edited in *Fian.* pp 22–7 (with addenda and corrigenda published in *ZCP* 8, 599 and *RC* 33, 98). For an alternate interpretation of stanza 3, see Hull, 'The quarrel'. [2] In this quarrel, Oisín and Finn refer to each other as *geilti*, arguing whether this is a more suitable appellation for an old or young man (*Fian.* pp 26–7). The figure of the *geilt* reappears in *fianaigecht* literature, but this would seem to be the earliest reference. [3] *Fian.* pp 22–3; Cross, 'A note on "Sohrab" and "Rustum" in Ireland', 178. The Welsh evidence has been briefly discussed by Jackson, *The international popular tale*, pp 70–1.

found in the *Shahnameh* 'Book of kings', authored by the poet Ferdowsi.[4] This was popularized in English in the nineteenth century with the publication of Matthew Arnold's long narrative poem on the topic.[5] This theme is also well known from the fragmentary German poem, the *Hildebrandslied*, concerning the encounter between Hildebrand and his son, Hadubrand,[6] and – among other sources in medieval Ireland[7] – from the conflict between Cú Chulainn and his son, Connlae, *Aided óenfir Aífe*.[8] The fourth reflex of this theme regularly included in comparative studies is the Russian oral epic narrative poem (*bylina*) concerning Il'ya of Murom's slaying of his son, Sokol'nik 'Falcon'.[9] Efforts have been made recently to expand the comparative corpus with Anna Ranero's inclusion of the tale of the combat between Arjuna and his son, Babhruvāhana, from the Sanskrit epic the *Mahābhārata*,[10] and Dean Miller's adducing of additional comparanda, some of them partial, from Ossetian, Old French, Norse-Icelandic and Armenian traditions.[11] Many of these parallels were previously noted by Murray Potter.[12]

The dating of the four central traditions to contain this theme (sketched in the previous paragraph) is of considerable interest. The most recent is that of Il'ya and Sokol'nik with 'about forty variants collected in the field during the last two hundred years' though the original lay 'is thought to be about fourteenth-century'.[13] Then there is Ferdowsi's 'Sohrab and Rustam' which dates to c.AD1000.[14] Next is the text of *Aided óenfir Aífe* which is generally dated to c.AD900.[15] Finally, there is

---

4 See Khaleghi-Motlagh, Khatibi and Omidsakar, *Abul'l-Qasem Ferdowsi. The Shahnameh*. A convenient text and translation of the 'Sohrab and Rustam' episode is to be found in Clinton, *The tragedy of Sohrab and Rostam*. **5** 'Sohrab and Rustum: an episode' in Arnold, *Poems*, pp 5–50. **6** Text in Braune (ed.), *Althochdeutsches Lesebuch*, pp 78–9 (and in multiple reprints since). Translation in Bostock, *A handbook on Old High German literature*, pp 44–7. See de Vries, 'Das Motiv des Vater-Sohn-Kampfes im Hildebrandslied'. **7** Cross, 'A note', 179–80, also points to the attestation of this theme in *Cath Maige Tuired* (ed. Gray) and *Fled Dúin na nGéd* (ed. Lehmann). Father and son relationships in medieval Irish tradition are further explored by Gray, '*Cath Maige Tuired*: myth and structure', 9–13 (vol. 19). **8** Meyer, 'The death of Conla'; van Hamel, *Compert Con Culainn and other stories*, pp 9–15. Translations conveniently available in Cross and Slover, *Ancient Irish tales*, pp 172–5 (repr. of Meyer's translation); Kinsella, *The Tain*, pp 39–45; Gantz, *Early Irish myths and sagas*, pp 147–52. For discussion, see d'Arbois de Jubainville et al., *L'épopée celtique en Irlande*, pp xxxii–xxxvi, 51–65 esp. 63–5; de Vries, 'Le conte irlandais Aided óenfir Aífe'; Findon, *A woman's words: Emer and female speech in the Ulster Cycle*, pp 84–106; Ó hUiginn, *Marriage, law and Tochmarc Emire*, pp 17–19; McCone, 'The death of Aífe's only son and the heroic biography'. **9** Plot summarized by Hatto, 'On the excellence of the "Hildebrandslied"', 826. A convenient English rendition of one version of the *bylina* is to be found in Hapgood, *The epic songs of Russia*, pp 206–13: 'Ilyá of Múrom and Falcon the hunter'. For discussion, see Miller, 'Cú Chulainn and Il'ya of Murom'; for various traditions concerning Il'ya, see Oinas, 'Russian byliny', pp 241–3. **10** Ranero, '"That is what Scáthach did not teach me"'; eadem, 'An old Indo-European motif revisited: the mortal combat between father and son'. **11** Miller, 'Defining and expanding the Indo-European *Vater-Sohnes-Kampf* theme'. As John Carey reminds me, Arthur's combat with Modred, which results in the latter's death, evolves into a father-son combat but does not seem to have been one originally. **12** Potter, *Sohrab and Rustum*. **13** Hatto, 'On the excellence of the "Hildebrandslied"', 826. **14** For the author, see Shapur Shahbazi, *Ferdowsi: a critical biography*. **15** Meyer, 'The death of Conla', 113; van Hamel, *Compert Con Culainn and*

the *Hildebrandslied*, the sole fragmentary copy of which is found on two leaves from an early ninth-century manuscript. John Knight Bostock argues that it 'was perhaps composed in Lombardy in the seventh or eighth century',[16] while Frederick Norman believes that 'the poem could have been current at a Langobard court any time after 600. It must have been produced well before 700'.[17] Thus, it is the oldest written attestation of the four.[18] All of these dates pertain solely to the extant literary texts; we have no way of establishing how long these traditions may have been extant orally or in earlier written versions that no longer survive, or even how pertinent dating concerns are to the whole issue.[19]

Kuno Meyer thought it most likely that the theme of the 'father-and-son combat' originated in Persia, made its way westwards to the Goths and other Germanic tribes, coming to Ireland through Anglo-Saxon influence 'during the seventh or early eighth century'.[20] Tom Peete Cross also subscribed to this theory, seeing a Persian origin for the theme, with subsequent transmission to and cultivation by the Germans, before it 'found its way into Irish literature from an Anglo-Saxon source'.[21] The dating of the various sources set out above adds no weight of support to this scenario; however, the 'supposition that the text [of the *Hildebrandslied*] was written at the abbey of Fulda, an English foundation with continuing English connections'[22] does give some support to the second part of the theory of Meyer and Cross that the narrative pattern would have been known in Anglo-Saxon England which could have been the source of its transmission to Ireland. Ultimately, however, though inherently possible, this theory remains in the realm of informed speculation.[23]

---

other stories, p. 9. For discussion, see Thurneysen, *Die irische Helden- und Königsage*, pp 403–12 §33. **16** Bostock, *A handbook on Old High German literature*, p. 81. **17** Norman, 'Hildebrand and Hadubrand', 334 (repr. in idem, *Three essays on the Hildebrandslied*, p. 48). **18** The tale of the combat between Arjuna and his son, Babhruvāhana, from the *Mahābhārata*, is obviously older but seems to differ substantially from these four traditions. For example, the son kills the father (which Ranero refers to as an 'inverted version') but he is brought back to life by Ulūpī, the serpent princess; she subsequently reveals that she staged the conflict to save Arjuna from an old curse. Compare the plot summaries provided by Ranero, '"That is what Scáthach did not teach me"', 246–7, and eadem, 'An old Indo-European motif revisited', pp 125–7. However, Ranero emphasizes the important supernatural elements in both stories, and the fact that of all the tales that might be thought to contain the Indo-European theme of the 'father-and-son combat', *Aided óenfir Aífe* and the *Mahābhārata* are the only two in which the heroes have divine ancestry. **19** I am thinking here of the observation of Jackson, *The international popular tale*, p. 15, regarding the distribution of the story known as 'The two brothers'. Though hundreds of versions have been collected in Europe, the 'fundamental kernel of the story was known already as early as about 1250BC in Egypt in the tale of Anupu and Bitiu which exists in a papyrus of that date'. However, Thompson, *The folktale*, p. 275, argues that 'though this tale [of Anupu and Bitiu] has some resemblance to the present day European story of The Two Brothers, the plot is essentially different and they probably do not have direct connection'. Thompson believes instead (p. 31) that 'The Two Brothers seems ... to have arisen in western Europe and very likely in northern France'. **20** *Fian*. p. 22. Thurneysen, *Die irische Helden- und Königsage*, p. 403, also suggests an external origin for this motif, with cultivation in Ireland beginning in the eighth century. **21** Cross, 'A note', 182. **22** Bostock, *A handbook on Old High German literature*, p. 75. **23** In *EIHM* p. 62 n. 3, T.F. O'Rahilly states that there is 'no justification' for this view; however,

Though this international theme is generally known as the 'father-and-son combat',[24] Dean Miller has cogently argued that its most important aspect is the death of the son, and not the actual conflict itself, because 'the normative non-generative sexual role of a hero is thus reset or re-established when he kills his own unwanted progeny' ensuring that his martial gifts 'are only temporarily transmitted to any son or heroic heir and then they are won back from that slain heir'.[25] The other defining characteristic of this combat is what Arthur Hatto has called the 'good' father slaying the 'good' son; there is no previous enmity between the two and both fulfil societal roles as warriors.[26] The important point is that the theme we are trying to isolate is not that contained in multiple examples of fathers and sons in combat but just those tellings where the father slays the son. Crucial to this is an analysis of the son's killing by the father as a regressive step for society, 'an aborting of forward temporal movement'.[27] In the case of *Aided óenfir Aife*, for example, society is seen to suffer as a result, as the Ulaid have no successor to Cú Chulainn. As Joan Radner has perceptively argued:

> thematically, the Ulster Cycle as a whole tends to present the tragic breakdown of those relationships on which early Irish society was founded: the relationship between host and guest, between kindred, between fosterbrothers, between men and women, between lords and clients and kings and overkings, between the human worlds and the gods.[28]

Thus, the theme of the 'father-and-son combat' fits very well within the presentation of the wider Ulster Cycle, and this appropriateness may well have inspired its usage.[29] Indeed, this context adds great pathos to the final scenes in *Aided óenfir Aife* when Connlae takes leave of the Ulster heroes, telling what great deeds he could have achieved in their honour.[30]

he never returned to the topic to present his arguments and evidence.   **24** Thompson, *Motif index of folk literature*, N 731.2: 'father-son combat'.   **25** Miller, 'Defining and expanding the Indo-European *Vater-Sohnes-Kampf* theme', 307 and 321.   **26** Hatto, 'On the excellence of the "Hildebrandslied"', 820.   **27** Miller, 'Defining and expanding the Indo-European *Vater-Sohnes-Kampf* theme', 320.   **28** Radner, '"Fury destroys the world"', 47.   **29** However, it is important to note that father-son conflicts which result in the death of the son are not confined to the Ulster Cycle. For example, the death of the physician, Míach, at the hands of his father, the Túath Dé Danann physician, Dían Cécht, in *Cath Maige Tuired* (ed. Gray, 32–3 §§33–5) seems to have been provoked by Míach 'implicitly condemning his father's skill by surpassing it' (Gray, *Cath Maige Tuired*: myth and structure', 9 [vol. 19]); this parallels Connlae's exhibition in front of the Ulaid which seems to demand a response from Cú Chulainn. With regard to Dían Cécht's killing of Míach, Gray (ibid.) notes that 'there is no suggestion that Dían Cécht's response is excessive'. The same might also be said about Cú Chulainn's slaying of Connlae; no member of the Ulaid presumes to criticize Cú Chulainn for his behaviour.   **30** Meyer, 'The death of Conla', 120–1: '*Dīa mbeinn-sea etraib co cend cōic mbliadan, no silfind-se firu in betha reimib for cach leth 7 congabthai rīghi co Rōim*, 'If I were among you to the end of five years, I should vanquish the men of the world before you on every side, and you would hold kingship as far as Rome'.

There is no doubting the structural similarities between the stories of Il'ya/Sokol'nik, Rustam/Sohrab, Cú Chulainn/Connlae, and Hildebrand/Hadubrand as they contain many elements in common, viz:

- the father leaves when the child is very young or before he is even born;
- the father gives the mother a token for the boy to wear: for Sohrab an amulet; for Connlae a thumb-ring; for Sokol'nik a golden ring. This element is not present in the *Hildebrandslied* though, in their meeting, Hildebrand tries to give Hadubrand spiral rings as tokens of favour;
- the father and son are thrown together without explicit recognition;
- an argument ensues;
- identities are revealed, at least partially: Il'ya reveals his identity to his son which in many versions leads Sokol'nik to kill his mother; Rustam acknowledges in speech that he recognizes Sohrab as his son; Cú Chulainn is advised by his wife, Emer, in a *roscad* that the foe he is going to face is his son, Connlae, but Cú Chulainn will not accept a woman's counsel;[31] Hadubrand refuses to accept Hildebrand's word that he is his father, believing him to be long dead;
- a fight ensues culminating in the death of the son: the *Hildebrandslied* breaks off, however, before the outcome of the battle is known;[32]
- the son's identity is then revealed by means of the token originally bestowed by the father.

Thematically and structurally, there must be some underlying shared tradition between these sources. The detailed correspondences between the surviving versions rule out the possibility of polygenesis. The question (as posed above) is whether we see this shared tradition as being transmitted to Ireland via Anglo-Saxon England, or whether we would be more inclined to see these tales as reflexes of an earlier Indo-European theme surviving in distinct Indo-European cultures.[33] Modern scholarship would tend to favour the latter scenario.

31 Findon, 'A woman's words: Emer versus Cú Chulainn in *Aided óenfir Aífe*', p. 145n., draws attention to the possibility that 'the *roscada* containing Emer's warning and Cú Chulainn's response were added later to *Aided óenfir Aífe*. Though this is worth pursuing further, these comparanda would render this hypothesis less likely. In *A woman's words: Emer and female speech in the Ulster Cycle*, p. 91, Findon notes that the other extant summaries of this narrative 'all omit Emer's intervention and speech. None of them mentions Emer at all, and since she alone seems to be able to discern Connla's true identity, all of the summaries assume that Cú Chulainn is ignorant and therefore not guilty of the crime of *fingal* [kinslaying]'. **32** See Bostock, *A handbook on Old High German literature*, p. 47: 'It is almost universally assumed that the poem had a tragic ending – the death of either the father or the son, or possibly both'; this position is supported by later works in the wider Germanic tradition which draw on this earlier material. However, Bostock notes that 'it is conceivable, in view of the near-perfect symmetry of the extant text, that nothing is lost, and that the poem treated an episode in a well-known story'. **33** Alfred Nutt argued for the second option in his

In a recent study, another twist has been added to the tale. Evidence has been assembled to show that the 'father-and-son combat' is found not just in twenty-five episodes in sources from twelve different Indo-European languages, but also in fourteen episodes from eight Arabic folk-epics. The conclusion of this study is worth quoting in some detail. It would see the theme of the 'father-and-son combat' as:

> an oral-compositional typescene in the Indo-European and Middle Eastern *Kulturbund*. The typescene consists of a 'core' scenario that is notably lacking in details: a heroic father begets a son on an exogamous mother, is separated from him during his early childhood, but meets him as a youth and fights him unawares. In the early Indo-European versions of this story, the identity of the son was not disclosed until after the father had dealt him a mortal blow, but in later Indo-European versions, and in all Arabic versions, the father-son combat ended in mutual recognition and reconciliation.[34]

Demarcation of the episodic nature of this theme suggests that the issues concerning the dating of the Cú Chulainn version of the 'father-and-son combat' may need to be revisited. While ascribing *Aided óenfir Aífe* to c.AD900 remains unchallenged, the dating of the oldest version of the related tale, *Tochmarc Emire*, is relevant here. Jimmy Miller has extended the work of Kuno Meyer and has assembled detailed evidence to back up Meyer's assertion that this text dates to the eighth century.[35] The first episode in our theme (the father leaves when the child is very young or before he is even born) is present in this version of *Tochmarc Emire*; the second (the father gives the mother a token for the boy to wear) may be present because what Cú Chulainn leaves for his unborn son is not a physical token but his name;[36] these factors may point towards the theme being present in Ireland at that time. Thus, we may prefer to understand *Tochmarc Emire* as a narrative tradition that naturally attracted the international theme of the 'father-and-son combat', which was subsequently realized fully in the tale we know as *Aided óenfir Aífe*. As we shall see below, however, a similar interpretation cannot be advanced with regard to the existence of this theme within the Finn Cycle.

'Problems of heroic legend', p. 128. **34** Anderson and Norouzalibeik, 'Father-son combat: an Indo-European typescene and its variations', 319. **35** Meyer, 'The oldest version of *Tochmarc Emire*', 438–9; Miller, 'The role of the female warrior in Early Irish literature', pp 160–72. **36** The earliest text to mention the thumb-ring and the *gessa* upon Connlae (not to yield to a single man, not to reveal his name to a single man, nor to refuse combat to a single man) is *Aided óenfir Aífe*; these elements are also present in the later version of *Tochmarc Emire*: see van Hamel, *Compert Con Culainn and other stories*, 55 §76.

APPLICATION OF THE THEME OF 'FATHER-AND-SON COMBAT' TO THE CONFLICT BETWEEN FINN AND OISÍN

The artificial nature of the confrontation between Finn and Oisín has justly been commented upon; this poem contains the only reference in the early tradition to disunity between Finn and Oisín. Kuno Meyer believed that this artificiality was the result of applying the Indo-European motif to a situation where it did not naturally belong with resultant consequences: 'the tragic issue was not adaptable to the Ossianic saga. So a humorous and burlesque treatment is substituted, such as we find occasionally in the literature of other nations'.[37] However, the supporting example cited by Meyer, surviving in the medieval French *chanson de geste*, *Macaire*, bears no resemblance to the detailed thematic structure outlined above.[38] Tom Peete Cross followed Meyer on this point arguing:

> Though it has been assumed that 'The Quarrel between Finn and Oisín' is merely an adaptation of the story as told of Cú Chulainn and Conlai, the occurrence of a similar burlesque and humorous treatment in versions outside Ireland render this hypothesis doubtful.[39]

Thus, he argues for two separate Irish treatments of a theme borrowed from abroad, both representing permissible variations present in other cultures. But the Middle English texts Cross draws attention to, representing 'burlesque and humorous treatment in versions outside Ireland', are in no way similar to the detailed theme of the 'father-and-son combat' that we have examined. The only consistent elements in texts such as *Sir Eglamour of Artois*, *Sir Triamour* and *Sir Degare*, which resonate with our international motif, are the facts that the fathers and sons are thrown together in combat situations without recognition.[40] Further variants of a 'father-and-son combat' found in other Middle English romances, such as *Reinbrun: Gij sone of Warwicke*, *Ipomédon* and *Torrent of Portyngale*, do not compare in detail with the treatment of the broader theme.[41]

Although material connected with the 'father-and-son combat' was obviously known in Ireland by the end of the Old Irish period at the latest, it does not seem to me to have informed the *fíanaigecht* poem concerning the conflict between Finn and Oisín, notwithstanding the assertions of previous scholars. It is worth emphasizing that this text predates the extant versions of Il'ya and Sokol'nik, the

---

37 *Fian.* pp 22–3. **38** See discussion in Potter, *Sohrab and Rustum*, pp 82–3. **39** Cross, 'A note', 178. **40** Severs, *A manual of the writings in Middle English, 1050–1500*, vol 1, pp 124–5 §79, 129–30 §82 and 140–1 §92. Cf. Hibbard, *Medieval romance in England*, pp 274–8, 283–9, 301–5. **41** For details, see Hibbard, *Medieval romance in England*, pp 140–2, 224–30, 279–82. However, these Middle English sources emphasize why Burrow, *Medieval writers and their work*, p. 8, from his standpoint as a Professor of English, made the observation that 'one of the most striking features of the European Middle Ages (after

Shahnameh, and *Aided óenfir Aife*. When we re-examine the central elements of the international theme outlined above, we find that with the exception of the father and son being thrown together without recognition (on one side in this case) and the ensuing argument, the Fenian text does not conform to any other aspect of the underlying story pattern. Furthermore, with the international motif, the son and father are either thrown together or the son comes to seek his father; the canonical examples do not show us the father seeking the son as happens in 'The quarrel between Finn and Oisín'. To argue that a father-son conflict, particularly one which does not result in the death of the son, could not arise in any other context in the literature of a nation is patently absurd; it is so obviously such a major issue in life as well as in literature.

The act of removing this international motif as underlying prop from our *fianaigecht* composition has one detrimental consequence: how else to account for the story's awkwardness, which manifests itself in two major ways? First, the cause and nature of the disagreement, itself atypical, alluded to in the prose introduction is unexplained and does not adequately function as a context for the ensuing dialogue. Second, the term used to describe this poetry is *oblirach* 'lampoon', which is a low-status title to give to any poetic composition associated with Finn; fortunately, the complexity of the ensuing verses gives lie to the *oblirach* reference.[42] These two problems also point to tensions between the prose introduction and the following stanzas but there seem to be no grounds, linguistic or otherwise, for assuming that they were anything but a unity from their conception.

The exclusion of outside influences results in the removal of the most discernible source of what have been seen as discordant elements within the text, the anomalous lack of unity between Finn and Oisín being the most obvious example.[43] Perhaps there were other, now lost, aspects of the early lore of Finn that provided a context for this situation or perhaps it was always exceptional.[44] Either way, I do not believe that the international theme of the 'father-and-son combat' can be profitably utilized in its analysis as the discrepancies involved create more problems than they solve.

---

about 1100) [is] that France dominates almost all departments of cultural and intellectual life'. **42** *Oblirach* is the composition of an *oblaire* 'lampooner', one of the three sub-grades of *fili* 'poet'. See Breatnach, *Uraicecht na ríar*, pp 112–13 §20: *Oblaire, cóic dréchta lais. Lethscrepul a díre*, 'An *oblaire*, he has five compositions. His honour-price is half a scruple'. **43** More typical of the harmonious relationship between the two is Finn coming to Oisín's aid in the *dinnšenchas* of Tipra Sengarman: see Stokes, 'The prose tales in the Rennes dindšenchas', §52 (*RC* 15, 446–8). **44** We must also factor into our considerations the loss of – and damage to – Medieval and Early Modern Irish-language manuscripts which may distort our understanding of the nature and extent of our native literature, including *fianaigecht*: for discussion, see Ó Corráin, 'Cad d'imigh ar lámhscríbhinní na hÉireann?'

AN ALTERNATIVE ANALYSIS OF THE TALE

There is a different approach, however, which allows us to situate 'The quarrel between Finn and Oisín' within broader Fenian tradition.[45] This approach is predicated on the nature of the riddling dialogue between father and son which is presented primarily as a contest between old and young. Such contests are not uncommon in early narrative literatures. For example, Tolkien describes *Beowulf* as:

> essentially a balance, an opposition of ends and beginnings. In its simplest terms it is a contrasted description of two moments in a great life, rising and setting; an elaboration of the ancient and intensely moving contrast between youth and age, first achievement and final death.[46]

Though our text in no way attains to the narrative sophistication of *Beowulf*, nevertheless it shares with it the broad outlines of the 'youth versus age' theme as articulated by Tolkien.

Though arguments are given on both sides, such as the wisdom and experience of age versus the dynamism and vitality of youth, the author of 'The quarrel between Finn and Oisín' is concerned to show the *fer líath* 'grey-haired man' as a match in every way for the *ócláech* 'young warrior'. This central concern surfaces repeatedly in the Finn Cycle.[47] In *Marbad Cúlduib*, for example, we see Finn cooking a pig with weapons in one hand because Oisín and Caílte have shown themselves, on previous days, unable to prevent the theft of a cooked animal.[48] When setting about his work, he quotes the maxim: *as aithe cach ndelg as sou*, 'sharper is each thorn that is younger'.[49] Finn then proceeds to underscore the irony of his utterance by slaying the Otherworld thief, Cúldub, a feat which

---

45 See Chapter Six (pp 91–3) for analysis of recurring themes in the early Finn material, though it is worth stating that thematic consistency is not necessarily to be expected in a tradition which is so fragmentary and diffuse. **46** Tolkien, 'Beowulf: the monsters and the critics', p. 28. **47** See discussion in Ó hÓgáin, 'Fionn féin: pearsa agus idéal', pp 150–2. **48** Interestingly, in 'The quarrel between Finn and Oisín', when Finn comes upon his son in the wilderness he is also cooking a pig, that most Fenian of all occupations outside of hunting (i.e., enjoying its fruits). **49** Hull, 'Two tales', 329, 331 (with references p. 331 n. 20). This maxim is also found in *Sermo ad reges* in Leabhar Breac, in a conversation between King David and his son Solomon: see Atkinson, *The passions and the homilies from Leabhar Breac*, p. 156, ll 4136–7 (trans. p. 406). Similarly, in *Esnada tige Buchet*, the maxim is put into the mouth of the king, Catháir Már, who explains to Buchet the hospitaller that because of his advanced age he has no power over his rapacious sons who have beeen abusing Buchet's hospitality (Greene, *Fingal Rónáin*, l. 505n.). However, as Greene points out (p. 43 n. 505), the use of the maxim here 'seems somewhat forced and rests on only one manuscript'. See discussion in O'Rahilly, *A miscellany of Irish proverbs*, p. 97 §304. This maxim is also re-used in a Fenian context as it is put into the mouth of the *fénnid*, Garad mac Morna, in *AcS* as he begs off playing *fidchell* with the women of the *fían* because of his advanced years: see Stokes, 'Acallamh', l. 1384 (= O'Grady, 'Agallamh', i, p. 124; Dooley and Roe, *Tales*, p. 43).

the younger Oisín and Caílte were unable to perform. Again, in *Tochmarc Ailbe*, the conflict between youth and age re-emerges when Ailbe, the youngest daughter of Cormac mac Airt, accepts Finn as her husband, preferring his age and experience to what youth has to offer.⁵⁰ Typical of her declamations is the following verse:

> Eol dam cinco·ranacc coill.
> as ferr ammes in odhchroind
> in flesc mæt ni·dlig a sesc.
> is suail for·bera forbeirt.
>
> I know, though I have not been to the wood,
> that the knotty tree's acorns are best.
> A flimsy sapling is not worth loving:
> scant will be its yield.⁵¹

These examples illustrate succinctly an alternative Fenian context within which we may analyse 'The quarrel between Finn and Oisín'; furthermore, Finn's lack of youth is also emphasized in later texts such as *Tóraigheacht Dhiarmada agus Ghráinne* and *Feis tighe Chonáin*. Although Finn is presented in these narratives as a grey-haired man of advancing years, it has been argued that there is a sense in which he never truly represents old age because in some ways 'Finn never really completes the passage into adulthood'.⁵²

CONCLUSIONS

Though aspects of our narrative may not resonate fully with other *fianaigecht* materials, the approach adopted here allows us to situate the conflict between Finn and Oisín within normative Finn Cycle materials. This youth versus age viewpoint helps establish the existence of a coherent tradition within which the dispute is no longer seen as completely anomalous. Ultimately, by excising the international theme of the 'father-and-son combat', we avoid the need to assume that this text is fundamentally different to other early extant *fianaigecht* sources.

---

50 This tale is analysed in detail in Chapter Eight. **51** Thurneysen, 'Tochmarc Ailbe', 264 § 8.10. I follow John Carey here who emends line 2 *odhcroind* to *odbchroind*. **52** Nagy, *The wisdom of the outlaw*, p. 148. In that sense *Tochmarc Ailbe* may be a slightly atypical *fianaigecht* tale, as it leads to marital happiness along with the birth of three sons, both markers of a successful transition into adulthood.

CHAPTER FIVE

The early tales set around the river Suir

There are three very early interconnected pieces of Fenian lore, which are probably to be dated to the eighth century,[1] in which the action is primarily situated on the banks of the river Suir around Cathair Dúin Iascaig (present-day Cahir, County Tipperary). The texts in question are *Bruiden Átha Í*, *Marbad Cúlduib*,[2] and 'Finn and the man in the tree'. These brief tales set in Déisi territory, taken together, give a fascinating insight into one early branch of *fíanaigecht* tradition.[3]

BRUIDEN ÁTHA Í

Bruiden Átha Í is a short bipartite tale that opens with Finn beheading Cuirrech Lifi in revenge for Cuirrech's decapitation of his wife, Badamair (presented as the eponym of a place, perhaps a chthonic goddess);[4] thus, this introductory section functions as the *dinnšenchas* of Cenn Cuirrig.[5] The subsequent narrative shows us Finn's attempts to make peace with Cuirrech's half-brother, Fothad Canainne, who agrees to come to an ale-banquet organized by Finn. As Fothad is under a *geis* only to drink ale in the presence of severed heads, Finn goes to a place where killing is allowed and slays the occupants of a passing chariot, Téite and her husband, Finn mac Regamain. He beheads Téite to fulfil the *geis* but, as she is Fothad's sister, this action only serves to increase the enmity between Finn and Fothad.

---

[1] The evidence for this proposed dating, and for other dates suggested throughout this work, is forthcoming in Murray, *The early Fenian corpus*. [2] I previously followed Meyer, 'Two tales', 245 (who printed the tale title as TUC*AIT* FHAGHB*ALA* IN FESA DO FINN INSO OCUS MARB*AD* CUIL DUIB), in seeing this original compound name (see Uhlich, *Die Morphologie*, pp 40–41 §31, 222) as two words, reflecting later scribal usage. However, examination of the manuscript, RIA MS D.iv.2, fo. 88rb10, shows that the reading is *marbad culduib* and confirms its continuing treatment as a compound. [3] It is suggested in Chapter Two, p. 56, that the growth of *fíanaigecht* into a quasi-national literature by the Early Modern Irish period may be in part due to the fragmentary nature of the early tradition. It is hoped that the evidence presented in Chapters Five and Six will go some way towards substantiating this claim. [4] This is expressed in an elliptical manner in the Yellow Book of Lecan version where the phrase *fri haigthi bana* 'with white faces' is used (Hull, 'Two tales', 323, 326). In the text in RIA MS D.iv.2, this striking image is replaced with the more prosaic *cin chinnu marbu ina fhiadnaise*, 'without dead heads in his presence' (Meyer, 'Two tales', 242, 244). [5] For more information on this placename, see *HDGP* 'B' s.n. Bodhamair.

The early tales set around the river Suir 75

This short tale resonates more fully with later Fenian tradition, and with medieval Irish literature generally, than any other early expression of *fíanaigecht*.[6] On a prosaic level, we can instance the re-use of some of its constituent elements in later texts; for example, the places it lists where killing is allowed[7] are also cited in 'The Irish ordeals'.[8] Furthermore, a brief outline of the death of Cuirrech is given towards the end of the *Acallam* in a dialogue between Oisín and Caílte at Tara.[9] However, it is in the transmission in later *dinnsenchas* collections of the story's Cenn Cuirrig element that we can see the full extent of its intertextual connections.[10]

The published prose part of the entry on Cenn Cuirrig from the *Rennes dinnsenchas* draws its information from the same tradition which underlies our text.[11] The thematic similarities and dissimilarities are here listed:[12]

- in *BÁÍ*, Cuirrech and Fothad Canainne are presented as uterine brothers while Téite is said to have the same father as Fothad; in *RD*, all three have the same mother.
- in *BÁÍ*, Cuirrech is named as the person who killed Dub, Badamair's foster-brother; in *RD*, it is said that Finn killed him and that he was Cuirrech's son-in-law. Both texts have the same information word for word at this point (see below) detailing the connection between Dub and Diarmaid.
- Finn beheads Cuirrech in both narratives, an action necessary for the onomastic tale to work but, in *RD*, Cuirrech does not decapitate Badamair.
- there is an itemization of places in *RD* through which Finn tracks Cuirrech that is not part of *BÁÍ*; this itinerary brings Finn northwards to the Barrow.[13]
- the second part of *BÁÍ*, which is not directly connected with the *dinnsenchas* of Cenn Cuirrig, is virtually unrepresented in *RD* with the exception of

---

6 Edited by Meyer, 'Two tales', 242–5; Hull, 'Two tales', 323–9; Baumgarten, 'Placenames', pp 7–10 (partial).   7 Hull, 'Two tales', 323–4, 326 (= Meyer, 'Two tales', 242, 244; Baumgarten, 'Placenames', pp 8–10).   8 Stokes, 'The Irish ordeals', p. 199. There may be a suspicion, however, that this passage did not originate as part of *Bruiden Átha Í* but is a later interpolation into the text because the prohibitions on slayings are said to be as a result of *cain Cormaic i n-Ere*, 'the law of Cormac in Ireland'. Such a national dimension would not be compatible with the early date assigned to the narrative. Baumgarten, 'Placenames', p. 17, suggests reading *caínchomrac* 'fair play, peace' here instead of *cain Cormaic*.   9 Stokes, 'Acallamh', ll 7919–27 (= O'Grady, 'Agallamh', i, p. 231, ii, p. 262; Dooley and Roe, *Tales*, p. 221).   10 It is quite possible that the outline of the story in *AcS* derives from *dinnsenchas* sources rather than from *Bruiden Átha Í* directly. However, it must be noted that Baumgarten, 'Placenames', p. 11 n. 31, posits a direct textual link between the *Acallam* and *Bruiden Átha Í*.   11 Stokes, 'The prose tales in the Rennes dindsenchas', §49 (*RC* 15, 443–4). For discussion, see Murray, 'The treatment of placenames in the early *fíanaigecht* corpus', pp 455–6.   12 In what follows, *BÁÍ* = *Bruiden Átha Í* and *RD* = *Rennes dinnsenchas* §49.   13 Perhaps the direction intended is towards the Curragh of Kildare, which is what Cuirrech Lifi would normally denote in a placename context. Perhaps this element is an integral part of the tradition as *Lifi* 'of the Liffey' is Cuirrech's epithet in *BÁÍ*. This might also explain the placename in the title of the narrative, as the only well-known Áth Í in Ireland is Athy, County Kildare, not far from the Curragh;

genealogical information concerning Téite and the fact that Finn was responsible for killing her and her husband. She was of interest to the author of the *Rennes dinnšenchas* because of her connection with the placename Óenach Téite (present-day Nenagh, County Tipperary).

Though the thematic resemblances involved might suggest that the author of the *Rennes dinnšenchas* had access to *Bruiden Átha Í*, the lack of direct linguistic borrowings and parallels, with two possible exceptions, go some way to rendering this less likely. If we do posit direct access to our *fianaigecht* source, then we must accept that it was drastically reworked and reshaped to suit its new context. The two direct linguistic comparisons that may be noted are between *Dub hua Duibne dia·raibi Diarmaid mac Duib maic Duibne* in *BÁÍ* ('Dub hua Duibne, from whom Diarmaid mac Duib maic Duibne was descended') compared with *Dub hua Duibne, dia roibe Diarmait mac Duib meic Duibne* in *RD*, and between *elli for Cuirreach* in *BÁÍ* compared with *eill for Find* ('an advantage over Find') in *RD*.

We also find a re-working of this narrative complex in the metrical *dinnšenchas* tradition.[14] Here the onomastic connection with Cenn Cuirrig is completely broken and it is in the context of Cuirrech Lifi, the Curragh of Kildare, that the material has been assembled. The opening verse of the poem derives from *Bruiden Átha Í*; unfortunately, we do not know whether it comes directly from the tale (my suspicion is that it does not) because this quatrain had an independent existence as witnessed by its presence in *Mittelirische Verslehren* where it is put into the mouth of Caílte and used to illustrate the metre *dían airšeng*.[15] Some of the remaining material in this short poem reflects an understanding of at least part of the underlying story pattern, derived perhaps from *Bruiden Átha Í* or, more likely, from a knowledge of the tradition preserved in the *Rennes dinnšenchas*, though this poetic version also has additional elements not present in the other two sources. Furthermore, the beheading of Cuirrech is also alluded to in various versions of a later Fenian lay concerning Caílte and the animals.[16] This literary re-working and transformation of tradition, most probably preserved both orally and in written format, serves as much to conceal as to reveal its sources; parallels between the extant narratives may be drawn but it remains difficult to make inferences regarding the exact nature of the relationships involved.

---

however, as Baumgarten ('Placenames', p. 11) notes, the age of the title 'is uncertain'. **14** *MD* iii, pp 234–5 (see notes on pp 519–20). **15** Thurneysen, 'Mittelirische Verslehren', p. 32 §3. **16** Ross, *Heroic poetry*, p. 40, no. IX, §§3–4 (= *DF* I, §vii, pp 19, 116; Ní Shéaghdha, *Agallamh na seanórach*, iii, p. 73 [cf. ibid., ii, pp 43, 45, 53]). See Meek, 'Development and degeneration in Gaelic ballad texts', pp 142–3.

MARBAD CÚLDUIB

Marbad Cúlduib follows on from *Bruiden Átha Í*.[17] Not only is it found immediately after it in both manuscripts to contain the tales, but the opening line of the narrative actually makes this connection explicit: *Feacht aili do [Fi]nd a Cind Curraig*, 'On another occasion Find was in Cend Curraig'.[18] The story relates how Finn kills the Otherworld thief, Cúldub, who comes every day to steal the pig which is being cooked by a member of the *fían*. Oisín and Caílte are unable to overcome this enemy and it is left to Finn to pursue Cúldub to his Otherworld abode, Síd Fer Femen, and to kill him at its entrance. Finn's thumb gets stuck in the door into the *síd*, between this world and the Otherworld. This then is said to be the origin of his 'thumb of knowledge':[19]

> Do·beir forgom fair oc techt isin sid co·raimid a druim trid. Aroisir a laim frisan ersaind coro·druid in comla ara ordain co·tard ina beolu. As·bert didiu alaile is de sin ro·bai fis ac Find, ar a ndechaid da mer isan sid is ed no·gebed ina beolu.

> He made a thrust at him as he went into the fairy mound, and thereby his back broke. His hand stuck fast against the door-post so that the door-valve closed on his thumb and he put it into his mouth. Therefore, some say that hence it is that Find obtained knowledge, for he used to put into his mouth the portion of his finger that had gone into the fairy mound.[20]

This alternative origin for Finn's acquisition of mantic abilities predates the earliest attestation of the standard account of how he became a seer by several centuries. The orthodox version is that Finn burned his thumb while cooking the 'salmon of knowledge' for his namesake, Finn Éices, that he put his thumb in his mouth to cool it down and thus attained prophetic function.[21] Our alternate version is not completely isolated, however, as this motif is also present in 'Finn and the man in the tree' (see below).[22]

The slaying by Finn of an Otherworld rival with a spear at the entrance to the *síd* is a recurrent theme in *fíanaigecht*: it is also present in *Macgnímrada Finn* and

---

17 Edited by Meyer, 'Two tales', 245–9; Hull, 'Two tales', 329–33. **18** Hull, 'Two tales', 329, 330. Cf. the version in RIA MS D.iv.2, however, which reads *Fecht do Find hua Baiscne i Cind Chuirrig*, 'Once Find O'Baiscne was at the Head of the Curragh': Meyer, 'Two tales', 242, 243. **19** See Carey, 'Obscure styles', 25–6. **20** Hull, 'Two tales', 330, 332 (= Meyer, 'Two tales', 246, 247). **21** Meyer, 'Macgnimartha Find', 201 §18 (= Meyer, 'The boyish exploits', 185–6 §18; Nagy, *The wisdom of the outlaw*, pp 213–14; *CHA* §93 p. 198). This version may have been influenced by the Norse story of Sigurd and the dragon, Fáfnir; for references, see Murray, 'Interpreting the evidence', p. 44 n. 76. For the international tale-type which may underlie the narrative, see Bruford, 'Oral and literary Fenian tales', pp 45–7. **22** There are two later versions of how Finn attained prophetic knowledge contained in *Feis tighe Chonáin*; these are discussed by

the *Acallam*. As Joseph Nagy has pointed out, there are obvious links between these episodes in the later narratives.²³ In *Macgnímrada Finn*, Áed mac Fidga is slain by Finn at Samain at the door of the *síd* with a poisonous spear he receives from the *féinnid*, Fíacail mac Conchinn;²⁴ in *AcS*, Finn kills Aillén mac Midna at Samain at the entrance to the *síd* with a poisonous spear he gets from the *féinnid*, Fíacha mac Conga.²⁵ Thus, what we see being recycled in the *Acallam*, harks back at least to Finn's boyhood deeds and may be traced back to our obscure text from the eighth century. Interestingly, in both these later examples, Finn is presented as a hero within society – in *Macgnímrada Finn* as an apprentice *fili* avenging the death of Oircbél the poet, in the *Acallam* preventing Tara from being burned – defending this world from the negative interference of the Otherworld.²⁶

Marbad Cúlduib is by far the earliest of the three texts to contain this motif of Finn's spearing of an Otherworld rival at a *síd* entrance. However, there is no textual link that might establish whether the relevant passages in these later Finn Cycle texts are drawn directly from *Marbad Cúlduib*; my suspicion is that they do not so derive but that similar traditions are being drawn upon, traditions which may have been significantly shaped and influenced by our early tale, however.²⁷ An anonymous poem in the Book of Leinster beginning *Échta Lagen for Leth Cuind* does provide a narrative link between the slaying of Cúldub and the killing of Áed:

> Aed mac Fidaig di láim Ḟind
> di ṡleig Fíaclaig meic Conchind ...
> Din tṡleig cétna romarb Find
> Cúldub mac Fidga forḟind.²⁸

> Áed mac Fidaig fell by Finn's hand
> by the spear of Fíaclach mac Conchind ...
> With the same spear Finn killed
> Cúldub mac Fidga the very fair.

Nagy, 'Liminality and knowledge', 141–2, and further contextualized by Ó Cionnfhaolaidh, '*Feis tighe Chonáin*: a window on the medieval *fiannaigheacht* tradition', Chapter Three.   **23** Nagy, *The wisdom of the outlaw*, pp 186–9.   **24** Meyer, 'Macgnimartha Find', 202–3 §§23–6 (= Meyer, 'The boyish exploits', 187–9 §§23–6; Nagy, *The wisdom of the outlaw*, pp 216–18; *CHA* §93 pp 199–201).   **25** Stokes, 'Acallamh', ll 1662–761 (= O'Grady, 'Agallamh', i, pp 130–2, ii, pp 142–5; Dooley and Roe, *Tales*, pp 51–4). Aillén's grave is also briefly mentioned in the lay 'The standing stones of Ireland': *DF* II, §xlii, pp 80–1 [stanza 49].   **26** Both these events are also described in the late Middle Irish poem beginning *A Rí Ríchid, réidig dam*: see *Fian.* p. 46 §§5–6, p. 48 §§13–15 (= *LL* iii, ll 18031–6, 18063–74). The reference here to the events surrounding Finn's killing of Aillén (though he is not named in the poem) at Tara proves that this tradition pre-dates the compilation of the *Acallam*.   **27** The points of correspondence between *Marbad Cúlduib*, *Macgnímrada Finn* and the *Acallam* are conveniently set out in *DF* III, pp lxiv–lxv. This theme has been explored in even greater detail by Scott, *The thumb of knowledge*, pp 16–44.   **28** *Fian.* p. xxiii §XX (= *LL* i, ll 7040–5).

There is a conflation of traditions here with Áed referred to as 'mac Fidaig' and Cúldub given Áed's regular patronymic. Clearly, the tradition of Finn killing an Otherworld rival with a spear was a persistent part of the Finn Cycle from the earliest cultivation of written *fianaigecht* sources right through to the compilation of the *Acallam*.

'FINN AND THE MAN IN THE TREE'

This is the only one of these three inter-related texts that has come down to us independently of the other two. In fact, it owes its survival to its being quoted in the medieval Irish law tracts.[29] This was a well-established tradition in both medieval Ireland and Wales as has been demonstrated by Robin Stacey who warns against the 'privileging of the lawbooks over the literary sources for historical sources ... [as] it may cause us to underestimate the extent to which the authors of the law tracts drew on traditional tales and characters in their writings'.[30] This observation is borne out by 'Finn and the man in the tree', found in the famous legal codex Trinity College Dublin MS H.3.18 as part of its introduction to the *Senchas már*.[31] This manuscript also contains another famous leading case, the tract known as *Echtra Fergusa maic Léti*, which is preserved in its discussion of distraint.[32] In our case, it is the prophetic gift known as *imbas forosnai* 'knowledge which illuminates' that our text is being used to illustrate.[33]

The tale itself is composed of two connected sections. The first comprises a short telling of the killing of Cúldub detailing Finn's attainment of his 'thumb of knowledge'. However, in this case it is a woman carrying a vessel of liquid who closes the door on his thumb which has led Nagy to speculate that 'presumably, some of the liquid in the woman's vessel spills on to his finger. Finn removes it and puts it in his mouth, thus ingesting the magical fluid'.[34] He reveals his mantic prowess by putting his thumb in his mouth and reciting a *roscad* full of

---

29 For the variety of material preserved in this way, see Dillon, 'Stories from the law tracts'; Qiu, 'Narratives in early Irish law: a typological study'. **30** Stacey, 'Law and literature in medieval Ireland and Wales', pp 67–8. For further discussion, see Owen, 'Royal propaganda: stories from the law-texts'; Breatnach, 'Law and literature in early medieval Ireland'; Stacey, 'Learning and law in medieval Ireland'. **31** Meyer, 'Finn and the man in the tree' (= *CIH* iii, pp 879.23–880.14). **32** Binchy, 'The saga of Fergus mac Léti' (= *CIH* iii, pp 882.4–883.22). Ironically, the legal principle discussed in the story is not *athgabál* 'distraint' but *díguin* 'violation of protection': see Binchy, 'The saga of Fergus mac Léti', 46, and *Críth gablach*, p. 83. **33** This aspect of Finn's poetic ability is dealt with more fully below in Chapter Twelve, pp 142–3. See Chadwick, 'Imbas forosnai'. **34** Nagy, 'Intervention and disruption in the myths of Finn and Sigurd', 126. Nagy makes this suggestion based on the parallel incident in the later *Feis tighe Chonáin* where 'Finn and his men try to enter to *síd* where the well of knowledge is located; one of the three women who are trying to close the door and keep Finn out is carrying a vessel full of liquid from the well, and some of the liquid splashes out of the vessel and into Finn's mouth, so that he acquires knowledge' (126 n. 12). For the text, see Joynt, *Feis tighe Chonáin*, §XX, ll 1331–76 at ll 1358–62. For discussion, see *EIHM* pp 326–7; Ford, 'The well of Nechtan', p. 70; Ó hÓgáin, *An file*, pp 211–15.

imbas forosnai. There are parallels between this *roscad* and that contained in *Marbad Cúlduib*: compare *Tair Femen fuigial formuig meis mui muic cetson sirchrand sirlúath laith find sra* [leg. *fri*] *aulad Cúlduib chanmae*[35] with *Mai muiced son dar Femen fugiath sir-chrand sir-luth laitho Find fri ulaid Cul Dub*.[36] The close textual correspondences here echo the thematic unity between the pieces and serve to reinforce their shared background for the reader.[37]

The second, longer part of the story tells of the *fían*'s capture of an unnamed women from Dún Iascaig, probably to be identified with Badamair who is carried off in *Bruiden Átha Í*. Though desired by Finn, she prefers his *gilla*, Derc Corra, but he refuses to sleep with her out of loyalty to his master. She turns Finn against Derc Corra by accusing him of violating her,[38] and he is sent into exile. In the woods one day, Finn and his followers see a man at the top of a tree with a blackbird on his shoulder that he is supplying with nuts; a bronze vessel containing a fish in his hand; a stag at the base of the tree which he is feeding with apples; and all of them drinking together out of the vessel.[39] Finn utilizes his prophetic ability to identify the man in a concluding *roscad* as his former servant, Derc Corra, as no-one else can pierce his disguise.

Following Kuno Meyer's reading of the first element of the man in the tree's name as Derg, Gerard Murphy interpreted his full name as Derg Corra mocu Daigre ('Red one of Corr (?) of the race of Flame') and saw in this a reflex of the fire motif which is often a constituent element of those presented as enemies of Finn.[40] However, John Carey has persuasively argued that the name should be read as Derc Corra (perhaps 'eye of a crane', 'cave of a peak', or 'hollow of a pool'), with the figure best understood perhaps as the personification of a place;[41] the gentilic – mocu Daigre – connects Derc Corra with Uí Daigre in County Tipperary.[42]

A very interesting interpretation of the text has been advanced by Kaarina Hollo. She reads the tableau being presented as 'a skilfully composed reflection upon the mystery and salvific power of Christ's crucifixion and the Eucharist that also reflects the tension between secular and monastic power in early medieval Ireland'. As she notes:

---

35 Meyer, 'Finn and the man in the tree', 346 (= *CIH* iii, p. 879.30–32). Meyer (p. 347) refers to this as 'untranslatable'. **36** Hull, 'Two tales', 330 (= Meyer, 'Two tales', 246). As Hull notes (p. 333n.) 'the text is, in general, too corrupt to warrant a translation'. **37** See Scott, *The thumb of knowledge*, pp 12–13 and Hull, 'Two tales', 333 n. 2. **38** For this interpretation, see Gwynn, 'Varia III, 3: "Finn and the man in the tree"'. **39** Carey, *Ireland and the grail*, pp 95–6, draws attention to the possibility that this narrative may underpin the Grail 'Continuation' attributed to Wauchier de Denain; furthermore, he states (p. 96n.): 'What the original significance of this tableau may have been is another question, very likely an unanswerable one'. **40** *DF* III, pp lv–lvi, lxiii–lxiv. This motif is discussed further in Chapter Twelve, p. 149. **41** Carey, 'Two notes on names', 120–3 at 122. **42** Uí Daigre held lands around the parish of Latteragh, in the barony of Upper Ormond, County Tipperary, approximately 60 km north of Cahir: Ó Riain, *Corpus*, p. 335.

The man in the tree is holding a vessel filled with water and sharing food and drink with a bird, a stag and a fish, the last contained in the vessel. The nut is first divided, then shared between the man and the bird. The apple is divided and shared between man and stag. The man then drinks from the vessel. The eucharistic overtones of this are inescapable.[43]

This case is strengthened by the use of the three genera of animals (*tria genera animantium*), that is, the image of a man in a tree (representing Christ on the Cross) sharing communion with creatures of the earth, air and water. Such crucifixion imagery is common across Europe in the early Middle Ages.[44]

The final rhetoric, or *roscad*, in the narrative has been scrutinized in some detail and both Vernam Hull and John Carey have established useful working translations of it.[45] It does not function as a further or fuller explanation of the process of *imbas forosnai* but comprises a description, which is also contained in the prose, of Derc Corra's actions in the tree. The eating of nuts with the blackbird is mentioned, consuming of apples is noted but with no reference to a stag, and the fish referred to is a salmon (in the prose it is a trout the first time,[46] a salmon the second). An explicit connection is being made between the actions of Derc Corra and the attainment of knowledge as there is a long association of nuts (particularly hazelnuts), water and salmon with the acquiring of *imbas*. The most famous example concerns the well of Segais;[47] the earliest reference to this is in 'The caldron of poesy', probably dating to the mid-eighth century, which describes:

> fáilte fri tascor n-imbais do-fuaircet noí cuill cainmeso for Segais i sídaib, conda·thochrathar méit moltchnaí iar ndruimniu Bóinde frithroisc luaithiu euch aige i mmedón mís mithime dia secht mbliadnae beos.
>
> joy at the arrival of *imbas* which the nine hazels of fine mast at Segais in the *síd*'s amass and which is sent upstream along the surface of the Boyne, as extensive as a wether's fleece, swifter than a racehorse, in the middle of June every seventh year regularly.[48]

There is a further early reference to Segais published as an addendum to this text which tells us that accessing *imbas* from hazelnuts that grow around this well facilitated Cormac mac Cuilennáin in becoming a great *fili*.[49] The same idea, that

---

43 Hollo, '"Finn and the man in the tree" as verbal icon', pp 61, 55.   **44** Ibid., pp 56–7, for discussion and examples.   **45** Hull, 'A rhetoric'; Carey, 'Obscure styles', 26–7.   **46** The word used is *brecc* (literally 'the speckled one'), the standard Irish word for a trout; however, the trout is a member of the salmon family so this interchange might not be of significance here.   **47** For discussion and references, see *EIHM* pp 322–3.   **48** Breatnach, 'The caldron of poesy', 66–7 §11.   **49** Ibid., 93. For another text connecting

hazelnuts contain great wisdom, is also present in the *Rennes dinnṡenchas* prose account of the origin of the river Shannon:

> Sinend … dodechaid do Tiprait Connla fil fo muir dia forcsin. Tipra sin fo 'tat cuill 7 imbois na heicsi .i. cuill crinmoind aiusa. [7 a n-aen uair bruchtais a meas 7 a mblath 7 a nduilli,] 7 i n-oen frois dofuitet forsin tiprait, co tuarcaib rigbroind chorcarda fuirri, [co cocnaid na bradana in mes, conad he sug na cno cuirthear suas ina mbolcaib corcardaib,] 7 bruinnit secht srotha éicsi as, 7 imsoat and afrithisi.
>
> Sinend … went to Connla's Well which is under the sea, to behold it. That is a well at which are the hazels and the inspirations (?) of wisdom, that is, the hazels of the science of poetry, and in the same hour their fruit, and their blossom and their foliage break forth, and these fall on the well in the same shower, which raises on the water a royal surge of purple. Then the salmon chew the fruit, and the juice of the nuts is apparent on their purple bellies. And seven streams of wisdom spring forth and turn there again.[50]

The central idea is that knowledge (*imbas*) is contained in hazelnuts,[51] and that it may be accessed directly by eating them, or alternatively by eating the salmon which feed on these nuts.[52] In the *dinnṡenchas* of Ráth Chnámrossa, Finn is able to distinguish between 'nuts of knowledge' (*cna rois*) and 'nuts of ignorance' (*cna amrois*) which come from Segais.[53]

CONCLUSIONS

The existence of this group of narratives associated with a very specific area of the country points to the localized literary cultivation of complex inter-woven *fíanaigecht* traditions in the eighth century. That these were not isolated tales is clear from their context with their cross-references to other materials as well as

---

Cormac mac Cuilennáin with the nuts of Segais, see Thurneysen, 'Zu Verslehre II', 268 §14; cf. Carey, 'Dán doiléir atá curtha i leith Chormaic mhic Cuileannáin'. **50** Stokes, 'The prose tales in the Rennes dindṡenchas', §59 (*RC* 15, 456–7). The poetic version is in *MD* iii, pp 292–5, ll 9–44. For discussion, see Ford, 'The well of Nechtan', pp 72–3. **51** See, for example, the phrase *a caillib crínmond*, 'from the hazels of poetic art', in *Imacallam in dá thúarad*: Stokes, 'The colloquy of the two sages', 18–19 §24. This is glossed in the Book of Leinster .i. *a noí collaib na Segsa*, 'from the nine hazels of the Segais' (*LL* iv, 24316). Boyle, 'Allegory, the *áes dána* and the liberal arts in Medieval Irish literature', 32, suggests that 'the severing of the nuts from their husks represents the breaking open of literal meaning in order to discover the hidden meaning inside'. **52** This of course ties up with the later better-known episode in *Macgnímrada Finn* of how Finn gained prophetic powers by eating the 'salmon of knowledge': Meyer, 'Macgnimartha Find', 201 §18 (= Meyer, 'The boyish exploits', 185–6 §18; Nagy, *The wisdom of the outlaw*, p. 214; *CHA* §93 p. 198); see discussion in Ó hÓgáin, *An file*, pp 233–42. **53** Stokes, 'The prose tales in the Rennes dindṡenchas', §31 (*RC* 15, 333–4).

The early tales set around the river Suir

their espousal of themes attested elsewhere in Fenian literature. As Rolf Baumgarten has asserted:

> These tales presuppose the existence at the time of other related ones, among other things because of the number of actors and persons introduced without comment, whose status would have been known (thematically or incidentally) from those other contexts.[54]

As we shall see in the next chapter, these tales represent only one localized story nexus among several; together they serve to demonstrate how widespread, though marginal, the written cultivation of *fíanaigecht* was in the Old Irish period.

---

[54] Baumgarten, 'Placenames', p. 15. This concept of an 'immanent narrative', i.e. one that was not related explicitly as a whole but one whose complete outline was known by the relevant audience, has been outlined by Clover, 'The long prose form', 23–7. Its relevance to medieval Irish narrative has been discussed by Poppe, *Of cycles and other critical matters*, pp 13–14 (see above Chapter One, p. 47 n. 185). The concept has been developed in detail by Foley, *Immanent art*. A similar idea underpins Nagy's discussion of the Ossianic controversy ('Observations on the Ossianesque', 437): 'First and foremost among Macpherson's tendencies as an adaptor was his casting or recasting the narrative or textual material in terms of fragments: waifs and strays that either he or the traditional, yet authorial, genius of Ossian (as impersonated by Macpherson) saw fit to bring together into an organic whole, which in an almost Platonic sense was supposedly always there, but awaited realization at the hands of a redactor, collector, or translator'.

CHAPTER SIX

Further early *fianaigecht* sources

Along with the Old Irish material connecting Finn with Déisi territory around Cahir, outlined in the previous chapter, there are further early texts which connect Finn with other specific locations around the country. These connections and sources are here detailed.

THE LAIGIN CONNECTION

In a genealogical poem attributed to Senchán Torpéist, which may date as early as the seventh century and which is probably the earliest extant reference to Finn, he is explicitly said to descend from Núadu Necht, ancestor of the Laigin:

> Find Taulcha
> tuath-cuire,
> Caílte crothsat
> cres ṁbodbae
> bārcaib di thonnaib.
> Trī hūi Baīscni
> būadach cuitechta
> cond ar ferga
> filset trī hūi Nuadat Necht.

> Find (and) Taulcha, an evil band, (and) Caílte caused warlike brandishing from ships/strongholds (and) waves/land. The three descendants of Baíscne, a victorious company; they turned on doglike wrath (= warriors), the three descendants of Núadu Necht.[1]

There seems to be deliberate confusion here between Finn mac Cumaill úa Baíscne and Finn fili mac Rossa Rúaid, one of the early Laigin kings who is listed in the genealogies as a great-grandson of Núadu Necht.[2] It has been surmised that this 'mistaken identification ... may have helped to give rise to one of the more persistent features of the Fenian tradition of Finn – that he is a poet who has visionary knowledge of events'.[3] Though it is hard to sustain this conclusion

---

[1] Corthals, 'The rhymeless "Leinster poems"', 121–2. [2] For example, see *CGH* p. 15 (117e28–31) and p. 335 (311ab50–52). [3] Dooley and Roe, *Tales*, p. xiv.

considering that nearly all the various early *fíanaigecht* sources mention Finn's mantic abilities, there seems to be clear grounds for suggesting that the rise in prominence of Finn Cycle narratives 'may owe something to the conflation of Finn with the Find File of earlier genealogical distinction'.[4]

T.F. O'Rahilly sees the process working the other way: instead of the conflation of a number of different characters under the name of Finn, he believes that there was an original single divine hero attested under various names throughout the country. Thus, he prefers to argue that 'there is no "confusion" between Finn *fili* and Finn mac Cumaill, who are always kept distinct, even though they are ultimately the same'.[5] The extent of Finn's Laigin connection is restricted to just one population group in *Tesmolta Cormaic 7 aided Finn*, where, among other pedigrees, he is said to be of Uí Thairsig (Úa Failge).[6] This affiliation is also mentioned in the *Acallam*,[7] while his father Cumall is said to belong to this people in *Macgnímrada Finn*.[8] The Laigin connection becomes the dominant one in later *fíanaigecht* sources with Finn and his *fían* based at the stronghold of Almu in Laigin territory;[9] with him named as doing great deeds on behalf of Laigin in the poem beginning *Échta Lagen for Leth Cuind* preserved in the Book of Leinster;[10] and with Finn and the *fían* playing a central role in defending Laigin against the imposition of the cattle-tribute, known as the *bóroime*, by the king of Tara.[11]

EARLY GENEALOGICAL ASSOCIATIONS

The genealogies preserve differing traditions concerning Finn mac Cumaill's ancestry. In the short genealogical poem mentioned above, Finn has a Leinster pedigree and he is also given a Laigin descent through his mother, Muirne, daughter of Tadg mac Núadat.[12] Elsewhere, he is bestowed with Érainn ancestors, notably Dáire mac Dedaid,[13] while the prose *banṡenchas* also gives his mother as

---

[4] Ibid., p. xvi. [5] *EIHM* p. 281. [6] O'Grady, 'Teasmolad Corbmaic', i, p. 92, ii, p. 99 (= Meyer, *Cath Finntrága*, p. 76). Interestingly, it is claimed in *Lebor gabála Érenn* that Uí Thairsig (along with Gabraige Succa and Gáileóin) are not Goídil but are of Fir Bolg stock: Macalister, *Lebor gabála Érenn*, iv, 13, 25. [7] Stokes, 'Acallamh', ll 6546–8 (= O'Grady, 'Agallamh', i, p. 216, ii, p. 245; Dooley and Roe, *Tales*, pp 183–4): '*can do Find mac Cumaill?*' '*Do Laignib*', ar Cailte. '*Cá tuath do Laignib?*' ar in rí. '*A Híb Tairrsig Laigen*', ar Cailte ('Where did Finn mac Cumaill come from?' 'From Laigin', said Caílte. 'From what Laigin people?', asked the king. 'From Uí Thairsig Laigen', said Caílte). [8] Meyer, 'Macgnimartha Find', 197 §1 (= Meyer, 'The boyish exploits', 180 §1; Nagy, *The wisdom of the outlaw*, p. 209; *CHA* §93 p. 194). [9] For discussion, see Parsons, 'Revisiting Almu in Middle Irish texts'. [10] *LL* i, ll 6980–7098. [11] Stokes, 'The borama', pp 44–51 §§23–36. Interestingly, although Finn fights on behalf of Laigin against Cairpre Lifechair who has assumed the kingship of Ireland (§22), he is nevertheless referred to as *rígḟénnid Érenn* (§24). O'Connor, *A short history of Irish literature*, p. 31, refers to *fíanaigecht* as 'very like the legendary history of the Lagin'. [12] Her pedigree is given, for example, in *Fotha catha Cnucha*: Hennessy, 'The battle of Cnucha', 88 (= *LU* ll 3157–61; Nagy, *The wisdom of the outlaw*, p. 219). [13] For example, see Meyer, 'Mitteilungen aus irischen Handschriften: Finns Stammbaum und die Fiana'.

Tarbga of the Érainn.[14] Furthermore, his own pedigree headed *Genelach Find meic hUmaill* is cited among *láechsluinte lagen*;[15] it is unclear from the manuscript layout whether it is to be understood as a subgrouping of Loígis,[16] who were vassals of Laigin but whose genealogical origin was Cruithin.[17] It would be unsurprising if it were thus as it would dovetail with later sources such as *Macgnímrada Finn*, where Finn is raised in Slíab Bladma, and with *Fotha catha Cnucha*, where he is reared in Temair Mairce, both in Loígis territory.[18]

FINN AND DÁL NARAIDE

There is a text from the Old Irish period, *Scél asa mberar combad hé Finn mac Cumaill Mongán*, which connects Finn to Ulster and more specifically to Dál nAraide, the major Cruithin population group in the country.[19] The Mongán in question was a historical figure, Mongán mac Fíachnai, king of Dál nAraide who died in 625. The story concerns an argument between Mongán and his poet, Forgoll. Because the king disagrees with him about where Fothad Airgtech was slain – with Forgoll claiming the event happened in Leinster – the poet threatens satire:

> As:bert in fili no-nd:n-aírfed dia áithgiud ocus no:aírfed a athair ocus a máthair ocus a senathair ocus do:cechnad fora n-usciu conna:gébthae íasc ina inberaib. Do:cechnad fora fedaib conna:tibértais torad fora maige, comtis ambriti caidchi cacha clainde.

> The poet said that he would satirize him for contradicting him and he would satirize his father and his mother and his grandfather and he would chant upon their water so that fish would not be caught in its river mouths. He would chant upon their woods so that they would not give fruit onto their plains, so that they would be barren henceforth of every produce.[20]

---

14 Dobbs, 'The ban-shenchus' [*RC* 48, 178, 213] (= *Fian.* p. xxix §XLVII: 'Tarbdha'). In *Macgnímrada Finn*, the wife of Cumall, before he elopes with Muirne, is named as Torba but she is not reckoned as Finn's mother: Meyer, 'Macgnimartha Find', 197 §1 (= Meyer, 'The boyish exploits', 180 §1; Nagy, *The wisdom of the outlaw*, p. 209; *CHA* §93 p. 194). **15** *CGH* p. 99 (128b9); Meyer, 'Find mac Umaill'. **16** Ó Cuív, *Catalogue of Irish language manuscripts in the Bodleian Library*, i, p. 192, treats them as separate from the Loígis genealogies. In his edition, O'Brien (*CGH* pp 99–100) places them under a 'Laigin' running header while indexing them (*CGH* p. v) under 'Loíchsi'; but avoids the issue in the later indexes (*CGH* p. 643). **17** *EIHM* p. 30 n. 5; Ó Murchadha, 'Early history and settlements of the Laígis', p. 35 and p. 54 n. 2. **18** Meyer, 'Macgnimartha Find', 198–200 §§4–12 (= Meyer, 'The boyish exploits', 181–4 §§4–12; Nagy, *The wisdom of the outlaw*, pp 210–12; *CHA* §93 pp 195–7); Hennessy, 'The battle of Cnucha', 90 (= *LU* ll 3187–93; Nagy, *The wisdom of the outlaw*, p. 220). **19** White, *Compert Mongáin*, pp 73–4, 79–81 (= Meyer, *The voyage of Bran*, pp 45–8, pp 49–52; Hull, 'An incomplete version', 416–17; *LU* ll 10938–98). For detailed analysis, see Nagy, *Conversing with angels and ancients*, pp 303–7. **20** White, *Compert Mongáin*, pp 73, 79 §3 (= Meyer, *The voyage of Bran*, pp 46–8; Hull, 'An incomplete version', 416; *LU* ll 10946–50).

Further early fíanaigecht *sources*

Mongán promises to bestow his queen, Breóthigern, upon Forgoll after three days to avert this satire. By that time, and foreseen by Mongán, a figure who also disagrees with the poet arrives in Mongán's fort from south-west Munster, perhaps from the abode of the dead.[21] He asserts that he killed Fothad Airgtech in the battle of Ollarba,[22] and proves this by revealing Fothad's grave, with a pillar at one end inscribed with details in *ogam*.[23] The story concludes with the revelation that the visitor from Munster is the revenant Caílte and that Mongán is in reality (a reborn?) Finn mac Cumaill.[24]

With *Scél asa mberar* we have Finn materials taken over into what was, at that time, a larger written tradition concerning Mongán, a text 'in which southern traditions are appropriated by a northern author'.[25] The relative lack of cultivation of Mongán literature from the late Old Irish period onwards should not blind us to the vigour and substance of the early corpus concerning him.[26] Proinsias Mac Cana sees this Mongán/Finn development as typical of 'east Ulster in the seventh century [which] was the focus of a remarkable phase of literary activity which handled traditional materials in a free, fresh and sometimes innovational style'.[27] Kim McCone is of the same opinion regarding the literary significance of East Ulster asserting that 'one can hardly help wondering whether this locality and its monasteries might have been the cradle of continuous prose and prosimetrum writing in Old Irish'.[28]

There are many comparisons which may be drawn between *Scél asa mberar* and early Finn Cycle materials. Briefly, we may note:

- Mongán and Finn both share the gift of mantic perception;
- Fothad Airgtech is drawn into Finn's ambit in this story; as we have seen, his brother, Fothad Canainne, is also brought into the Fenian Cycle;

[21] The abode of the dead was known as Tech nDuinn ('The house of Donn') and was said to be located off the Bear peninsula. For discussion, see Meyer, 'Der irische Totengott und die Toteninsel', 537–43. [22] Ollarba: river Larne, County Antrim. [23] See Carey, 'The testimony', where he assembles evidence to show that *ogam* inscriptions could be used as legal proof, and could function as 'the correction of the living by the dead' (p. 4). In this example we have 'double' testimony, as the *ogam* inscription identifies the body in the grave and also establishes the veracity of the evidence provided by the visitor from Munster. [24] Ó Briain, 'The conception and death of Fionn Mac Cumhaill's canine cousin', p. 198, refers to *Scél asa mberar* as 'an embryonic *Acallam na senórach*' believing that it 'must have influenced the development of the *Acallam*'; cf. Carey, 'Suibne Geilt and Tuán mac Cairill', 104–5. This tale is also discussed by Toner in the context of the limitations of poetic authority, and how such authority should not be confused with truth: 'Authority, verse and the transmission of *senchas*', 75–7. [25] Carey, 'On the interrelationships', 77. [26] Mongán is the central figure of four inter-related Old Irish texts (*Compert Mongáin, Scél asa mberar, Scél Mongáin, Tucait baile Mongáin*) and he plays an important part in *Immram Brain*: see White, *Compert Mongáin* (= Meyer, *The voyage of Bran*, pp 42–58; Hull, 'An incomplete version'; Mac Mathúna, *Immram Brain*, pp 472–9; *LU* pp 333–7). He is also the main character in two other texts: *Compert Mongáin ocus serc Duibe Lacha do Mongán* (Meyer, *The voyage of Bran*, pp 58–84) and Knott, 'Why Mongán was deprived of noble issue'; see White, *Compert Mongáin*, pp 41–4. Further miscellaneous early references to Mongán are assembled in Meyer, *The voyage of Bran*, pp 84–90. [27] Mac Cana, '*Fianaigecht* in the pre-Norman period', p. 88. [28] McCone,

- this would seem to be the earliest text in which Caílte's ability from which he got his epithet, *coslúath* 'swift of foot', is implicitly being referenced with his dash from south-west Munster to the River Larne;[29]
- Mongán is also bound up with the *fían*: in *Immram Brain* he is described as being *la fénnid(i)* 'with *fían-warrior/s*';[30] and in the poem beginning *Fíanna bátar i nEmain*, his death at the hands of the *fían* of Cenn Tíre is mentioned.[31]

This tradition linking Caílte with the killing of Fothad Airgtech at Ollarba is an enduring one in the Fenian Cycle. For example, it is mentioned in the poem beginning *Eól dam i ndairib dréchta*,[32] and again in the lay known as 'The shield of Fionn';[33] it is also cited in the annalistic tradition.[34] Furthermore, a battle at Ollarba becomes known as one of the three battles which brought about the downfall of Finn and his *fían*.[35] Overall, it is clear that North of Ireland characters and locations formed an important part of early *fíanaigecht* tradition.

FINN AND CORCU LOÍGDE

Links between *fíanaigecht* and south-west Ireland primarily concern Finn and Lugaid Mac Con, the legendary king of Ireland of Corcu Loígde descent.[36] We know from early sources that there was an important *fían* associated with Mac Con; for example, there is mention of *fían maicc Maicc Con* in Tírechán's *Collectanea* which might be a scribal error for *fían Maic Con*.[37] There are also relevant references in *Sanas Chormaic* s.vv. *mugéme*,[38] and *rincne*.[39] This latter entry constitutes a short retelling of an incident in *Scéla Mośauluim*. Here Finn slays Ferchess, in revenge for his killing of Lugaid Mac Con, because he was his *fían*-warrior (*ar is Find ba fhénnid do suidiu*).[40] As Sharon Arbuthnot has pointed

---

Echtrae Chonnlai, p. 119. **29** This defining characteristic of Caílte is also found in Welsh literature where he is called Scilti Scawntroet 'Caílte light-foot': for discussion, see Sims-Williams, *Irish influence on medieval Welsh literature*, pp 173–80. **30** The plural reading is from Mac Mathúna, *Immram Brain*, p. 42 §56; the singular from Meyer, *The voyage of Bran*, p. 26 §56. Neither translates as '*fían*-warrior/s': Mac Mathúna (p. 55) chooses 'warriors' while Meyer (p. 27) opts for 'champion'. **31** Stokes, 'On the deaths', 310 §29 (= *LL* i, ll 4095–6); the other half of the same quatrain concerns Finn's death. See also ibid., 322 §28 and 328 §27. **32** Meyer, 'Mitteilungen aus irischen Handschriften: *Do chomramaib Laigen inso sís*', 118 §18. **33** *DF* I, §xvi, pp 37, 138. **34** *AFM* 285 (i, pp 120–1). **35** Stokes, 'Acallamh', ll 1–10 (= O'Grady, 'Agallamh', i, p. 94, ii, p. 101; Dooley and Roe, *Tales*, p. 3). **36** This section draws on the fuller discussion in Ó Muirigh, 'Fionn, fian agus Corca Laoidhe'. In *Macgnímrada Finn*, some of Finn's exploits bring him to West Munster, primarily into Cíarraige terrritory: see Meyer, 'Macgnimartha Find', 200 §§13–14 (= Meyer, 'The boyish exploits', 184 §§13–14; Nagy, *The wisdom of the outlaw*, p. 212; *CHA* §93 p. 197). **37** Bieler, *The Patrician texts*, pp 154–5, §40.7 (= *CHA* §99 p. 212). That the second *maicc* is most likely a case of dittography is pointed out in *EIHM* p. 202 n. 1. **38** Meyer, 'Sanas Cormaic', pp 75–7 §883 (= Stokes, *Three Irish glossaries*, pp 29–30; O'Donovan, *Sanas Chormaic*, pp 111–12). **39** *Fian*. pp xx–xxi (= Meyer, 'Sanas Cormaic', p. 97 §1084; Stokes, *Three Irish glossaries*, pp 38–9; O'Donovan, *Sanas Chormaic*, pp 142–3). **40** O Daly, *Cath Maige Mucrama*, l. 681 (= *Fian*. p. 38).

Further early fíanaigecht *sources*

out with regard to Ferchess, 'his name seems to be understood as a compound of *fer* "a man" and *ces* "a spear", and, whenever this figure appears, violent action involving spears seems bound to ensue'.[41]

Kuno Meyer follows Heinrich Zimmer in seeing this Finn episode 'as a later insertion';[42] however, the fact that these events are also present in verses in *Scéla Moṡauluim*, which may be as old as AD 700, would tend to negate this opinion.[43] If this date be accepted, then the material associating Finn with Corcu Loígde is contemporary with the oldest of the various other traditions discussed here. Furthermore, it is suggested below that Finn and *fíanaigecht* may also be connected with Corcu Loígde through the character of Fothad Canainne.[44] Finn, as we have seen, is presented as the *fénnid* of Lugaid Mac Con in *Scéla Moṡauluim*; in *Bruiden Átha Í* (and later in the *Acallam*), Fothad is said to be a son of Lugaid. Both are associated with the Cailleach Bérre, who has been shown by Tomás Ó Cathasaigh to be the archetypal sovereignty goddess,[45] intimately bound up with Corcu Loígde.[46] As Pádraig Ó Riain has pointed out to me, the literary connections between Finn, Corcu Loígde and the Cailleach Bérre are also preserved in later Irish tradition in the poem beginning *A aencheard Bhérre*.[47]

FINN AND MIDE

In many Middle Irish sources, Finn is intimately bound up with Mide and, more particularly, with Tara. It is tempting to see this connection as arising from the nationalization of the Finn Cycle, which was underway by the tenth century. This process is best exemplified by the portrayal of Finn that begins to emerge at this period, as leader of the *fían* of Ireland under the king of Tara, Cormac mac Airt. The first text to explicitly connect Finn with Cormac would seem to be 'Finn and Gráinne', dating perhaps to the tenth or eleventh century.[48]

There is evidence to suggest, however, that Finn's connection with Mide may not have originated with his emerging role as leader of Cormac mac Airt's *fían* but may have been traditionally considered a constituent part of his 'biography', particularly in tales concerning his death. For example, the earliest references we have to Finn's demise are in the fragmentary text concerning his death, *Aided Finn*, and in two poems attributed to Cináed úa hArtacáin (†975). In *Aided Finn*, he dies on the banks of the Boyne and is found by the three sons of Uirgriu, and

---

41 Arbuthnot, 'Finn, Ferches and the *rincne*: versions compared', p. 64.   **42** *Fian*. p. xxi.   **43** Murray, 'A reading from *Scéla Moshauluim*', 200 n. 22.   **44** See Chapter Thirteen, pp 156–7.   **45** Ó Cathasaigh, 'The eponym of Cnogba', 30, 33–8; see Radner, 'The hag of Beare'.   **46** For example, as Ó Coileáin, 'The structure of a literary cycle', 109, has argued, the famous 'Lament' associated with the Cailleach may well be interpreted as a reflection of the waning power of Corcu Loígde due to Eóganacht expansion.   **47** Found in Leabhar Ua Maine, fo. 146vb26–147va51 (as yet unpublished).   **48** Meyer, 'Finn and Grainne';

by Aiclech mac Dubdrenn who beheads him.[49] The first of the two úa hArtacáin poems found in *Senchas na relec* concerns the graveyard at Brug na Bóinne and notes Finn's death at the hands of the Lúaigne (*for fein Lúaigni lond*).[50] The second, beginning *Fíanna bátar i nEmain*, again mentions the Lúaigne and locates his slaying at a ford on the river Boyne.[51] Thus, the killing of Finn by the Lúaigne is a consistent, if not exclusive, part of Fenian tradition.[52]

For T.F. O'Rahilly, the Lúaigne, whom he believed later Gaelicized their name as Luigne, were 'a section of the Ernean population of the Tara district whom the Goidelic conquerors of the Eastern Midlands enrolled as vassal-allies and fighting-men' and notes that 'tradition consistently represents [them] as defenders of the Tara monarchy against its enemies'.[53] Thus, Finn's new role in medieval Irish literature as leader of the *fían* of the king of Tara may be interpreted as usurping the earlier literary role of the Lúaigne who were reckoned as the *fénnidi* of Cormac's grandfather, Conn Cétchathach.[54] This development seems to represent the continuation of a long-established literary opposition between Finn and the Lúaigne. The other texts that also explore this issue, *Macgnímrada Finn* and *Fotha catha Cnucha*, postdate the earliest reference to Finn's death by over a century and thus may not constitute independent sources for the ongoing feuding between Finn and the Lúaigne. That the opposition between Finn and the Lúaigne predates the earliest extant narratives concerning his death becomes clear when one examines the tale known as 'Finn and the jester' preserved in *Sanas Chormaic* under the lemma *orc tréith*.[55] This short story, dating perhaps to the ninth century, tells how Finn's jester, Lomnae, comes upon Finn's female companion, an unnamed woman of the Luigne, sleeping with the *fénnid* Cairpre, who pleads with him to keep her secret:

> Teccomnacuir didiu Find fecht n-and i Tethbai cona féin 7 luidh for cūairt selgae 7 dorrūaraid Lomnae i fuss. A mbūi side oc imt[h]echt ammuigh co farnic Corpri fēinnid i lligi la mnāi Find i tāidhe. Roguid didiu an ben do Lomnae a dīchlidh 7 ba saoth lais-som brath Find.

Corthals, 'Die Trennung'.   **49** Meyer, 'The death of Finn mac Cumaill'; this is discussed in Chapter Ten, pp 126–7. See the detailed discussion in Parsons, 'Breaking the cycle?' and the convenient list of references in her Appendix (pp 91–6 at pp 91–3).   **50** *LU* l. 4152; cf. *Fian.* p. xxii §XIII.   **51** Stokes, 'On the deaths', p. 310 §29 (= *LL* i, ll 4097–8).   **52** See Chapter Ten, pp 124–6.   **53** *EIHM* p. 391.   **54** This is explicitly stated in *LL* facs. p. 386b49–51: *ro boi righfianus eirenn acu geinmháir co rus dilgenn finn mac cumaill iat iar tain 7 is iat ro batar tuailngigh catha la conn cétchathach*, 'they had the royal *fianas* of Ireland for a long time until Finn mac Cumaill destroyed them afterwards, and it is they who were the battle chiefs of Conn Cétchathach' (cf. *ZCP* 8, 599). Similarly, Finn's destruction of the Lúaigne of Tara (Lúaigne Temrach) is noted in *Timna Cathaír Máir*: Dillon, *Lebor na cert*, pp 168–9.   **55** *Fian.* pp xix–xx (= Meyer, 'Sanas Cormaic', pp 86–8 §1018; Stokes, *Three Irish glossaries*, pp 34–5; O'Donovan, *Sanas Chormaic*, pp 129–31; Russell, 'Poets, power and possessions', pp 39–40). A Middle Irish verion of this tale is published

Further early fianaigecht *sources*

> Once Find came into Tethba with his *fían* and went hunting and Lomnae remained behind. When he was going out, he saw Cairpre the *fénnid* secretly lying with Finn's woman. The woman beseeched Lomnae to conceal it but it would grieve him to betray Find.[56]

When Lomnae makes this deceit known to Finn in an *ogam* riddle carved on a switch, the woman has her lover kill and behead the jester in revenge. Finn comes across the headless body, divines its identity through the mantic practice known as *teinm laído*,[57] finds Cairpre and his fellow warriors in company with Lomnae's talking head – which is on a spit by the fire as fish is being cooked[58] – and then kills him. This is the sole example in the early *fíanaigecht* material of the Lúaigne being called by their later name, Luigne; it also provides another example of the ongoing feud between them and Finn.

Finally, from a Mide perspective, it is worth noting that two of the three battles that brought about the end of the *fían*, namely the battles of Gabar and Comar, are located within its borders;[59] this is unsurprising considering that they were fought against king Cairpre Lifechair, son of Cormac mac Airt.

SHARED THEMES AMONG THE EARLY SOURCES

Though these various Old Irish and early Middle Irish compositions are connected with various parts of the country, this does not mean that they are completely independent of each other. In fact, there are enough thematic similarities between these sources to suggest that, however we conceptualize the relationships, much of this extant material seems to reflect widespread shared traditions. These correspondences are here outlined in brief:

1 *Treachery of women*
Early *fíanaigecht* sources are pretty consistent in attributing a treacherous nature to women. Téite in *Bruiden Átha Í* is mistakenly thought by her husband to be the cause of his death; Finn's paramour attempts to seduce his *gilla* in 'Finn and the man in the tree' and succeeds in having him banished from Finn's retinue; his chosen lover betrays him with another man in 'Finn and the jester' and helps bring about the death of Lomnae. Similarly, the wife of Ailill Flann Becc betrays

by Dillon, 'Stories from the law tracts', 48–9, 58–61 §IX (= *CIH* vi, pp 2115.38–2116.27). **56** *Fian*. p. xix (= Meyer, 'Sanas Cormaic', p. 87 §1018; Stokes, *Three Irish glossaries*, p. 34; O'Donovan, *Sanas Chormaic*, p. 130). **57** See *EIHM* pp 336–40; Carey, 'Obscure styles', 24–5. **58** A similar tableau of severed head and fish is found in a story concerning Finn's demise: see Meyer, 'The death of Finn', 464–5; cf. Chapter Ten, p. 126. **59** Stokes, 'Acallamh', ll 1–2 (= O'Grady, 'Agallamh', i, p. 94, ii, p. 101; Dooley and Roe, *Tales*, p. 3). Gabar: the Gowra valley near Tara, County Meath; Comar: near Clonard, County Meath, probably at the confluence of the river Boyne and the Clonard or Kinnegad river (see *HDGP*

him in *Reicne Fothaid Chanainne*.⁶⁰ It is also significant that in most of these narratives the women are not even named.

2 *Finn's inability to form lasting relationships with women*

Alongside this presentation of women as treacherous are the repeated instances in the early sources of Finn's inability to form permanent relationships with members of the opposite sex. Thus, in 'Finn and the man in the tree', 'Finn and the jester', and 'Finn and Gráinne', the women he has chosen as partners do not reciprocate his desire and all pull away from him; these parallels have prompted Joseph Nagy to refer to the character of Derc Corra from 'Finn and the man in the tree' as 'arguably a multiform of the figure of Diarmait'.⁶¹ As John Carey has noted, 'Find's own identity as a roving warrior-hunter opens up to him the possibility of a multitude of sexual relationships, but at the same time dooms all such relationships to impermanence'.⁶² Such a multitude of relationships is explicitly mentioned in 'Finn and the jester' where it is said that whatever hill or forest Finn frequented, 'there used to be an appointed woman awaiting him in every territory in closest proximity to him'.⁶³ It also seems evident that part of Finn's incapacity with women is due to his position as an eternal *gilla* in society, never fully entering the adult world.⁶⁴

3 *The gaining of inspiration*

Finn's ability to gain insight is repeatedly stressed in the early sources; he 'wins knowledge in liminal situations and is marked as a liminal figure by the acquisition of knowledge'.⁶⁵ For example, Finn's getting and using of this gift is one of the central themes in *Marbad Cúlduib* and 'Finn and the man in the tree'. Similarly, in 'Finn and the jester' and *Scéla Mos̄auluim*, we see Finn's recourse to his prophetic capacity to illuminate the course of events. Even with Finn's brief appearance in *Reicne Fothaid Chanainne*, it is his mantic abilities which are mentioned.⁶⁶

'Cóbh – Cutloch', s.n.). **60** See below, Chapter Thirteen, pp 153–5. **61** Nagy, *Mercantile myth*, p. 16. Diarmaid is, of course, an important Fenian character, one of the central figures in *Tóraigheacht Dhiarmada agus Ghráinne*; for details, see Chapter Seven. **62** Carey, 'Nōdons, Lugus, Windos', p. 115. This is frequently the situation in the Fenian lays also; one might instance Finn and Daolach who had a short-lived relationship until her death in 'The naming of Dún Gáire' (*DF* II, §xxxviii, pp 28–9 [stanza 28]) and the impermanence of the union between Finn and Scáthach in 'Caoilte's urn' (*DF* I, §xvii, pp 42–4, 145–8). **63** *Fian.* p. xix: *nobith ben aurdalta ar a chind in cach thīr ba nessam dō* (= Meyer, 'Sanas Cormaic', p. 87 §1018; Stokes, *Three Irish glossaries*, p. 34; O'Donovan, *Sanas Chormaic*, p. 130). **64** See Nagy, *The wisdom of the outlaw*, pp 124–63. A *gilla* in medieval Irish society was a youth who was old enough to bear arms but who had not yet reached the age of manhood (*óclachas*). The term (anglicized in Scots as 'ghillie' or 'gillie') was also frequently used of those who were in positions of service to others; for example, messengers, attendants and servants. **65** Nagy, 'Liminality and knowledge', 142. **66** See below, Chapter Thirteen, p. 154.

4 Severed heads

It is striking that so many of the early *fíanaigecht* sources use the motif of the severed head. Although this is also common in medieval Irish literature outside of the Fenian Cycle,[67] it has a pronounced usage in early Finn tales. Thus, the decapitated heads of Cuirrech and Téite in *Bruiden Átha Í*, of Lomnae in 'Finn and the jester',[68] and of Finn himself in traditions concerning his death,[69] all point to the importance of this motif. Some of these heads also get to speak after separation from the body and in these circumstances their words are seen to have more weight and authority. Similarly, in *Reicne Fothaid Chanainne*, it is Fothad's severed head which recites the all-important poetic composition or *reicne*.[70]

Other themes which appear in numerous early sources include hunting with dogs;[71] raiding; cooking (particularly pigs); the portrayal of other *fíana*; the presence of an Otherworld thief; and the conflict between old and young. Many of these have proved very durable, featuring prominently in later Finn Cycle narratives, particularly the *Acallam*.

CONCLUSIONS

It is possible to draw tentative conclusions about the cultivation of the earliest strands of *fíanaigecht* based on the foregoing presentation. We have seen that the Old Irish Fenian sources connect Finn with Loígis and Dál nAraide (Cruithin peoples), with Laigin, and with Déisi and Corcu Loígde (Érainn population groups),[72] and that the later death tales, among other sources, say that Finn is of Uí Thairsig descent (Laigin) and that his mortal enemies are Lúaigne (Érainn). Traditionally, none of these materials were seen to connect Finn with the dominant Goídil as Cruithin, Érainn and Laigin are all seen by O'Rahilly as pre-Goidelic Celtic settlers in Ireland;[73] more recently, however, scholars such as John Koch would incline to the view that the Érainn were Goídil in origin.[74] Though one should not overemphasize the point, there may be some support here for

---

67 For example, the best-known examples of talking severed heads are those of Donn Bó in *Cath Almaine* (ed. Ó Riain, ll 147–64) and of Sualtaim in *Táin bó Cúailnge* (ed. O'Rahilly, ll 3442–8). **68** For discussion, see Clancy, 'Fools and adultery', 110–12; Carey, *Ireland and the grail*, pp 256–8. **69** See below, Chapter Ten, pp 125–7. **70** On severed heads, see Nagy, *Conversing with angels and ancients*, pp 158–63, 299–303. **71** See the brief humorous lament for the ill-judged Fenian hunt of the boar of Druim Leithe in Meyer, *The triads of Ireland*, pp 30–1, §236. On the importance of hounds to the *fénnidi*, see Chadbourne, 'The beagle's cry'; eadem, 'The voices of hounds'. For Bran, the most famous of all Finn's hounds, see Ó Briain, 'The conception and death of Fionn Mac Cumhaill's canine cousin'. The story of how Bran and Sceolang became hounds is related in Joynt, *Feis tighe Chonáin*, §XI–XVII, ll 698–1140 (cf. O'Kearney, '*Feis tighe Chonain Chinn-Shleibhe*', 159–67). **72** This final grouping also links Finn with Fothad Canainne: see Ó Muirigh, 'Fionn, fian agus Corca Laoidhe'. **73** *EIHM* pp 15–17. **74** See the convenient summary of his views in 'Ériu, Alba, and Letha', 22–3.

Eoin MacNeill's belief that the Finn Cycle originated as 'the hero-lore of a subject, not of a ruling race'.[75]

It is suggested above in Chapter Two that a contributing factor to *fianaigecht* emerging as a truly national literature in the Middle Irish period was the very widespread and fragmentary nature of the early tradition, which means that it was being cultivated at numerous diverse places throughout the country and so had a chance to develop in more than one location. Our analysis of the themes which are shared across these early sources points to the cultivation countrywide of similar types of material associated with Finn. It seems impossible to say whether these traditions were associated with diverse settings because material concerning an earlier divine hero fragmented and was separately cultivated, or whether traditions about different *fían*-leaders became subsumed into the narrative cycle associated with one of their number: either way, we are clearly dealing with 'a multiplicity of Finns'.[76] Whatever its origins, however, by the end of the Middle Irish period, the Finn Cycle belonged to all the peoples of Ireland, its 'nationalization' part of 'a sequence of profound socio-political, cultural and religious change which extended from about the tenth century to the end of the twelfth'.[77]

---

[75] See above, Chapter Two, p. 51. Mac Neill arrived at this conclusion, however, by mistakenly arguing that 'the Fenian epic originated among the Galeoin who dwelt in the neighbourhood of Almu': *DF* I, p. xxxii. [76] McQuillan, 'Finn, Fothad, and *fían*', 4. [77] Mac Cana, '*Fianaigecht* in the pre-Norman period', p. 99.

CHAPTER SEVEN

The background to *Tóraigheacht Dhiarmada agus Ghráinne*

What may be the best-known and best-loved Fenian tale, *Tóraigheacht Dhiarmada agus Ghráinne*, is a substantial narrative that details the love of Gráinne for the *fian*-warrior, Diarmaid ua Duibhne.[1] Betrothed to a no-longer young Finn, she forces Diarmaid to elope with her against his wishes and consequently Finn devotes his time to pursuing them, even inviting foreigners from overseas into the country to aid him.[2] After numerous close shaves, peace is finally made between the parties by Diarmaid's foster-father, Aonghus of Brugh na Bóinne. However, Finn later inveigles Diarmaid into hunting the magic boar of Beann Ghulban, which results in his death. As he lies dying, Finn refuses to give him a drink from his hands which would keep him alive.[3] The story ends with Gráinne gathering Diarmaid's family together, exhorting them to avenge their father.

Notwithstanding its centrality to Fenian tradition, the *Tóraigheacht* does not date to the medieval Irish period.[4] The earliest manuscript to contain this text is RIA MS 24 P 9, written by Dáibhidh Ó Duibhgeannáin in 1651; the narrative is present in a further forty manuscripts that date to the eighteenth and nineteenth centuries (between 1718 and 1850). Even though the manuscript tradition of the *Tóraigheacht* is late, its editor Nessa Ní Shéaghdha believes that the story was in existence, substantially in its present format, in the fourteenth century.[5] She bases this opinion on the fact that some of the poetry in the collection known as *Duanaire Ghearóid Iarla*, preserved in the Book of Fermoy, shares a background and context with the *Tóraigheacht*;[6] this material was composed in the second half of the fourteenth century by Gearóid Iarla, the third earl of Desmond (†1398).[7] Furthermore, as pointed out by Ruairí Ó hUiginn, the reference in the text to

---

1 The standard edition is that of Ní Shéaghdha, *Tóruigheacht*; previously edited by O'Grady, *Tóruigheacht Dhiarmuda agus Ghráinne*. **2** This is in contrast to the regular presentation of Finn as defender of Ireland against attack from without: see Ó hUiginn, '*Tóruigheacht Dhiarmada agus Ghráinne*', 161. **3** Finn's withholding of the drink is reminiscent of Lug's repudiation of the sons of Tuireann who wish to borrow the pig skin of the king of Greece which would heal their mortal wounds: see below, Chapter Twelve, p. 150. **4** This chapter draws freely on the 'Introduction' to Ní Shéaghdha, *Tóruigheacht*, pp ix–xxxi and Ó Cathasaigh, 'Tóraíocht'. **5** Murphy, *Ossianic* lore, p. 12, remarks concerning the *Tóraigheacht*: 'The only complete telling of the tale which has been preserved can hardly ... be older than the fourteenth century, and may not be much older than the earliest extant text of it'. **6** Ní Shéaghdha, *Tóruigheacht*, pp xiii–xiv. **7** Edited by Mac Niocaill, 'Duanaire Ghearóid Iarla'. The question of its autorship has been re-examined by

Clann Riocaird (*go rángadar go Doire Dá Bhaoth a gceart-lár Chloinne Ricaird*, ll 265–6) would also point towards a similar date of composition.[8]

Though the extant *Tóraigheacht* is quite late in date, we know that a tale concerning Diarmaid and Gráinne was current in tenth-century Ireland because of the existence of the title *Aithed Gráinne la Diarmaid* in the medieval Irish tale-lists.[9] A number of early Diarmaid and Gráinne narratives have survived, mainly from the Middle Irish period. Because we have no surviving copy of the *Aithed*, however, we cannot be certain if any of these materials derive from it.

COMPARISONS BETWEEN THE *TÓRAIGHEACHT* AND EARLIER SOURCES

Though all early and late versions of the tale share many features, themes and a basic structure in common, there are important differences between the contexts of the tale as presented in the *Tóraigheacht* (and in *Duanaire Ghearóid Iarla*) as compared with the earlier sources (detailed below). These differences may be briefly enumerated here:[10]

- in 'Finn and Gráinne', Gráinne is married to Finn while in *Tochmarc Ailbe* she is named as his former wife; such a marriage in not mentioned in the *Tóraigheacht* nor in *Duanaire Ghearóid Iarla*;
- in 'Finn and Gráinne' and *Tochmarc Ailbe*, though their separation creates problems, there is no emphasis on any personal acrimony between Finn and Gráinne on its account; in the *Tóraigheacht* and in *Duanaire Ghearóid Iarla*, the personal antipathy caused by their parting is foregrounded;
- there is a strong Munster element in both the *Tóraigheacht* and *Duanaire Ghearóid Iarla* which is not found in 'Finn and Gráinne' and *Tochmarc Ailbe*. Diarmaid and Gráinne's itinerary brings them to Limerick and Sliabh Luachra in the *Tóraigheacht*; in his position as earl of Desmond, it is no surprise to see Gearóid mac Muiris focusing on the Munster aspect of this narrative tradition in his *duanaire*.

The fundamental difference between the older fragments and the later tradition, however, is that the Middle Irish materials contain no mention of Diarmaid's

---

Mac Mathúna, 'An fhilíocht a leagtar ar Ghearóid Iarla i Leabhar Fhear Maí'. **8** Ó hUiginn, '*Tóruigheacht Dhiarmada agus Ghráinne*', 160. The earliest annal reference to Clann Riocaird dates to 1213 though it is more regularly attested from the fourteenth century onwards. For details, see *HDGP* 'Clais an Chairn – Cnucha', s.n. **9** Mac Cana, *The learned tales*, pp 46, 57: *A. Grainne re Diarmait / A. Grainde re Diarmaid* (List A); *Aithi Graine ingine Corbmaic la Diarmaid ua nDuibne / A. Graine ingine Cormaic ri Diarmaitt hua nDuibne / Aithed Granne ingine Corbmaic la Diarmaid ua Duibhne* (List B). Ó hUiginn, '*Tóruigheacht Dhiarmada agus Ghráinne*', 161, notes that *tóraigheacht* tales become common in the Early Modern Irish period but are not given as a tale-type in the tale-lists. **10** For what follows, see Ní Shéaghdha,

death by the magic boar. This is first mentioned in the literature in *Acallam na senórach*:[11]

> Ocus luidhset as sin rompo co Leacht na muice [co Beind nGulban,] áit ar' marbh an muc Diarmait ó Duibhne.[12]

> And they departed then for Leacht na Muice, to Beann Ghulban, the place where the pig killed Diarmaid ua Duibhne.

and again:

> do Lighi in Ḟeindida, in bail ar' marb in mucc doilfi drái[d]echta Diarmait húa Duibne.[13]

> to Lighe an Ḟéinnidha, the place where the magically-formed pig killed Diarmaid ua Duibhne.

Though these references are brief and pithy, it is clear that the author expects his audience to know what they relate to. Nevertheless, as is apparent from these quotes, no explicit link is made between Diarmaid's demise and his elopement with Gráinne. This connection is noted for the first time in the poem beginning *Éuchtach inghen Díarmatta*,[14] whose composition Murphy has tentatively placed at 'some date between 1250 and 1400'.[15] Furthermore, the outline structure of the *Tóraigheacht* is present in the opening eight verses of this poem, further evidence that the storyline was extant in something like its current form by the fourteenth century.[16]

THE EXTANT MEDIEVAL IRISH SOURCES FOR THE DIARMAID AND GRÁINNE STORY[17]

1. 'Finn and Gráinne': This is the title given by Kuno Meyer to a short text from the Book of Lecan, which gives an account of Finn's wooing of Gráinne.[18] To

---

Tóruigheacht, pp xii–xiii; Ó Cathasaigh, 'Tóraíocht', pp 34–6. **11** Of course, 'the reliability of material is not necessarily dependent on the date of the language, and the general assumption that it is, is an unfortunate legacy of a scholarship built on a linguistic foundation': Ó Coileáin, 'The structure of a literary cycle', 89. **12** Stokes, 'Acallamh', ll 1514–15 (= O'Grady, 'Agallamh', i, p. 127, ii, p. 138; Dooley and Roe, *Tales*, p. 47). **13** Stokes, 'Acallamh', ll 6895–6 [cf. trans. p. 257] (= Dooley and Roe, *Tales*, p. 194). **14** *DF* I, §xviii, pp 45–7, 149–51. **15** *DF* III, p. 40; perhaps, this composition might be more closely dated to 1300–50. **16** A poem on the death of Diarmaid, dating perhaps to the fifteenth century and preserved in the Book of the Dean of Lismore, has been edited, translated and analysed by Meek, 'The death of Diarmaid' (see also Lloyd, Bergin and Schoepperle, 'The death of Diarmaid', 162–8). It makes no mention of a relationship between Diarmaid and Gráinne (who does not feature in the composition). **17** The sources itemized here have been discussed in detail by Ní Shéaghdha, *Tóruigheacht*, pp x–xii and by Ó Cathasaigh, 'Tóraíocht', pp 33–7. See also Lloyd, Bergin and Schoepperle, 'The reproach of Diarmaid', 41–4; Meek, 'The death of Diarmaid', 337–8. **18** Meyer, 'Finn and Grainne'; Corthals, 'Die Trennung'.

avoid having to accept his advances, she sets Finn an impossible task: the collection of a pair of every wild animal in Ireland. However, her plan backfires when Caílte completes the task on his behalf and arrives in Tara with the animals;[19] she is then betrothed to Finn. At a subsequent feast of Tara, however, Finn overhears Gráinne saying to her father that she hates him; they separate consequently. There is no mention of Diarmaid in the narrative, which probably dates to the tenth or eleventh century.

2. *Tochmarc Ailbe*: In this story, we see Finn in exile because of Gráinne's elopement with Diarmaid with resultant tensions between him and Cormac mac Airt, Gráinne's father. Cormac makes peace with Finn who is divorced from Gráinne. Finn then pursues Gráinne's younger sister, Ailbe, who is happy to accept his advances. We hear no more subsequently in *Tochmarc Ailbe* of what becomes of Gráinne and Diarmaid.[20] The text likely dates to the early Middle Irish period.

3. In the commentary to *Amra Coluim Chille*, there are two stray verses which concern Diarmaid and Gráinne. In the first, which may date to the ninth or tenth century, Gráinne tells Finn of her love for another:

> *Ut dixit Gráinne ingen Chormaic fri Finn*
> Fil duine
> frismad buide lemm díuterc,
> día tibrinn in mbith mbuide,
> huile, huile, cid díupert.
>
> As Gráinne, daughter of Cormac, said to Finn
> There is one on whom I should gladly gaze, to whom I would give the bright world, all of it, all of it, though it be an unequal bargain.[21]

Gerard Murphy thought that this might be 'the earliest reference extant to Gráinne's love for Díarmait', though of course he is not explicitly named therein;[22] furthermore, we cannot be certain that the title and the verse were originally a unity.

---

19 Caílte's feat with the wild animals is also well-attested in later sources; for references, see *DF* III, pp 18–19 and Meek, 'Development and degeneration in Gaelic ballad texts', pp 141–2. Murphy notes that this 'version of the theme resembles the international folktale of the rabbit-herd, who, with the help of his magic pipe, calls rabbits together, and thereby wins a princess as his bride': *DF* III, p. 19 n. 2. To continue the folklore comparison: mention must be made of Caílte's role in this story which is so similar to that of the magic helper in later Fenian lore. Murphy has pointed out that 'these Fionn helper-tales have a generic resemblance to the folktale, told in many countries, of the Skilful Companions … who arrive to help a folktale hero in performing a task or winning a bride': *DF* III, p. xiii. Cf. *DF* III, Appendix A, pp 177–88: 'Orally preserved Fionn helper-tales'. A further comparison (in a wooing-tale context) may also be drawn: in *Tochmarc Emire*, Cú Chulainn is sent by Conchobur to collect the flocks and wild animals of Slíab Fúait (van Hamel, *Compert Con Culainn*, p. 65 §89). **20** *Tochmarc Ailbe* is the subject of the next chapter. **21** Murphy, *Early Irish lyrics*, pp 160–1 (= Stokes, 'The Bodleian Amra Choluimb Chille', 156–7). **22** Murphy, *Early Irish lyrics*,

The second verse, tentatively dated to the eleventh century, is thought to have been spoken by Diarmaid, even though the narrator is not identified. The mention of a kingdom (l. 2) might refer to Gráinne in her role as Cormac's daughter; thus, it could conceivably be addressed to her by Finn before she elopes with Diarmaid. This is less likely, however, as it extols the decision she has made, presumably her choosing of the outdoor life with the *fian*:

> Is maith do chuit, a Gráinne
> is ferr duit inda ríge
> serccoll na cailech feda
> la banna meda míne.
>
> Good is your portion, o Gráinne,
> it is better for you than a kingdom
> the meat of the wood grouse
> with a drop of sweet mead.[23]

4. *Úath Beinne Étair*: Dating perhaps to the eleventh century, this untitled prose narrative, which contains a poem of nine quatrains, describes an incident occurring in a cave on the Hill of Howth that may have formed part of a larger composition concerning the elopement of Diarmaid and Gráinne. Finn nearly catches up with the pair but Diarmaid's foster-father, Aonghus from Brugh na Bóinne, comes to their rescue. There is no story title given in either of the manuscripts. Ní Shéaghdha has followed earlier scholarship in equating this narrative with *Úath Beinne Étair*, a title preserved in one of the medieval Irish tale-lists, presumably because of the opening line of the text:

> Fechtus dio raiuhe Diarmait mac Duinn i Duipne ind uaim Penni hEdair ier mbreith Grainde ingine Corbmaic aur aithed o Find.
>
> Once Díarmaid, son of Donn, grandson of Duibhne, was in the cave of the Hill of Howth after carrying off Gráinne, daughter of Cormac, in elopement from Finn.[24]

Ní Shéaghdha believes that in origin 'it is probably an episode from the lost tale, *Aithed Grainne ingine Corbmaic le Diarmaid ua nDuibne*';[25] in favour of this conjecture, we see that the word *aithed* 'elopement' is also contained in the opening line.

p. 236. However, if we accept that the poem beginning *Úar in lathe do Lum Laine* (no. 5 below) refers to Gráinne and Diarmaid, Murphy's statement may not be true as that poem is at least as old, if not older, than this verse. **23** Stokes, 'The Bodleian Amra Choluimb Chille', 264–5. **24** Ní Shéaghdha, *Tóruigheacht*, pp 130–1; for discussion, see Meyer, 'Uath Beinne Etair', 125–8. **25** Ní Shéaghdha, *Tóruigheacht*, p. 130.

5. *Úar in lathe do Lum Laine*: A poem of nine quatrains, preserved in the Book of Leinster, which takes the form of a dialogue between Tethna (presented as a daughter of Cormac mac Airt) and an otherwise unidentified lover, Lom Laine. Eugene O'Curry argued that in the 'absence of any direct historical reference to the occasion of its composition, I am inclined to believe, from the allusions in it, that it was written on the occasion of the elopement of King Cormac's elder daughter, *Grainné*, with … Dermot O'*Duibhné*'.²⁶ Máirín O Daly agreed with O'Curry's position noting that 'the circumstances indicated are so reminiscent of the story of Gráinne, not the Tóraigecht but the earlier and less romantic version in *ZCP* i 458, that I am inclined to regard "Tethna" and "Lom Laine" as pseudonyms for Gráinne and Díarmait'.²⁷

If this reasoning is accepted, this ninth-century poem would be the oldest written source extant, along with the verse beginning *Fil duine* (see above no. 3), for the Diarmaid and Gráinne story. Verses 2 and 3 of *Úar in lathe do Lum Laine* are also to be found in *Baile binnbérlach mac Búain* where verse 2 is credited to Gráinne's sister, Ailbe, in a gloss in the Harleian MS 5280 version of the tale: *Et amail adbert ingen Cormaic ui Quinn [.i. Ailbi]*.²⁸ This strengthens the Fenian links of this poem.

THE *TÓRAIGHEACHT* AND LATER MANUSCRIPTS: AN ALTERNATIVE INTERPRETATION

In scholarly approaches to this narrative complex, primacy has been given to the earliest manuscript witness to the *Tóraigheacht*, that is, RIA MS 24 P 9. However, an alternative interpretation of the relationship between this version and later texts of the narrative (particularly the longer version in RIA MS 23 L 37, written in 1737–8) has been advanced by Caoimhín Breatnach. Rather than prioritizing the shorter text of MS 24 P 9, and perceiving it as closer to a no-longer extant earlier *Tóraigheacht*, he would see its lack of consistency and narrative discrepancies as reflecting the possibility that it is an abridged version of an earlier narrative. What gives weight to Breatnach's suggestion is the fact that the three subsequent narratives in the manuscript can all be shown to have undergone this process of abridgement; there is specific evidence in one of these texts, *Tromdháimh Ghuaire*, that it was the scribe of the manuscript, Dáibhidh Ó Duibhgeannáin, who was responsible for the omission of a couple of its poems. Furthermore, '[i]ncomplete text and blank spaces left at the end of both

---

26 O'Curry, *Manuscript materials*, p. 467. **27** O Daly, 'Úar in lathe', p. 99. **28** Meyer, 'Scél Baili binnbérlaig', 223 (he added the omitted 'Ailbi' in the corrigenda in *RC* 17, 319); see Murray, 'Some thoughts on *Baile binnbérlach mac Búain*'.

Tromdháimh Ghuaire and the "Second vision of Adamnán" suggest that these texts were incomplete in Ó Duibhgeannáin's exemplar'.[29]

What weighs against this approach somewhat, however, is the emphasis placed therein upon on the significance of the 'narrative discrepancies' in the earliest text of the *Tóraigheacht*. It starts from the unproven assumption that such 'discrepancies' in the RIA MS 24 P 9 text need explication, and is largely based on a comparison with the longer later version in RIA MS 23 L 37 where some of the inconsistencies are resolved, thus rendering the narrative more 'coherent'. However, this attaches an importance to the concept of 'coherence' that is not sustained in any analysis of medieval textuality, including medieval Irish textuality. As John Dagenais has argued in another context, 'when we choose "coherence" or "intelligibility" as the *sine qua non* for undertaking work on medieval texts, pretending that these were qualities they once possessed but have now lost, we are simply choosing not to look at medieval texts'.[30] Notwithstanding these caveats, however, Breatnach's fresh approach must make us wary about making any facile assumptions about the relationships between earlier and later manuscript versions of the *Tóraigheacht*.

MYTHOLOGICAL ASPECTS OF THE *TÓRAIGHEACHT*

It has long ago been suggested that Diarmaid and Gráinne were initially mythological characters:

> That Diarmaid originally was a deity is not open to doubt. He is to be identified with the well-known god Donn, the Lord of the pagan Irish Happy Otherworld … Gráinne likewise is a mythical personage. Her name may mean 'the hateful goddess', which would well describe her true nature. Although there is but little trace of her real nature in the literary *Pursuit*, I think Gráinne really is the ugly goddess: the loathsome crone, who becomes a radiantly beautiful maiden when she marries the sacred King in many Irish stories of kingship.[31]

Though I cannot adhere to all the detail of this formulation, and am unwilling to go too far down this road in pursuit of deformed or transformed mythology,[32]

---

29 Breatnach, 'The transmission and text of *Tóruigheacht Dhiarmada agus Ghráinne*', p. 150.   **30** Dagenais, *The ethics of reading in manuscript culture*, p. 111.   **31** Breatnach, 'Tóraigheacht Dhiarmada agus Ghráinne', p. 146. If this interpretation is accepted, then as Henar Velasco López has pointed out in a paper to the medieval Irish seminar in UCC, titled 'Classical and Irish mythology: Adonis, Diarmaid and the wild boar', Diarmaid's rejecting of Gráinne may be understood as a rejection of sovereignty. She returned to this topic at the XIII International Congress of Celtic Studies in Bonn in a presentation on 'Diarmaid, Adonis and the wild boar'; I wish to thank Prof. Velasco López for providing me with a copy of this talk.   **32** Recently,

there are certainly aspects of the tale with strong Otherworldly resonances. For example, the fact that Diarmaid and the boar are destined to have the same lifespan would point in this direction. This feature of the story may have originated with Diarmaid as the possessor of an external soul, a common motif in Irish and international fairy tales and folklore. Similarly, there are Otherworldly connections through Aonghus an Bhrogha of the Túatha Dé Danann who is presented as Diarmaid's foster-father; it is he who saves the lives of Diarmaid and Gráinne on numerous occasions and who also brokers the peace between them and Finn.[33]

Another indicator that we might be dealing here with material of an ultimately mythological origin is the question of whether this story should be considered a reflex of the Indo-European 'Myth of the rival wooers'.[34] We have many famous love-triangles in medieval Irish literature, such as Noísiu/Derdriu/Conchobur in *Longes mac nUislenn*, Cano/Créd/Marcán in *Scéla Cano*, and Fergus/Medb/Ailill in *Táin bó Cúailnge*.[35] However, it is very difficult to assess what debt, if any, these treatments owe to the earlier Indo-European myth. Joseph Nagy has recently commented on what he terms the 'Celtic "love triangle"' and argues that such tales may be best understood as offshoots or multiforms 'of a *generating narrative matrix* in Celtic tradition, probably traceable back to Indo-European'.[36]

With regard to the *Tóraigheacht*, however, a fruitful comparison has been drawn between the presentation of Diarmaid, Gráinne and Finn and the most famous example of the 'Myth of the rival wooers', that detailing the love of Aphrodite, goddess of love, for the mortal Adonis in defiance of her lover Ares, god of war. In consequence:

> Ares sent a wild boar, or himself assumed the shape of a wild boar, which fatally wounded Adonis while he was hunting. Similarly Finn was believed to have arranged the boar-hunt to allure Diarmaid to his death at the year's end. Both Adonis and Diarmaid went hunting against his mistress's will.[37]

however, John Carey ('The death of Diarmaid'), in an intriguing and wide-ranging re-analysis of the tale, has advanced the hypothesis that a version of the myth of Attis, consort of the Phrygian mother-goddess Cybele, 'was transmitted by the Galatians of Asia Minor to the Celts of the West'. He suggests that 'the story which was told of the divine youth Attis in Anatolia came to be told of the "Divine Youth" Maponos in Britain, and was eventually attached to the figure of Diarmaid in Ireland and subsequently Scotland'. I wish to thank Prof. Carey for providing me with a pre-publication copy of his paper. **33** The creation of the truce between Diarmaid and Finn is described in Ní Shéaghdha, *Tóruigheacht*, pp 78–9 (ll 1353–80). **34** Mention should also be made here of the medieval Welsh Otherworld figure, Gwynn ap Nudd, who may ultimately share a Celtic mythological origin with Finn. Gwynn figures in a supernatural love-triangle with Creiddylad daughter of Llud Llaw Ereint and her husband, Gwythyr uab Greiddawl (see discussion below, Chapter Twelve, pp 145–6). **35** Hull, *Longes mac nUislenn*; Binchy, *Scéla Cano meic Gartnáin*; O'Rahilly, *Táin bó Cúailnge, recension 1*. **36** Nagy, 'The Celtic love-triangle revisited', p. 225 (italics in the original). **37** Rees and Rees, *Celtic heritage*, p. 295; cf. *DF* III, p. xxxvi n. 1.

The background to Tóraigheacht Dhiarmada agus Ghráinne

If the episodes being compared here are original to the *Tóraigheacht*, and not later borrowings from the Greek myth of Adonis,[38] then there is a strong case to be made for seeing it as containing elements of a shared myth,[39] a myth with its roots outside of the Indo-European world.[40]

When we move our focus to the medieval, we find that the Tristan stories are the best-known sources to contain a love triangle, detailing the passion of Tristan for Iseult, wife of his uncle Mark. The connections between these stories and the Celtic tales that may underlie them have often been examined, but the relationship is much disputed.[41] Historically, the most influential treatments of this topic within Celtic Studies have been those of Gertrude Schoepperle and Rachel Bromwich.[42] Nessa Ní Shéaghdha showed herself to be an adherent to their school of thought, which saw marked Irish influence on the Tristan stories with the belief that some of the material borrowed is preserved in the *Tóraigheacht*, particularly.[43] More recently, however, Oliver Padel has questioned some of these assumptions arguing instead for the genesis of the Tristan stories in Cornwall;[44] his re-assessment has been substantially accepted by Bromwich who now sees the early evolution of the tradition as occurring in Wales and Cornwall.[45] Padel has further argued that the similarities between both sets of material may be due to the borrowing of some of the Tristan material into the *Tóraigheacht*, rather than the other way around.[46] This reinterpretation has had the advantage of removing some of the chronological problems associated with the initial argument of Irish influence on the continental material as the Tristan stories predate the literary *Tóraigheacht*, with which the direct comparisons were being made.

THE END OF THE TALE

Two distinct features of the tale's ending merit comment here. First, we read of Aonghus' response to Diarmaid's death. He refuses to release the body to anyone else, deciding instead to re-animate the corpse:

> '7 ó nach éidir leam a aithbheódhughadh arís cuirfead anam ǽarrdha ann ar chor go mbia ag labhairt ream gach laoi'.
>
> 'and since I cannot revive him again, I will put an aerial life into him so that he will talk to me every day'.[47]

---

38 Frazer, *Apollodorus: the library*, iii §xiv, 4; see Velasco López, 'Adonis y el jabalí'. **39** See Krappe, 'Diarmuid and Gráinne', 351–60. **40** For discussion, see Carey, 'The death of Diarmaid'. **41** See now the comprehensive treatment in Theuerkauf, 'The Celtic dragon slayer'. **42** Schoepperle, *Tristan and Isolt*; Bromwich, 'Some remarks'. **43** Ní Shéaghdha, *Tóruigheacht*, pp xxvi–xxix. **44** Padel, 'The Cornish background'. **45** Bromwich, 'The *Tristan* of the Welsh'. **46** Padel, 'The Cornish background', 56–7. **47** Ní Shéaghdha, *Tóruigheacht*, p. 100 (ll 1753–5).

As John Carey has pointed out, this is similar to Servius' account of the Adonis myth where after his death 'the *imago* of Adonis [is] brought back "so that he might be believed to live"'.[48] Second, Nessa Ní Shéaghdha notes that there are five different endings contained in the extant manuscripts of the *Tóraigheacht*. The oldest manuscript, RIA MS 24 P 9, concludes with Gráinne assembling Diarmaid's children and imploring them to seek revenge against Finn and his *fian*:

> 'Marbhaidh mná 7 mion-daoine
> ar olc re Fionn na Féin[e],
> ná dénaidh feall ná meabhail,
> dénaidh deabhaidh 7 éirghe'.

> 'Kill women and children
> to spite Fionn of the Fiana,
> do not do treachery or deceit,
> make strife and arise'.[49]

According to Ní Shéaghdha, the full implication of this ending is revealed when read in conjunction with the poem beginning *Éuchtach inghen Díarmatta*, mentioned above, which recounts the battle between Finn and Diarmaid's children, where Finn is badly wounded and Diarmaid's daughter, Éuchtach, is slain. Ní Shéaghdha believes that 'this is undoubtedly a more fitting ending to the tale and may perhaps have been the original ending'.[50]

LATER VERSIONS OF THE TALE

Substantial quantities of folktales concerning Diarmaid and Gráinne have been collected in Scotland and Ireland. In a significant number of these, the outline is similar to that presented in the *Tóraigheacht*, pointing to the intertwining of the oral and literary traditions.[51] However, many of these folktales contain elements which are not found in earlier written versions. Examples such as the portrayal of Diarmaid as a great lover and Gráinne as a *femme fatale*, tales which show the lovers able to outwit Finn by using his thumb of knowledge against him, and stories that show Diarmaid possessing a *ball seirce* 'love spot' making him

---

48 Carey, 'The death of Diarmaid'.   **49** Ní Shéaghdha, *Tóruigheacht*, pp 102–5 (ll 1815–18).   **50** Ibid., p. xviii. Again, this may put an undue emphasis on the importance of 'coherence'.   **51** Further discussion in Bruford, *Gaelic folk-tales and mediaeval romances*, pp 106–9, who emphasizes the importance of the earlier ballad tradition to the oral lore collected about Diarmaid and Gráinne. Mícheál Briody points out to me that since the publication of the studies of Bruford and Ní Shéaghdha, more than a hundred further versions of the story have been added to the catalogue of the Irish Folklore Commission, with less than a

The background to Tóraigheacht Dhiarmada agus Ghráinne

irresistible to the women who see it, are all well represented in folk tradition; later versions also give various endings to the tale ranging from the marriage of Gráinne and Finn, to his murdering her, to his marriage to Ailbe.[52] There are also a number of later Fenian lays concerning Diarmaid and Gráinne, many of which have particular incidents from the narrative, especially the death of Diarmaid, as their subject matter.[53]

CONCLUSIONS

While the importance of the written *Tóraigheacht* helped to substantially 'fix' the story's outline of events in Gaelic culture, it is possible that some of the extant later materials may derive from earlier tellings of the tale.[54] The vibrancy of the later tradition, allied to the scope and size of the literary version, show us the extent to which the tale of this love triangle has gripped generations of Gaels on both sides of the North Channel. Its very potency as a narrative has led Donald Meek to suggest that 'the traditional rivalry of Fionn and Diarmaid may well suggest that Diarmaid once occupied a place in the Celtic pantheon which even the growing importance of Fionn could not wholly supersede'.[55] The roots of the story, stretching back to the Middle Irish period at least, demonstrate the longevity of this narrative concerning the elopement of Diarmaid and Gráinne. The human themes of love, jealousy, betrayal and loyalty have also served to ensure its central place in Gaelic tradition.

---

third moderately lengthy; many consist of single episodes only. **52** Ní Shéaghdha, *Tóruigheacht*, pp xviii–xxvi. **53** For example, see Campbell, *Leabhar na féinne*, pp 153–64; An Seabhac, *Laoithe na féinne*, pp 275–7. **54** See the examples cited in Ní Shéaghdha, *Tóruigheacht*, p. xxii. **55** Meek, 'The death of Diarmaid', 335. Cormier, 'Open contrast', 598, believes that the text bears witness to 'a personal feud or struggle between Fionn and Diarmaid, the prize being possibly the respect and loyalty of the warriors – or dominance over them'. Gillies, 'Heroes and ancestors', investigates the curious fact that the Campbell earls of Argyll claimed descent from Diarmaid.

CHAPTER EIGHT

Tochmarc Ailbe

Tochmarc Ailbe is a substantial Middle Irish text concerned with the wooing by Finn mac Cumaill of Ailbe, daughter of Cormac mac Airt and sister of Gráinne. With a few notable exceptions, it has been largely ignored by scholarship since it was edited and translated by Thurneysen in 1921.[1] Considering that it is one of the longest Finn Cycle tales to pre-date the *Acallam*, this neglect of the *Tochmarc* is noteworthy. The narrative follows on from the tradition of Gráinne's elopement with Diarmaid. At the beginning of the tale, we see Finn estranged from Cormac mac Airt because of this event. However, peace is made between Finn and Cormac, Gráinne and Finn divorce peacefully, and we see Cormac encouraging any of his other daughters to become Finn's partner. Ailbe, Cormac's youngest daughter, visits the druid, Cithrúad, to ask in a *roscad* what is in store for her and in his short reply he tells her that her future husband will appear in Tara within twenty-four hours.[2] She then drinks a draught of ale provided by the druid that allows her to see her future husband in a sleep-induced dream: she recites the substance of that vision to Cithrúad in a poem of fifteen verses.

The next scene begins with Cormac hosting the Feast of Tara. Everyone arrives paired off excepting Finn. In a poetic dialogue of twenty verses between father and daughter, Ailbe reveals that she is falling in love with Finn and Cormac plays devil's advocate, questioning her to make sure that life with the old *fían*-warrior is what she truly wants. Then Cormac goes to meet Finn and when he asks him what particular skill he is bringing to the occasion, he points to his ability with proverbs and difficult speech. Though Cormac says that that is a skill only for brats and girls, Finn remains unoffended; perhaps because this is a skill worth having in the story as all competition therein is of a verbal nature. Finn then initiates a riddling dialogue with Ailbe.[3] This begins with Finn addressing the

---

[1] Thurneysen, 'Tochmarc Ailbe'. A recent partial translation into English has been provided by Ní Dhonnchadha ('From: Tochmarc Ailbe (The wooing of Ailbe)', in *The Field Day anthology of Irish writing*. Throughout, I utilize the text provided in Thurneysen's edition but use a new (as yet unpublished) translation of the full text made by my colleague, John Carey (I wish to thank him for providing me with a copy of this). [2] This *roscad* was left untranslated by Thurneysen but is now edited and translated in Corthals, 'Ailbe's speech to Cithruad (*Tochmarc Ailbe*)'; cf. idem, 'Ailbe zoekt een Man'. [3] Later independent versions of the riddling dialogue between Ailbe and Finn are extant. In 1804, Alexander and Donald Stewart (*Cochruinneacha taoghta de shaothair nam bard Gaëleach*, pp 545–7) made available a version they collected orally in the Scottish Highlands; in 1872, John Francis Campbell (*Leabhar na feinne*,

assembled ladies with a question: 'What lake is wider than any sea?' and Ailbe responds 'Dew is wider'.[4] This is the first in a sequence of thirty such riddles asked by Finn and answered by Ailbe.[5] Impressed by her aptitude and intellect, he proposes marriage and describes the charms of the outdoor life in a fourteen-verse performance. Ailbe accepts his invitation to 'a safely exuberant life in the green woods, not the dangerous excitement he knew as a young warrior'.[6] Finn pays seven *cumala* as her bride price,[7] and the tale ends with a list of blessings that follow their union including the birth of three sons.[8]

The story, which begins by highlighting the societal strife between Cormac and Finn because of Gráinne's rejection of Finn, ends with a happy resolution as Finn finds contentment with Ailbe.[9] Similarly, the love triangle is configured differently in this tale, one side being occupied by Ailbe's father and not by a rival suitor. This text is also exceptional in other ways. Though parts of it are consistent with many other aspects of medieval Irish literary culture,[10] there are unique facets of the narrative. To highlight this more fully, I will here contrast *Tochmarc Ailbe* with *Tóraigheacht Dhiarmada agus Ghráinne* and with the most famous of all medieval Irish love triangle stories, *Longes mac nUislenn*;[11] this Ulster Cycle tale details the elopement of Conchobur's ward, Derdriu, with Noísiu and his brothers, the sons of Uisliu, their return and treacherous slaying in revenge by Conchobur, and the subsequent tragic death of Derdriu.

pp 150–1) published copies from two eighteenth-century Irish manuscripts noting that 'These Questions are current in the Scotch Islands'; and, in 1986, Brian Ó Cuív ('Miscellanea 2: Agallamh Fhinn agus Ailbhe') discussed these various sources and printed an earlier version of the riddles from a seventeenth-century manuscript. See now Innes, 'Fionn and Ailbhe's riddles between Ireland and Scotland'. **4** Thurneysen, 'Tochmarc Ailbe', 270 §10.1: '… *Cia lind as lethi cac rian?*' – '*Leithi drucht*' or Ailbi. **5** These are subjected to scrutiny by Melia, 'What are you talking about? *Tochmarc Ailbe* and courtship flytings', and Eson, 'Riddling and wooing in the medieval Irish text *Tochmarc Ailbe*'. Eson (p. 113) refers to the riddling between Finn and Ailbe as 'a sophisticated tug-of-war, resulting in their acquisition of knowledge, wisdom and domestic tranquility'. **6** Ní Dhonnchadha, 'from: Tochmarc Ailbe (The wooing of Ailbe)', p. 207. **7** This is equivalent to the honour price of a *rí túaithe* (see Binchy, *Críth gablach*, p. 18, §31). For discussion of bride-price (*coibche*), see Eska, *Cáin lánamna*, pp 14–15. **8** Both the dialogue between Cormac and Ailbe, and the riddling between Ailbe and Finn, are examples of *stichomythia* (defined as 'an arrangement of dialogue in drama, poetry, and disputation, in which single lines of verse or parts of lines are spoken by alternate speakers'), which was widespread in ancient Greek tradition. It was also not uncommon in medieval Ireland; in the Finn Cycle, the best-known early example is found in 'The quarrel between Finn and Oisín': see above, Chapter Four. **9** In fact, Finn's marriage to Ailbe survived as an alternate ending to *Tóraigheacht Dhiarmada agus Ghráinne* in two oral versions of the story recorded in Donegal and Kerry: see Ní Shéaghdha, *Tóruigheacht*, p. xxii. **10** For example, Melia, 'What are you talking about? *Tochmarc Ailbe* and courtship flytings', pp 198–9, shows how *Tochmarc Ailbe* adheres to the narrative pattern of other wooing tales (*tochmarca*). **11** In what follows, TA = *Tochmarc Ailbe*, LMU = *Longes mac nUislenn*.

POINTS OF DISSIMILARITY BETWEEN *TOCHMARC AILBE* AND *LONGES MAC nUISLENN* / *TÓRAIGHEACHT DHIARMADA AGUS GHRÁINNE*

1 *Presentation of women*

In *LMU*, the only characteristic of Derdriu that is consistently stressed is her beauty: she is said to be 'by far the most beautiful girl who [ever] had been in Ireland'.[12] Similarly, in the *Tóraigheacht*, Gráinne is described as 'the woman of the finest shape and form and speech of the women of the whole world'.[13] These very formulaic words represent the most significant aspect of womanhood stressed in either of these two narratives.

By contrast, it is a feature of *TA* that women are presented in a very positive light throughout. Thus, for example, Ailbe and her sisters are said to be unmatched 'in the working of gold and silver, in intelligence and beauty and ancestry, in understanding and elegance and poetry'.[14] Furthermore, in the riddling dialogue, Ailbe is presented as the intellectual equal of Finn, similar to the description of Emer when being wooed by Cú Chulainn.[15] This rounded presentation of womanhood is atypical of *fíanaigecht* literature where negative portrayals of women tend to dominate.[16] There is very restricted verbal word-play in *LMU* between Derdriu and Noísiu:

> 'Is cáin', ol-se-sseom, 'in t-samaisc téte sechunn'! 'Dlegtair', ol-si-si, 'samaisci móra bale na bít tairb'.
>
> 'Fair', he said, 'is the heifer that goes past me'. 'Heifers', she said, 'are bound to be big where bulls are not wont to be'.[17]

However, this dialogue is concerned with nature and not with the learning of the educated such as is found in Ailbe's answers and in her earlier dealings with the druid, Cithrúad, where her words are used as the basis of the *fili*'s composition.

2 *Paternal character*

In *LMU*, though Conchobur is Derdriu's guardian and is effectively *in loco parentis*, he has her reared 'in a court apart ... in order that no man of the

---

12 Hull, *Longes*, pp 45, 62 §6 (= *EIMS* p. 260): *ingen as mór-áillem ro boí i n-Hērinn*.   **13** Ní Shéaghdha, *Tóruigheacht*, p. 2 (ll 25–6): *an bhean as feárr dealbh 7 déanamh 7 úrlabhra do mhnáibh na cruinne go cóimhiomlán*.   **14** Thurneysen, 'Tochmarc Ailbe', 262 §7: *oc imert oir 7 airgit 7 ar ceill 7 crut 7 cenel, ar ergna 7 urlabra 7 filidheacht*.   **15** Interestingly, as a counterpoint to this, one might note the observation of Kaivola-Bregenhøj, *Riddles*, p. 161, that riddling is culture-specific and that 'riddles are not an intellectual exercise. Riddles have to be learned'. I wish to thank Sandra Buckley for bringing this work to my attention.   **16** On this topic in the earliest Finn Cycle texts, see Chapter Six, pp 91–2.   **17** Hull, *Longes*, pp 46, 63 §9 (= *EIMS* pp 260–1).

Ulstermen might see her up to the time that she should spend the night with Conchobur'.¹⁸ Thus, although the druid, Cathub, prophesies that bloodshed and strife will follow Derdriu throughout her life, the prospect of her great beauty is sufficient reason for Conchobur to raise her to be his consort, despite this not being in the best interests of society. In the *Tóraigheacht*, Cormac is presented as having very little influence over his daughter Gráinne: she has refused all who have asked for her hand in marriage, to her father's dissatisfaction.¹⁹

We have a completely atypical picture of fatherhood presented in *TA*: it is the most positive picture of a male parent known to me from medieval Irish literature. First, Cormac gets great satisfaction from spending time with Ailbe and her sisters. Thus, we read that 'it was a custom of Cormac's, when the disputes of the men of Ireland weighed upon him, to go out and gaze on his daughters; for his love of them was great'.²⁰ Second, even though it is in his interests for one of his daughters to marry Finn and cement the relationship with his *fían*-leader, he interrogates Ailbe closely to ensure that this union is what she truly desires;²¹ only when convinced of this is he happy to allow Finn to woo her. Finally, Cormac gives his consent to the marriage and in return receives Ailbe's full bride-price and Finn as a son-in-law, thus ensuring a good outcome for himself, his daughter, his *fían*-leader and for society in general.²²

3 *Maturity more important than looks*
What draws Derdriu to Noísiu in *LMU* is his physical attractiveness: 'hair like the raven, and a cheek like blood, and a body like snow'.²³ In the *Tóraigheacht*, Gráinne professes that she has loved Diarmaid for a long time because of his physical prowess.²⁴ By comparison, what is stressed by Ailbe in *TA* is Finn's maturity and experience. The following verse which she recites is typical of her attitude:

> Fer liat go luime a ræe.
> he bis co ceill tæbtana
> as foirfi gach dal fors·mbi.
> anas in læch giallch–i.²⁵

18 Hull, *Longes*, pp 45, 62 §6 (= *EIMS* p. 260): *i llis fo leith … connach·acced fer di Ultaib cosin n-úair no·foad la Conchobor.* **19** Ní Shéaghdha, *Tóruigheacht*, p. 4 (ll 47–52). **20** Thurneysen, 'Tochmarc Ailbe', 262 §7: *fa bes do Cormac, an tan no·gabdis caingni fer nErenn fris, orus imach fairccsin na hinginraide dogres ar met a seirci leis.* **21** Ibid., 262–8 §§1–21. **22** Ibid., 280 §13: *Luid iarum in ingen co Find do deoin Cormaic iar sin 7 icaid Find .uii. cumola 'na tocra.* **23** Hull, *Longes*, pp 45, 63 §7 (= *EIMS* p. 260): *in folt amal in fiach ocus in grúad amal in fuil ocus in corp amal in snechta.* **24** Ní Shéaghdha, *Tóruigheacht*, pp 10–12 (ll 172–88). **25** Thurneysen, 'Tochmarc Ailbe', 264 §8.4. The final word in verse in Thurneysen's edition shows dittography: *giall\llch–i*; he suggests reading as *giallchuiri* 'of the hostage troop'. I follow John Carey who emends to *gillachta*.

> A grey man, with a short span,
> has a lean-ribbed wit.
> Finer is every assembly over which he is
> than the warrior who is still a boy.

That looks may not be the most important consideration in *TA* is evident from the main character's epithet, Ailbe Gruadbric 'Ailbe of the speckled cheek'. Freckles are generally not presented as a sign of good looks in medieval Ireland though the central character in *Echtrae Chonnlai* is called 'O ruddy Connlae of the speckled neck', and is presented there as being of beautiful appearance.[26]

4 *Importance of duty*

In *TA*, duty is presented as more important than passion. Thus, Ailbe is shown throughout as a dutiful daughter to Cormac, and though desire is invoked between herself and Finn, her need to love him out of respect for her father is also mentioned:

> Demin lim cid edh do·gneind.
> femedh for læc liat-cind
> nim·cacrad mo popo de.
> ar teacht docum glanfeinde.[27]
>
> I am certain that if I were
> to refuse the grey-headed warrior
> my dear father would not love me because of it,
> because of going to the pure *fían*.[28]

In contrast, Gráinne ignores her duty towards her betrothed in the *Tóraigheacht*, preferring to coerce Diarmaid into eloping with her.[29] Similarly, Derdriu sets aside the perceived obligations towards her guardian, Conchobur, in *LMU* by shaming Noísiu into running away with her.[30] In these tales, the men in question would prefer to do their duty towards their leaders but they are placed in situations where it would be more dishonourable for them to shun the women's advances.

26 McCone, *Echtrae Chonnlai*, p. 121 §5: *a Chonnlai Rúaid muinbric*. I wish to thank Patrick Zecher for reminding me of this. **27** Thurneysen, 'Tochmarc Ailbe', 266 §8.18. **28** A caveat to such statements of filial duty must be entered here. Later in the text (Thurneysen, 'Tochmarc Ailbe', 280 §13.4–5), Ailbe says: '... *do·denum ne menmu Cormaic abus' or in ingen, 'acht con·dernum indni bas mait lind ar tus'* ('... let us do what suits Cormac now', said the girl, 'so long as we do what suits ourselves first'). **29** Ní Shéaghdha, *Tóruigheacht*, pp 10–14 (ll 162–241). **30** Hull, *Longes*, pp 46, 63–4 §§9–10 (= *EIMS* pp 260–1). The fact that Derdriu has been raised from birth to become Conchobur's consort, without the opportunity to give her explicit consent to this arrangement, makes this situation different to the others being discussed. It also

5 Lack of treachery

In *LMU* there is treachery involved. The sons of Uisliu are given guarantees by Conchobur, king of the Ulaid, that it is safe for them to return to Ireland from Scotland. Despite the presence of guarantors, the promise is violated and Conchobur along with Eógan mac Durthacht, king of Fernmag, have the brothers slain.[31] Similarly, in the *Tóraigheacht*, Finn's treachery brings about Diarmaid's death. Such duplicity is not a facet of *TA*.

6 Lack of violence

Violent death is a regular outcome of tales with a love triangle. As we have seen, in *LMU* the sons of Uisliu are killed on their return to Emain Macha in revenge for Noísiu's elopement with Derdriu and this leads to a great slaughter of the men of Ulster. In *TA*, however, Finn and Gráinne part peacefully.[32] This may be contrasted with the *Tóraigheacht*; initially the main protagonists part peacefully but Finn's revenge on the hunt comes many years later and Diarmaid dies as a consequence.[33] In the longer term, within their respective story cycles, the ultimate outcomes of these events are also different for society: the slaying of the sons of Uisliu leads to the exile of Fergus mac Róich and three thousand of the Ulaid warriors in Connacht; in contrast, the peaceful resolution in *TA* leads to Ailbe becoming Finn's wife with Cormac's blessing.

7 Lack of tragedy

The events in *LMU* end on a tragic note when Derdriu commits suicide rather than allow herself to be shared between Conchobur and Eógan, who is being thus rewarded for the part he played in the treacherous death of the sons of Uisliu.[34] Similarly, the *Tóraigheacht* ends in tragedy with the death of Diarmaid; further tragic outcomes are also present in some of the various manuscript and folklore versions of the tale.[35] In comparison, *TA* ends on an upbeat note: Finn and Ailbe marry, she bears him three sons, and he experiences three wonders including his hair turning yellow.[36]

8 Presentation of kingship

Not only is Cormac presented as an ideal father in *TA*, the decisions he makes in the text constitute part of his portrayal as an ideal king. For example, in

---

strengthens the reading of the Ulster Cycle as exemplifying a society in decay: see Radner, '"Fury destroys the world"'. **31** Hull, *Longes*, pp 47–8, 64–5, §§13–15 (= *EIMS* pp 262–3). **32** Thurneysen, 'Tochmarc Ailbe', 254 §2: *ro·scarad Graindi tre coru fris*. **33** Ní Shéaghdha, *Tóruigheacht*, p. 94 (l. 1672). **34** Hull, *Longes*, pp 51, 69 §19 (= *EIMS* p. 267). **35** Typical variations include Gráinne spending the rest of her days in mourning, her inciting of Diarmaid's children to violence, Finn's murder of Gráinne, her being buried alive or burned: see Ní Shéaghdha, *Tóruigheacht*, pp xvii–xviii, xxiv–xxvi. Cf. the poem beginning *Éuchtach inghen Díarmatta* (*DF* I, §xviii, pp 45–7, 149–51). **36** Thurneysen, 'Tochmarc

supporting Ailbe's choice he is also able to restore Finn to his societal position where he can 'help youths to make the transition from childhood to adulthood'.[37] In contrast, Conchobur's decision in *LMU* to raise Derdriu to satisfy his own desires even though it is prophesied that she will cause great distress to the Ulaid is a failure of leadership. As Máire Herbert has noted, 'by arrogating to himself control of Deirdre's life, the king exceeds the limits of just authority' and 'as a result of the king's ill-judgement, societal cohesion was rent apart'.[38]

Neil Buttimer's description of *Ces Ulad* as a 'narrative ... centrally concerned with a transgression of the boundary between private and public spheres' is applicable here.[39] In *TA*, Cormac's advice in private to his daughter not to marry Finn is bad for society (as such an alliance would be for the public good); however, he is happy to reason with Ailbe, to change his mind and this leads ultimately to good results for society. This may be contrasted with Conchobur's public actions in *LMU* in removing the threat of Derdriu from society; however, he infringes correct behaviour in private and this leads ultimately to problems that spill over into the public sphere.

POINTS OF SIMILARITY BETWEEN *TOCHMARC AILBE* AND OTHER MEDIEVAL IRISH NARRATIVES

Though these contrasting presentations point to the freshness of viewpoint evident in *TA*, nevertheless much of the story's framework and context is similar to what can be found in other tales from medieval Ireland, including *LMU* and the *Tóraigheacht*. These points of comparison include:

1 *Life out of doors*
In *TA*, when Finn proposes marriage to Ailbe and describes the charms of the life she will have, the primary emphasis is on what the outdoor lifestyle has to offer. For example, he tells her that she can look forward to:

Ailbe', 282 §15.   **37** Nagy, *The wisdom of the outlaw*, p. 63 (cf. Breatnach, Review of Nagy, *The wisdom of the outlaw*, 157). Two societal roles are explicitly attributed to Finn in *TA*. (**1**) as a refuge for those who had fallen out with Cormac; see Thurneysen, 'Tochmarc Ailbe', 254 §1: *Et cec an tra do feraib Eirenn no·bid for dimfeirg on ri, is a tig Find no·bidis, comdis sidhaighthi fri Cormac* ('And any one of the men of Ireland who was outlawed by the king would be in the house of Finn, until they should be reconciled with Cormac'); (**2**) finding suitable marriages for members of the *fiana*; see Thurneysen, 'Tochmarc Ailbe', 268 §9: *'Do·rradhusa emh' ol Find 'tri cæga tocmarc todui co se do ingenaib flatha fer nErenn 7 Alban 7 ron·dilsidis* (recte *nos·dilsidis*) *uile do fianaib Erenn'* ('"I have made", said Finn, "thrice fifty wooings of choice to the daughters of the princes of Ireland and Scotland and they all gave themselves to the *fianna* of Ireland"'). This positive presentation of Finn is consistent across the entire tale.   **38** Herbert, 'The universe of male and female', pp 55, 58; see also eadem, 'Celtic heroine? The archaeology of the Deirdre story'.   **39** Quoted from Baumgarten (ed.), *Newsletter of the School of Celtic Studies* 9, p. 14.

> Colcad cailli clumglasi.
> suide for fertruib fuireach
> esteacht fri gair ndubglasi.
> gæt glan tre dairbri nduillech.⁴⁰
>
> A bolster of the green-feathered woods,
> sitting on lookout mounds,
> listening to the noise of a dark brook,
> the clean wind among leafy oaks.

This verse is characteristic of Finn's eulogizing of the open-air existence of the *fénnid* which he is offering.⁴¹ Similarly, in a poem of fourteen quatrains in *LMU*, when Derdriu is declaiming how happy she was in the company of Noísiu and his brothers, three of the verses recited tell of the joy of living in the forest. Typical of these is the following:

> Ō ro·sernad Noísi nár
> ˙Fulocht for feda fian-chlār,
> Ba millsiu cach bīud fo mil
> Ara·rālad mac Usnig.
>
> As often as modest Noisiu had spread out
> The cooking hearth on the martial plain of the forest,
> Sweeter was always than each honeyed food
> What the son of Uisliu had contrived.⁴²

Though the virtues of life al fresco are not explicitly lauded by Gráinne in the *Tóraigheacht*, that similar traditions do pertain to the Diarmaid and Gráinne saga is clear from the verse preserved in the commentary to *Amra Coluim Chille* beginning *Is maith do chuit, a Ghráinne*. Therein, 'the meat of the wood grouse with a drop of sweet mead' (*sercoll na cailech feda la banna meda míne*) is favourably compared with possession of a kingdom.⁴³ These evocations of life out of doors are typical of much medieval Irish literature in general, and of *fíanaigecht* in particular.

2 The riddling dialogue

As noted above, the interplay of words between Finn and Ailbe is primarily used in *TA* to demonstrate the intellectual parity of the two participants. This type of

---

40 Thurneysen, 'Tochmarc Ailbe', 278 §11. **41** The extent of this poetic praise of life in the woods is notable. The closest parallel would seem to be the famous poem known as 'King and hermit': Murphy, *Early Irish lyrics*, pp 10–19. **42** Hull, *Longes*, pp 48, 66 §17d (= *EIMS* p. 264). **43** Discussed above,

conversation is not unique to *TA*, however, as it occurs elsewhere in the literature. The most famous comparable example is Cú Chulainn's wooing of Emer in which similar use is made of riddling and opaque speech.⁴⁴ Cú Chulainn is greatly impressed by Emer's intellectual ability, and asks her to marry him saying, 'For I have not hitherto found a maiden capable of holding converse with me at a meeting in this wise'.⁴⁵ A further aspect of this type of dialogue is also mentioned by Cú Chulainn when questioned by his charioteer, Láeg: 'it is for this reason that we disguised our words, lest the girls should understand that I am wooing her'.⁴⁶ This can also enhance our understanding of the passage in *TA*. Not only is it used to establish the intellectual credentials of Ailbe, it also serves to conceal Finn's wooing of her until he declares publicly, in simple language, his desire to marry her: wider society only needs to know what is going on when there is something concrete to reveal.

3 Youth versus age

In contrast with *LMU* and the *Tóraigheacht*, *TA* shows us Ailbe's preference for an old and wise man rather than a young and callow youth. As noted previously, this presentation is paralleled elsewhere in the Finn Cycle. For example, in 'The quarrel between Finn and Oisín' and in *Marbad Cúlduib*, favourably comparing age with youth is also an important theme.⁴⁷ *TA* also gives us a very positive presentation of Finn in later maturity, in contradistinction to his portrayal as a malicious old man in a number of sources including the *Tóraigheacht*.

4 The feast of Tara

The description of *feis Temro* 'the feast of Tara' in *TA* is very similar to that contained in *Di ṡuidigud tellaig Temra* and indeed may be its source as it seems clear that its composition may be placed earlier. Thus, lines in *TA* such as:

> feo[i]l derg dina do beraib ia[i]rn, firbroccoid 7 nua cormu 7 a sean do fianuib 7 dimbfergaib; druith 7 deogburedo occ roind 7 ag dail doib.⁴⁸
>
> red meat moreover on iron spits, true bragget and new and old ale for *fianna* and brigands; jesters and cupbearers carving and pouring for them.

may be compared with similar ones in *Di ṡuidigud tellaig Temra*:

Chapter Seven, p. 99 §3.   **44** There is also a very brief riddling exchange between Derdriu and Noísiu (noted above, p. 108 §1).   **45** Van Hamel, *Compert Con Culainn*, p. 30 §26: '*Ar ní fúarus sa cosse ben follongad ind airis dála imacallaim fon samail seo frim*' (trans.: Meyer, 'The wooing of Emer', 150; repr. Cross and Slover, *Ancient Irish tales*, p. 160).   **46** Van Hamel, *Compert Con Culainn*, p. 32 §28: '*is airi ro celsem ar cobrai arná tuictis na hingena conid oca tochrai atúsa*' (trans.: Meyer, 'The wooing of Emer', 151; repr. Cross and Slover, *Ancient Irish tales*, p. 161).   **47** For discussion, see Chapter Four, pp 72–3.   **48** Thurneysen,

> Feóil derg dano do beraib íaraind 7 fírbrocúit 7 núa corma 7 assen do fíandaib 7 díbergachaib, 7 druith 7 deogbairi ic roind 7 dáil dóib.
>
> Then red meat from spits of iron, and bragget and new ale and milk water (?) for warriors and reavers: and jesters and cup-bearers carving and serving for them.[49]

It would seem that *TA* is either the origin of these lines in *Di śuidigud tellaig Temra* or else that both texts are drawing on the same, or very similar, source materials.

CONCLUSIONS

The points of dissimilarity between *TA* on the one hand and *LMU* and the *Tóraigheacht* on the other far outweigh the comparisons which may be drawn between them. Though *LMU* predates *TA*, it does not seem to have affected its composition. There is only one possible echo of the imagery of *LMU* within *TA*. This is where Cormac says to his daughter:

> Ro·cuala decair aniu.
> madin moc iar n-eirgeíú
> samaisc sech in tarb rus·car.
> tren rot·ucai dond rodamh.[50]
>
> I have heard a hard thing today,
> soon after rising in the morning
> a heifer leaves the bull who loves her;
> headlong you would give yourself to the great ox.

This is reminiscent of the exchange between Derdriu and Noísiu in *LMU*:

> 'Is cáin', ol-se-sseom, 'in t-śamaisc téte sechunn'!
> 'Dlegtair', ol-si-si, 'samaisci móra bale na·bít tairb'.
> 'Atá tarb in chóicid lat', or-se-sseom, '.i. rí Ulad'.
> 'No·togfainn-se etruib far ṅdis', or-si-si, 'ocus no·gēbainn tarbín óag amalt-so'.

'Tochmarc Ailbe', 262 §6.   **49** Best, 'The settling of the manor of Tara', 124–5.   **50** Thurneysen, 'Tochmarc Ailbe', 264 §8.7.

'Fair', he said, 'is the heifer that goes past me'.
'Heifers', she said, 'are bound to be big where bulls are not wont to be'.
'You have the bull of the province', he said, 'namely, the king of the Ulstermen'.
'I would choose between the two of you', she said, 'and I would take a young bullock like you'.[51]

It seems unlikely that the author of *TA* was drawing directly on *LMU* here though the imagery may have been deliberately used to evoke the earlier text. On the other hand, the *Tóraigheacht*, which postdates *TA*, does not textually resonate with it at all.

This analysis shows that *TA* both stands apart from and yet adheres to traditional medieval Irish story patterns. Though it contains sufficient shared materials for aspects of the tale to be profitably compared with other narratives from the same period, it has a freshness and distinctiveness all of its own. Its author combined a number of elements to strike a new tone in Middle Irish literature; however, there is no evidence to suggest that this fresh outlook had any influence on other compositions. Its isolation in modern scholarship is paralleled by its isolation in its own era: in a sense, the gauntlet was thrown down by its author but the challenge was not accepted by his contemporaries.

---

[51] Hull, *Longes*, pp 46, 63 §9 (= *EIMS* pp 260–1). See above p. 108 §1.

CHAPTER NINE

Finn's boyhood deeds

Of all the varying aspects of Finn mac Cumaill's biography, the element that has been best analysed and evaluated is that concerning his boyhood deeds. There are various editions and translations of the central text, *Macgnímrada Finn*, in print,[1] and Finn's youthful exploits are the subject of one of the few book-length treatments of any facet of *fíanaigecht* literature;[2] they are also well treated in numerous other shorter studies.[3] The following chapter draws freely upon this earlier scholarship.

Dating in the main to the end of the Middle Irish period, the extant prosimetric narrative *Macgnímrada Finn* is preserved (incomplete) in only one manuscript: Bodleian Library, Oxford, MS Laud 610. The structure of the text and the dating of its constituent elements point to its composite nature,[4] concerning itself as it does with various inter-related stories from Finn's childhood such as his father's death and his subsequent rearing by two *banfénnidi*, Bodbmall and Líath Lúachra; his early displays of great fighting and hunting ability; his attainment of poetic function; his acquiring of the new name of Finn; and his killing of an Otherworld attacker. These disparate, though related, elements would seem to have been forged together to create a continuous narrative, perhaps modelled on *Macgnímrada Con Culainn* (for which, see below). Various themes are present in the text which I outline briefly here.

THEMATIC CONCERNS IN *MACGNÍMRADA FINN*

The death of Finn's father, Cumall, at the battle of Castleknock is the opening episode in *Macgnímrada Finn*; this information is also furnished in the closely related tale *Fotha catha Cnucha*.[5] These narratives furnish a reason for the enmity between Finn and Uirgriu whose sons ultimately slay Finn: however, the extant

---

1 O'Donovan, '*Mac-gnimartha Finn*'; Comyn, *Mac-ghníomhartha Fhinn*; Meyer, 'Macgnimartha Find' (corrigenda: *Archiv für celtische Lexicographie* 1, p. 482); Meyer, 'The boyish exploits'; Nagy, *The wisdom of the outlaw*, pp 209–18; *CHA* §93 pp 194–201. **2** The publication in question is Nagy, *The wisdom of the outlaw*. **3** Many of these are conveniently listed in *DF* III, pp xxxiv–xxxv, 31–4. **4** This has been commented upon by Nutt, 'The Aryan expulsion-and-return formula', 19; Brown, 'The Grail and the English *Sir Perceval*' (1920–21), 223; Nagy, *The wisdom of the outlaw*, p. 7 ('more accurately described as a series of tales'). To take just one small example: one of its constituent poems, the famous *Cétamon*, dates to the Old Irish period: see edition by Carney, 'Three Old Irish accentual poems', 41–3. **5** Hennessy, 'The battle of Cnucha' (= *LU* ll 3135–219; Nagy, *The wisdom of the outlaw*, pp 218–21). The relationship

versions of these texts postdate the earliest of Finn's death tales which may account for the harmony between the sources. Similarly, events related in *Macgnímrada Finn* and *Fotha catha Cnucha* account for the feuding between Finn and Goll mac Morna as, in the battle of Castleknock, Cumall kills Goll's father, Dáire, and Goll kills Cumall in revenge. Goll 'one-eyed' acquires his name in the battle when he loses his eye. As we shall see below,[6] enemies of Finn tend to be depicted as burners and/or as having only one eye. Goll fits into both categories because of his physical incapacity and because his name was originally Áed ('fire'). Interestingly, there seems to be only one very brief reference to him extant that may predate *Macgnímrada Finn*.[7]

An element that first comes to attention in *Macgnímrada Finn* is the *corrbolg*, generally translated 'cranebag' and described as the bag containing Cumall's treasures. The only other contemporary mention of the *corrbolg* I am aware of occurs in the poem beginning *A Rí Ríchid, réidig dam* attributed to Gilla in Choimded úa Cormaic (*fl.* 12th century?) which reads:

> Tricha sét, nī gāes fir buirb
> tall Find a crāes in chorrbuilg

> Thirty jewels – it is not the wisdom of an ignorant man – Finn took out of the jaws of the crane-bag.[8]

As we shall see below, the Fenian episodes in *A Rí Ríchid, réidig dam* and *Macgnímrada Finn* are drawing on the same traditions. There is also a later Fenian lay beginning *Ceisd agam ort a Cháoilte*, dated by Gerard Murphy to 'the 13th century, or perhaps the very late Middle Irish period',[9] which has the *corrbolg* as its focus. Therein we are told that it was made from the skin of a crane, transformed from a woman, by Manannán mac Lir and the treasures it contains are listed.[10] These traditions are sustained into the Modern Irish period with the composition of such long and famous Fenian lays as that beginning *A chorr úd thall san léana*, better known as 'Oisín and the crane'.[11] As Joseph Flahive has pertinently observed, the 'crane motif is one with many echoes'.[12]

There are a number of other elements in *Macgnímrada Finn* that resonate clearly within *fianaigecht* in general, and which have all been comprehensively

---

between *Macgnímrada Finn* and *Fotha catha Cnucha* has been examined in detail by Scott, *The thumb of knowledge*, pp 49–53, 62–8, 81–2. There is a later narrative about this battle, known as *Cath Cnucha*, which includes mention of Finn's conception. This tale has not been edited but summaries of it are printed in O'Grady and Flower, *Catalogue of Irish manuscripts in the British Library (formerly British Museum)*, i, pp 516–17, ii, 397–8. **6** See Chapter Twelve, pp 149–50. **7** Meyer, 'Mitteilungen aus irischen Handschriften: Cath Sléphe Cáin inso'. **8** *Fian.* pp 50–1 §28. **9** *DF* III, p. 20. **10** *DF* I, §viii, pp 21–2, 118–20. **11** Ní Shéaghdha, *Agallamh na seanórach*, iii, pp 85–110. **12** See Flahive, 'Revisiting the Reeves

discussed heretofore. For example, Demne (as Finn was originally called) earns himself the epithet *máel* 'bald' before he is re-named as Finn. It has been suggested that this 'loss of hair indicates the extra-social and peripheral nature of the hero and perhaps also his initiation into the élite ranks of professional "knowers", which include druids, poets and other craftsmen'.[13] His attainment of poetic function by burning his thumb on the 'salmon of knowledge' is the best-known episode in the narrative; once again, *Macgnímrada Finn* is the earliest source for this crucial element of Finn's biography.[14] The slaying by Finn of an Otherworld rival with a spear at the entrance to the *síd* is a recurrent theme in *fíanaigecht*, occurring here and also in *Marbad Cúlduib* and in the *Acallam*.[15] The explicit connecting of Finn with the Laigin population group, Uí Thairsig, is also found elsewhere.[16] Taken together, the assembly of all these major Finn Cycle features in one composite text render it the most important witness to Finn's youthful exploits.

MACGNÍMRADA FINN AND *MACGNÍMRADA CON CULAINN*

One of the major points of departure for those wishing to study *Macgnímrada Finn* is its relationship with the earlier material concerning the boyhood deeds of Cú Chulainn.[17] Joseph Nagy has pointed to the intimate relationship that exists between the materials outlining the childhood feats of these two important medieval Gaelic heroes. He suggests that the impetus for writing down *Macgnímrada Finn* 'may have been suggested … by the existence of a similar collection of stories about the boyhood exploits of the Ulster hero Cú Chulainn'.[18] Elsewhere he has outlined the four story patterns that both sets of narratives have in common:

> '1. The young hero approaches society from the outside. He defeats members of his age-group, and consequently his relationship[s] to society, his fosterers, and his *männerbund* are defined.
> 2. He goes out of his normal environment to save members of his *männerbund* or to avenge them. He accomplishes his mission at the instigation of a woman, and he wins valuable objects for his *männerbund*.

Agallamh', pp 173–6 at p. 173.   **13** Nagy, 'Demne Mael', 11. See below, Chapter Twelve, p. 140, for further discussion.   **14** See above, Chapter Five, pp 77–82, where the earliest stories to contain mention of his attainment of his 'thumb of knowledge' are discussed.   **15** Also discussed above, Chapter Five, pp 77–9.   **16** See Chapter Six, p. 85; cf. Ó Briain, 'Ginealach "Geinealach Oisín"', pp 270–2.   **17** Examined by Rees and Rees, *Celtic heritage*, pp 249–53.   **18** Nagy, *The wisdom of the outlaw*, p. 7. The earliest and fullest version of *Macgnímrada Con Culainn* is contained in O'Rahilly, *Táin bó Cúailnge, recension 1*, ll 398–824.

3. While society is helpless, the young hero alone defends it from an attack.
4. He defies or deprives a druidic figure, who in turn defines his heroic destiny'.[19]

These basic patterns also encapsulate specific details common to both such as the means by which they attain their new names and the important roles that female warriors play in their martial training.[20] These parallels have been seen by Nagy as:

> striking evidence for a strong link between the two narrative traditions – a link which is possibly the result of literary remolding of oral narratives, or, as I think more likely, an indication of basic story patterns which generated heroic narrative in archaic Irish myth.[21]

Whatever about the various possible interpretations of the Cú Chulainn boyhood tales,[22] there is a strong case to be made that the sole surviving text of *Macgnímrada Finn*, as it stands, is modelled on literary versions of *Macgnímrada Con Culainn*. Late Middle Irish authors, blessed with a wealth of oral resources concerning Finn and his childhood feats, did not have far to look for well-known examples on which to fashion their composition. For example, Finn's first hunt is described in *Macgnímrada Finn* in the following terms:

> Tanic in mac i n-a aenur imach i n-araile la and ocus idcondairc na lachain forsin (loch). Tarlaic urchur fuithib ocus ro tescair a finnfad ocus a heteda di, co tocuir tamnell fuirre ocus ro gab-som iarum ocus ros fuc leis dochum na fianboithi. Conid hi sin cétsealg Find.
>
> On a certain day the boy went out alone, and saw ducks upon a lake. He sent a shot among them, which cut off the feathers and wings of one, so that a trance fell upon her; and then he seized her and took her with him to the hunting-booth. And that was Finn's first chase.[23]

Such descriptions recall Cú Chulainn's special skill in hunting birds, in making off with them while still alive,[24] and leave no doubt as to the remarkable prowess of both heroes.

---

19 Nagy, 'Heroic destinies', 39.   **20** For discussion of this issue, see Miller, 'The role of the female warrior in Early Irish literature'.   **21** Nagy, 'Heroic destinies', 39.   **22** On the various versions of *Macgnímrada Con Culainn*, see Melia, 'Parallel versions'.   **23** Meyer, 'Macgnimartha Find', 199 §6 (= Meyer, 'The boyish exploits', 182 §6; Nagy, *The wisdom of the outlaw*, p. 211; *CHA* §93 p. 196).   **24** See the description in O'Rahilly, *Táin bó Cúailnge, recension 1*, ll 781–9.

It would seem to me that literary modelling is the most obvious explanation for the detailed structural parallels which exist between the portrayals of the childhoods of Finn and Cú Chulainn. Thus, though I would subscribe to Nagy's view that common story patterns underlie the different narratives under scrutiny, the structural similarities between these textual traditions strongly suggest that the author of *Macgnímrada Finn* drew on a directly comparable narrative complex known to him, that of *Macgnímrada Con Culainn*, in the construction of his account.[25] The fact that these are the only tales in medieval Irish titled *macgnímrada* 'boyhood deeds' may also point in the same direction.

Such use of a pre-existing story pattern from without *fíanaigecht* highlights once more a significant aspect of *Macgnímrada Finn* adverted to at the beginning of this discussion. Its creation seems to represent a bringing together in the late Middle Irish period of previously unassociated items of Fenian lore. As John Carey has pointed out to me, the inconsistencies in the text and its shifting geographical focus would also bear out this interpretation; thus, when the author set out to write a comprehensive account of Finn's youth, it would appear that he had only fragmentary and contradictory anecdotes to draw upon in assembling his narrative. The borrowed *macgnímrada* structure facilitated him in his attempts to meld these elements together into a whole, elements which bear witness to the nature of Fenian tradition at the time of the composition of *Macgnímrada Finn*.

OTHER MATERIALS CONCERNING FINN'S BOYHOOD DEEDS

Apart from *Macgnímrada Finn*, there are further sources that contain information on aspects of Finn's childhood exploits. The oldest of these, which is preserved in the Book of Leinster, is the Finn episode in the poem beginning *A Rí Ríchid, réidig dam* (mentioned above):[26] this is roughly contemporary with the *Macgnímrada* as both date to the late Middle Irish period. Robert Scott argues that in this poem 'practically the whole of the story preserved in *Macgnímartha Finn* is told in detail, even to the quotation of some verses that actually occur in the prose story'.[27] Gerard Murphy is more circumspect in his analysis of their relationship pointing to the fact that the Finn stanzas 'refer to many of the

---

25 It is notable that Ulster Cycle characters and concerns feature in the Finn Cycle while the reverse does not happen. For example, Cú Chulainn is name-checked in *Áirem muintire Finn* (O'Grady, 'Airem muintiri Finn'), and he is also mentioned twice in the *Acallam* with his horses referenced once (Stokes, 'Acallamh', ll 2316, 2559, 5740 [= O'Grady, 'Agallamh', i, pp 145, 151, ii, pp 161, 167; Dooley and Roe, *Tales*, pp 71, 78, 160]). Furthermore, the story of Creidne – which concerns a female *fénnid* – has an Ulster Cycle rather than a Finn Cycle context: see *Fian.* pp xi–xii (trans. Ní Dhonnchadha, 'Creidne the she-warrior'). **26** *Fian.* pp 46–51 (= *LL* iii, ll 17726–8170 at ll 18015–126). **27** Scott, *The thumb of knowledge*, p. 49.

[boyhood] incidents but cannot be said to relate them', preferring to believe that 'oral versions, resembling the modern oral versions and differing in certain details from the Macgnímartha, were current at all periods'.[28] Nevertheless, there is no doubt that the detailed comparison undertaken by Scott conclusively shows that both texts draw upon the same body of tradition.[29]

There are further later sources concerned with Finn's childhood deeds.[30] In the *Acallam*, the incident previously alluded to concerning Finn's slaying of Aillén,[31] the burner of Tara, occurs when Finn is only ten years of age and constitutes good evidence of his early martial valour.[32] Indeed, by performing this task he attains the leadership of the *fían* (previously held by his father) from Goll mac Morna, a position he maintains until death.[33] We also possess a Fenian lay beginning *Sgríobh sin a Bhrógainn sgribhinn*, dated by Gerard Murphy to *c*.1400,[34] which is exclusively concerned with Finn's boyhood.[35] Murphy notes that it relates these episodes so tersely that it 'appears to be referring to incidents that are well known rather than relating them'.[36] Rather than seeking to create an oral/literary dichotomy here, however, it might be better to think of a vigorous tradition encompassing both modes of expression with each informing and colouring the other in ways that cannot now be accurately quantified or measured.

Modern folktales also tell of efforts to kill Finn in his youth, events which are hinted at but not described in the medieval *macgnímrada*. One such account reads:

> Rugas ar a' mac ann sin agus chas siad istigh i gcornán flainnín é, agus nuair chas, bhí aill mhór as cinn cuain fairrge a bhí ann. Thug siad lób é in sin, agus ghabh siad suas ar bhárr na haille, agus rugadar ar choirnéal an chornáin flainnín agus sgaoil siad amach é ins an bhfarraige. Rinne a shean-mháthair corr-éisg di héin, agus ghabh sí síos. Rug sí air agus chuir sí faoi n-a sgiathán é. Thug sí léi é go ndeachaidh sí go Coill na Creatallaidh.[37]

> They seized the boy then and put him into a bale of flannel and, when put, there was a large cliff over a harbour there. They took him with them then, and went up to the cliff-top, and they caught hold of the corner of the bale

---

28 *DF* III, pp xxiv–xxxv.   **29** Scott, *The thumb of knowledge*, pp 55–61.   **30** For example, Finn's account of why he is obliged to make his 'Jump' every year decribes events from his youth: Joynt, *Feis tighe Chonáin*, §III, ll 154–204 (cf. O'Kearney, '*Feis tighe Chonain Chinn-Shleibhe*', 128–33). See discussion in Ó Cionnfhaolaidh, '*Feis tige Chonáin*: a window on the medieval *fiannaigheacht* tradition', pp 23–5; Nagy, 'Tristanic, Fenian, and lovers' leaps', pp 163–5.   **31** See above, Chapter One, pp 39–40.   **32** Stokes, 'Acallamh', ll 1662–761 (= O'Grady, 'Agallamh', i, pp 130–2, ii, pp 142–5; Dooley and Roe, *Tales*, pp 51–4).   **33** Stokes, 'Acallamh', ll 1762–7 (= O'Grady, 'Agallamh', i, pp 132–3, ii, p. 145; Dooley and Roe, *Tales*, pp 54–5).   **34** *DF* III, p. 31.   **35** *DF* I, §xv, pp 33–4, 133–4.   **36** *DF* III, p. xxxiv.   **37** An Chraoibhín, 'Báirne mór', 189–90.

of flannel and released it into the sea. His grandmother transformed herself into a crane and flew down. She caught hold of him, put him under her wing and took him with her to Cratloe Wood.

Stories such as these are also bound up with traditions concerning Finn's death (see next chapter); however, there are many other folk versions of his *macgnímrada* which do not contain such accounts of his attempted killing.[38]

CONCLUSIONS

Taken together, the existence of a large body of folklore concerning the boyhood deeds of Finn mac Cumaill,[39] coupled with the extant Middle and Modern Irish compositions, constitute good evidence for sustained interest in this topic across the span of a millennium. That this should be so is not the least surprising, as evidence concerning the make-up of the 'heroic biography' has shown us that the suitable presentation of 'the youth of the hero' is fundamental to creating and sustaining the complete picture of the hero.[40] The most important early text, *Macgnímrada Finn*, gathers together numerous boyhood incidents that were current in the Middle Irish period; many of these are also referred to in *Fotha catha Cnucha* and in the poem beginning *A Rí Ríchid, réidig dam*. Though it is probable that the sole extant text of *Macgnímrada Finn* owes a large debt to the various episodes that constitute *Macgnímrada Con Culainn*, the vitality of the later material points to a vibrant oral tradition current alongside the literary narratives. As Gerard Murphy justly argues: 'It is unthinkable that the modern story-tellers of Ireland and Scotland derived their versions of the tale from the single poorly constructed Middle Irish version, or from the brief references in the poems'.[41] The boyhood deeds of Finn moved fluidly across these boundaries and to compare all these different tellings 'is to open up the vast network of Fenian story centred on this figure'.[42]

---

38 For example, see Ó Muirgheasa, 'An dóigh a chuaidh Fionn i dtreis'. **39** Many of the published versions of these folktales are conveniently listed in *DF* III, p. 32 n. 2. See further, Ó Duilearga, *Leabhar Sheáin Í Chonaill*, pp 198–202, 427, and Ó hÓgáin, *Myth, legend and romance*, pp 216–18, s.n. 'Fionn mac Cumhaill'. **40** See discussion in Ó Cathasaigh, *The heroic biography of Cormac mac Airt*. **41** *DF* III, pp xxxiv–xxxv. **42** Nagy, *The wisdom of the outlaw*, p. 8.

CHAPTER TEN

The death of Finn

There are various traditions concerning the death of Finn mac Cumaill, some of which are attested from the Middle Irish period while others survive only in modern folk tellings.[1] However, no materials from the Old Irish period are extant that bear witness to stories concerning his demise.[2] There are two early and interrelated accounts of his death which seem to underlie all other tellings;[3] I will deal with these first.

EARLY TRADITIONS: PART ONE

This version of how Finn mac Cumaill died is attested in numerous Middle Irish sources. The basic outline of events is that Finn was killed in a battle against Lúaigne Temrach at Áth Brea on the Boyne.[4] His killers are often named as the sons of Uirgriu and/or Aiclech mac Dubdrenn, and his decapitation is frequently mentioned.[5] This account is to be found in the following sources:

1. In a poem contained in *Senchas na relec*, attributed to Cináed úa hArtacáin (†975), there is a brief reference to 'the death of Finn by the *fían* of fierce Lúaigne'.[6]

2. In a *fíanaigecht* poem also attributed to Cináed úa hArtacáin beginning *Fíanna bátar i nEmain* are found the lines:

> la féin Luagne aided Find
> oc Áth Brea for Boïnd.[7]
>
> Finn's death was at the hands of the *fían* of Lúaigne
> at Áth Brea on the Boyne

---

1 For a fuller treatment of the material discussed in this chapter, see Parsons, 'Breaking the cycle?'. **2** See references in Scott, *The thumb of knowledge*, pp 68–9; Parsons, 'Breaking the cycle?', pp 91–6. **3** See *DF* III, pp xli–xlii. **4** A battle by Finn at Áth Brea is mentioned in a lay on 'The naming of Dún Gáire' (*DF* II, §xxxviii, pp 26–7) but there is no mention of Finn's death there. **5** The name is variously written *mac Dubdrenn* 'son of dark encounters' and *mac Du(i)brenn* 'son of black (spear)-points', both appropriate for the one who beheads Finn. There is a Dubdrenn named as Cormac mac Airt's steward in *Finnsruth Fíthail* where the name's appearance 'is perhaps intended to reflect some kind of antagonism toward the warrior class on the steward's part': Carey, 'The testimony', 8. **6** *LU* l. 4152: *écht Find for féin Lúaigni lond*; cf. *Fian.* p. xxii §XIII. **7** Stokes, 'On the deaths', 310 §29 (= *LL* i, ll 4097–8). See above, Chapter Six, p. 90.

The death of Finn

The version of this poem contained in British Library MS Egerton 1782 has the following additional verse:

> Ro bith Finn dna, robith Finn,
> ba do goeib gomach guin,
> do thall Aicclech mac Duibrenn
> a chenn do mac Murni muin.[8]

> Finn was slain then, Finn was slain,
> it was with spears, a venomous killing,
> Aiclech mac Duibrenn
> beheaded the fair son of Muirne.

3. In a poem beginning *Annálad anall uile*, attributed to Gilla Cóemáin (*fl.* 1072), we find the following reference:

> co torchair Find leo, cíar fell
> do rennaib trí mac Urgrenn.

> until Find fell by them – though it was treachery –
> by the spear-points of the three sons of Urgru.[9]

4. This mention of the sons of Uirgriu is echoed in the *Annals of Tigernach* which reads:

> Fínd hua Baiscne decollatus est o Aichleach mac Duibdrenn 7 o maccaib Uirgrend do Luaignib Temrach oc Ath Brea for Boínd.[10]

> Finn the descendant of Baíscne was beheaded by Aiclech mac Dubdrenn, and by the sons of Uirgriu of the Luaigni of Tara, at Áth Brea on the Boyne.

5. There is a further quatrain containing similar information cited in the margins of the Book of Leinster:

> Ro díchned Find ba fer tend,
> ó Acclech mac Duibdrend
> is ro benad de a chend
> o maccaib anaib Urgrend.[11]

---

8 Ibid., §30 (= Meyer, 'The death of Finn mac Cumaill', 462 n. 3). This verse is also contained in the second fragment of the early tradition concerning Finn's 'Jump': see below, p. 127 §1.   **9** Smith, *Three historical poems*, pp 198–9 §29 (= *LL* iii, ll 15522–3); cf. *Fian.* p. xxvi §XXXV and Stokes, *The tripartite Life*, ii, p. 536 §29.   **10** Stokes, 'The annals of Tigernach' [*RC* 17, 21] (= Murphy, *The annals of Clonmacnoise*, p. 61; *AFM* 283 [i, pp 118–19]; cf. *LL* i, ll 4097–8).   **11** *LL* iii, 21833–6 [marg.] (= *Fian.* p. xxv §XXVII).

> Finn was beheaded, he was a strong man,
> by Aiclech mac Dubdrenn
> and he was decapitated
> by the fiery sons of Uirgriu.

6. *Tesmolta Cormaic 7 aided Finn*: This late Middle Irish text, most likely composite, begins with extensive praise of Cormac mac Airt before going on to describe Finn's death, foretold through his mantic abilities, in his old age at the hands of the sons of Uirgriu and Aiclech mac Dubdrenn of Lúaigne Temrach.[12] As we shall see in the next section, this text would seem to be the link between the two early traditions concerning his killing.

EARLY TRADITIONS: PART TWO

There is a second tradition concerning the death of Finn, that is also attested from the Middle Irish period. It seems to be a development and refinement of the earlier account, noted above. A basic narrative was assembled by Kuno Meyer out of two fragments from separate manuscripts – Bodleian Library, Oxford, MS Laud 610 and British Library MS Egerton 92 – believing that these constitute 'the beginning and end of an *Aided Finn* story, while the connecting piece is lost'.[13] Therein we see Finn, in his old age, deserted by his retinue. He decides to go to his 'Jump', that is, a place on the river Boyne where he was wont to leap across the river, to see if he still retained his physical abilities. On his way, he encounters a woman (referred to as a *cailleach* 'hag' in the second fragment) and the prophecy of his death by drinking from a horn is mentioned. He goes to his 'Jump', dashes his head off a rock and is killed. Uirgriu's three sons and Aiclech mac Dubdrenn come upon his body. Aiclech beheads him and, as fish is cooked and divided later at an encampment, the severed head speaks of what has happened.[14]

Fragment 1 breaks off with Finn meeting the woman on the way to his 'Jump' and fragment 2, which does not immediately follow on, begins with the prophecy of his death. As Meyer has noted, what the missing section contained may be inferred from *Tesmolta Cormaic 7 aided Finn* where Finn's wife, the prophetess Smirgat, foretells that if he drinks from a horn his life will come to an end.[15] He then drinks from a spring at Adarca Iuchna ('The Horns of Iuchna') and the prophecy is fulfilled.[16] At the beginning of fragment 2, Finn appears to be

---

12 O'Grady, 'Teasmolad Corbmaic' (= Meyer, *Cath Finntrága*, pp 72–6). **13** Meyer, 'The death of Finn mac Cumaill'. **14** See Baumgarten, 'Placenames', pp 21–3, for an investigation of the 'creative literary etymologizing' inherent in this reconstructed narrative. **15** Meyer, 'The death of Finn mac Cumaill', 463. **16** O'Grady, 'Teasmolad Corbmaic', i, p. 91, ii, p. 98 (= Meyer, *Cath Finntrága*, p. 74). As Baumgarten, 'Placenames', p. 22, points out, Adarca Iuchna may refer to Iuchna, daughter of his inveterate enemy, Goll

acknowledging the truth of this situation to the hag. As Meyer suggests, the two fragments seem to constitute the beginning and end of a single text, perhaps originally called *Aided Finn* though there is no indication of a title in either source. The opening piece from Laud MS 610 directly follows *Tesmolta Cormaic 7 aided Finn* in the manuscript; the section from Egerton MS 92 has no such Fenian context.

OTHER TRADITIONS

Our early sources contain information about other traditions in medieval Ireland detailing how Finn met his death, including:

1. In the British Library MS Egerton 1782 version of *Fíanna bátar i nEmain*, the verse cited above (p. 125 §2), is glossed: *la Aiclech mac Duibrenn dorochair Finn ac Ath Brea ós Boaind 7 ní a mBeola Broghoige a Luachair*,[17] 'Finn fell by the hand of Aiclech mac Duibrenn at Áth Brea above the Boyne, and not in Beóla Brogaige in Luachair'. The substance of this gloss is also to be found in *AcS* where it is clear that an alternate tradition is being cited connecting Finn's death with Lúachair in Kerry: *nogu bhfuair bás 7 aidhed a n-Aill in bhruic a Luachair Degadh* ('until he died in Aill in Bruic in Lúachair Degad').[18]

2. In the Book of Leinster poem beginning *A Rí Ríchid, réidig dam*, we read that Finn was buried in Ard Caille in north Cork:

> I nArd Chaille, cāilti clē,
> i Múscraigi trī Maige,
> a chend síar ri Liaic Sinnaig,
> adnacht Find cu flathminnaib.
>
> In Ard Caille, sinister harsh fate!
> in Muskerry of the three plains,
> his head west against the Fox Stone,
> Find with princely treasures was buried.[19]

I am not aware of any other extant references to this tradition.

3. The Early Modern Irish text, 'The chase of Síd na mBan Finn',[20] reworks earlier traditions of Finn's death within a new context, that of the hunting of the

---

mac Morna. In the 'Lament for the fiana' (*DF* I, §xix, pp 47–9, 151–3), she is credited with the killing of Finn; see *DF* III, pp 42–3. **17** Meyer, 'The death of Finn mac Cumaill', 462 n. 1. **18** Stokes, 'Acallamh', ll 1766–7 (= O'Grady, 'Agallamh', i, pp 132–3, ii, p. 145; Dooley and Roe, *Tales*, pp 54–5). Finn's death is noted elsewhere in *AcS* but with no further mention of context or location. For further references, see Parsons, 'Breaking the cycle?', pp 94–5. **19** *Fian.* pp 46–7 §1 (= *LL* iii, ll 18015–18). **20** *Fian.* pp 52–99; the section concerning his death occupies pp 68–99 and the translation is reprinted in

great boar of Formáel.²¹ For example, characters from older stories, such as Aillén mac Midna from *AcS*, reappear in it in a friendlier guise.²² Notable Lúaigne Temrach enemies are named for the first time, such as Fer Taí and his son Fer Lí who play such a pivotal role in this battle.²³ The story breaks off incomplete as the five sons of Uirgriu are in the process of slaying Finn at Áth Brea.

As is obvious from the foregoing, not only were alternate versions of Finn's death present in medieval Ireland, but we know that some such accounts were known to the author of *Tesmolta Cormaic 7 aided Finn*, as he feels the need to assure us that what he has written down is the 'correct' account: 'this then is the Death of Finn according to the truth of history, as the learned relate'.²⁴

LATER MATERIALS

For the most part, modern folklore concerning Finn's death preserves tales which provide both a continuation of and a disjunction with earlier traditions. For example, Dáithí Ó hÓgáin points to the fusion of originally separate versions of the death of Finn into one inclusive narrative:

> An alternative account ... was still common until recent times in oral tradition. According to this he had once been challenged by an otherworld woman to leap backwards and forwards across either the Boyne river or from one cliff to another in Luachair Deaghadh (south-east Kerry). The woman enjoined on him to do this jump once every year, and when he grew old and attempted it he fell and was killed.²⁵

In this case, the survival of material concerning his 'Jump' has been interwoven with the early tradition that his death may have occurred in Kerry; variant versions were also collected in Scotland where in one example Finn falls and is beheaded after being challenged to leap backwards.²⁶

Cross and Slover, *Ancient Irish tales*, pp 424–38. A new edition of this text is being prepared by Martina Maher.   **21** There is a late lay, 'The chase of Slievenamon', unconnected with this prose, concerning a hunt at Síd na mBan Finn, published in *DF* II, §lviii, pp 216–21, and in An Seabhac, *Laoithe na féinne*, pp 118–19; it contains no reference to Finn's death, however. Hunting at Síd na mBan Finn is also mentioned in *AcS*: for example, see Stokes, 'Acallamh', ll 619–20 (= O'Grady, 'Agallamh', i, p. 107, ii, p. 116; Dooley and Roe, *Tales*, p. 21).   **22** *Fian*. pp 54–7, §§4–5: here called Máillén mac Midhna, he hosts a great feast for Finn and his *fían*; see *DF* III, pp 197–8.   **23** The wife of Fer Taí, and mother of Fer Lí, is Iuchna, daughter of Goll mac Morna (see above n. 16). For the Lúaigne, see Chapter Six, pp 89–91.   **24** Meyer, 'The death of Finn mac Cumaill', 462–3 (= O'Grady, 'Teasmolad Corbmaic', i, p. 92, ii, p. 99; Meyer, *Cath Finntrága*, p. 76): is í sin iarum Aided Finn iar fírinne in senchasa amail adfiadat na heólaig.   **25** Ó hÓgáin, *Myth, legend and romance*, p. 218, s.n. 'Fionn mac Cumhaill'. This is very similar to what is found in Joynt, *Feis tighe Chonáin*, §III, ll 154–204 (cf. O'Kearney, 'Feis tighe Chonain Chinn-Shleibhe', 128–33).   **26** Campbell, *Leabhar na feinne*, p. 195.

CONCLUSIONS

It is no surprise that multiple traditions concerning Finn's death are extant when one considers the important place he occupies in Gaelic culture. Furthermore, as Proinsias Mac Cana has argued, 'it is in his death that the hero finally attains his apotheosis. In the creation of the heroic identity of the hero it is in a sense ultimately more important to be killed than to kill'; consequently, '*oitte/aideda* "death-tales" are at the very core of the heroic ethos'.[27] The essence of the account attested from the earliest sources, that is, his death and subsequent beheading at the river Boyne, has persisted in modern folklore but other elements have also become common, such as the alternate tradition that his place of death was in Kerry rather than in Meath. What all of these pieces attest to is the vigour of *fianaigecht* with the renewal, expansion and reinforcement of these death tales over the centuries.

---

27 Mac Cana, *The learned tales*, p. 29.

CHAPTER ELEVEN

The early tradition of Fenian lays

The majority of *laoithe fianaigheachta*, Fenian lays (or ballads), were probably written after 1200 and so lie outside the scope of the present study. However, significant numbers are tentatively dated to the Middle Irish period and represent an important corpus of *fianaigecht* material to engage with here. There are two major early collections of Fenian lays; interestingly, although these two sources together 'provide a total of 96 complete ballad texts, they have only 4 full texts in common'.[1] First, we have those preserved in Scotland in the early sixteenth-century manuscript, The Book of the Dean of Lismore, written in non-Gaelic orthography by James McGregor, assisted by his brother Duncan and others.[2] However, these poems do not date to before 1200: 'the period of composition of the full corpus of bardic verse in [the] B[ook of the] D[ean of] L[ismore] extends from the thirteenth century to the early sixteenth, but the ballads appear to be, for the most part, fifteenth-century in their present forms'.[3] Second, there are the lays preserved in UCD Archives, Franciscan MS A 20(b), a manuscript compiled in Ostend in Belgium in 1626–7 by Aodh Ó Dochartaigh for Captain Somhairle Mac Domhnaill; this collection is known as Duanaire Finn.[4] It has long been recognized that certain of these compositions are from the Middle Irish period though the question of their exact dating is a somewhat thorny issue.

DATING OF THE DUANAIRE FINN CORPUS

In the course of outlining his methodology for dating the compositions in Duanaire Finn, Gerard Murphy ascribes fourteen poems, out of a total of sixty-nine, to the late Middle Irish period and a further twenty-three to an 'intermediate period' (*c*.1200–*c*.1250).[5] Murphy was rightly tentative in his approach, noting that 'insufficient evidence, deliberate linguistic archaism, and corrupt transmission of the text, in many cases render the conclusions ...

---

[1] Meek, '*Duanaire Finn* and Gaelic Scotland', p. 23. [2] This Fenian corpus was edited by Ross, *Heroic poetry*, but there are fundamental problems with his edition. For the scribes and orthography of the manuscript, see Meek, 'The Scots-Gaelic scribes'. Normalized versions of two of the Fenian poems from the Book of the Dean of Lismore are presented in Meek, 'The banners of the *fian* in Gaelic ballad tradition', and idem, 'The death of Diarmaid'. [3] Meek, '*Duanaire Finn* and Gaelic Scotland', p. 20. [4] Edited by MacNeill and Murphy, *DF* I–III. See Ó hUiginn, '*Duanaire Finn*: patron and text'; idem, 'Somhairle Mac Domhnaill agus *Duanaire Finn*'; idem, 'Captain Somhairle and his books revisited'. [5] *DF* III, pp cvii–cxvii at pp cxvi–cxvii.

doubtful'.⁶ Donald Meek has noted that 'although Murphy's criteria for dating the poems on linguistic grounds are currently being reassessed, the broader picture seems convincing'.⁷

A major part of this reassessment is John Carey's re-examination of a number of the lays in Murphy's edition; he concludes that 'several of the poems may well date from the eleventh century, and some may conceivably be as old as the later tenth' which, as the author notes, would make them contemporary with the earliest Gaelic narrative poetry.⁸ Furthermore, his analysis of the poem known as 'The headless phantoms', an earlier version of which is also extant in the twelfth-century Book of Leinster, shows how completely the later rendering in Duanaire Finn has been modernized, and how this reworking camouflages its earlier composition date. Indeed, he argues that if the Book of Leinster text had not survived, 'The headless phantoms' could not 'persuasively be dated earlier than the thirteenth century, and even a later date would be difficult to rule out'.⁹ Carey's conclusions regarding the poetry in Duanaire Finn are worth quoting in full:

> any estimate of date must take into account the possibility that a poem's first composition may have taken place even earlier than the surviving evidence attests; more specifically, when only one or two features in a poem point clearly to a later date, we are entitled to suspect that these may have entered the text in the course of its transmission.¹⁰

As Geraldine Parsons has pointed out, one important implication to derive from this is that 'the dividing line between the earlier prose-dominated corpus and the later one, which is traditionally seen to be initiated by the earliest *Duanaire* items, needs to be reassessed'.¹¹ Furthermore, if these revised dates are accepted, it would suggest that the origins, if not the growth, of the medieval Irish ballad tradition pre-dated the rise of western European balladry.¹²

DELINEATING THE CORPUS

Where Murphy sees the use of deliberate linguistic archaisms suggesting that some of the poems may be more recent than the dates he assigns to them, Carey proposes that deliberate modernization was also being utilized with certain compositions suggesting that such poems may be older than Murphy thought.

6 Ibid., p. cxvi. 7 Meek, '*Duanaire Finn* and Gaelic Scotland', p. 20. 8 Carey, 'Remarks on dating', p. 18. 9 Ibid., p. 17; see below pp 134–5. 10 Ibid., p. 18. 11 Parsons, Review of Carey, *Duanaire Finn: reassessments*, 72. 12 For discussion, see Murphy, *Ossianic lore*, pp 19–21; Tristram, 'Early modes of Insular expression', p. 440: 'It was only in the wider context of the rise of West European balladry in the eleventh and twelfth centuries that the Gaelic world developed a real taste for narrative verse'. See, however, the cautionary comments of Ó Háinle, '"Scéala Catha Cronnmhóna"', pp 332–4.

Without in-depth forensic re-examinations of each of the sixty-nine poems, however, it is not feasible to suggest new dates of composition for them. Furthermore, other manuscript versions of some of the lays which Murphy did not examine may also throw further light on the date of composition.[13]

The more conservative approach, which I take here, is an overview of the fourteen poems that Murphy assigns to the Middle Irish period. Though more compositions from Duanaire Finn probably date to the pre-Modern period, Meek is surely right in noting that Murphy's 'broader picture seems convincing'. At the very least, examination of the entire corpus by a single scholar leads to a relative chronology between the texts themselves, a relative chronology that cannot be gainsaid unless bettered by another single scholar or, preferably, a team of scholars working together. Of the seventeen poems which Murphy dates completely or partially to '*c*.1200' (*DF* III, pp cxvi–cxvii), elsewhere he dates five of them to the Middle Irish period;[14] when one realizes how slender the dating criteria are, however, such fluctuation is completely understandable.[15] I have decided to focus here solely on the fourteen lays that Murphy assigns to dates between *c*.1100 and *c*.1175.

(a) *DF* §i 'The abduction of Eargna'
This is a poem of 44 stanzas, beginning *Eól damh senchus Feine Finn* (*DF* I, pp 1–3 [text], pp 95–8 [trans.]). It is recited by Dubdét to Patrick, and concerns the abduction by the *fénnid* Conán of Eargna, daughter of Áed Rinn mac Rónáin, a cousin to Finn and one of his warriors.[16] Áed has sworn publicly to kill anyone who would marry Eargna. There are strong legal overtones in this composition

---

[13] However, Flahive, 'The shield of Fionn', in an edition and examination of the Leabhar Ua Maine version of the lay beginning *Uchán a sgíeth mo ríogh réil*, only otherwise preserved in Duanaire Finn (listed below p. 135 §(g)), has shown that the detailed additional evidence presented does not materially affect Murphy's dating of the text to the late Middle Irish period. [14] §iii 'The rowan-tree of Clonfert' is placed among those poems of the 'intermediate period' and is assigned a date '*c*.1200', while elsewhere in the same volume, in his detailed analysis of the poem, Murphy states that 'the language of the greater part of the poem is Middle Irish ... [and that it is] probable that the original poem dates from the 12th century' (*DF* III, p. cxvi; pp 10–12 at p. 10). Similarly, §xii 'The household of Almha' is also given a date '*c*.1200' and is elsewhere dated 'to the Middle Irish period ... to the end of the 12th century' (*DF* III, p. cxvi; pp 23–4). Alongside §iii and §xii, the first sixteen stanzas of §xxii are elsewhere dated to the twelfth century (*DF* III, p. 49; cf. Ó Briain, '*Duanaire Finn* XXII', pp 54–5), while the original stanzas of §xliii 'The womenfolk of the fian' and the brief three-stanza poem §xlvi 'The kinship of Fiamhain with Oisín' are assigned to the Middle Irish period (*DF* III, pp 100–1, 107). Such minor inconsistencies in treatment are largely due to the length of time Murphy spent working on the third volume. His linguistic analysis was completed in 1927 but the volume was not published until 1953: see *DF* III, pp iv–v. [15] Indeed, it must be acknowledged that very precise dating, based exclusively on linguistic criteria, is practically impossible in the Irish language. For a discussion of some of the issues involved, see Carey, 'Remarks on dating', and Murray, 'Interpreting the evidence'. [16] Other versions of this narrative are extant: see Stern, 'Le manuscrit irlandais de Leide', 3–22 (corrigenda in *ZCP* 13, 194) and *MD* iv, pp 350–67; cf. *DF* III, pp 3–6.

The early tradition of Fenian lays

with Oisín referred to (§1) as law-giving (*ilreachtach*); Finn paying Áed wergeld (*éric*) for slaying his father (§5); Eargna being willingly abducted (§17) by Conán (a recognized category of union in medieval Ireland)[17] before being forcibly taken by Oisín who had fallen in love with her (§22); and Finn inciting Áed (§27) to seek his daughter's bride-price (*tinnscra*) to avenge his dishonour although Finn had encouraged Conán in private to seek Eargna. Conán beheads Áed in single combat but dies a year later from the wounds he receives in the fight.

(b) *DF* §v 'The bathing of Oisín's head'
This is a poem of 41 stanzas, beginning *A bhen dén folcadh mo chinn* (*DF* I, pp 14–17 [text], pp 111–14 [trans.]). It shows us Oisín looking back on his glory days in the *fian* acquiring treasures, but also admitting the negative aspects of their lives, in this case focusing on the argument that separated him from Caílte. The poem has an elegiac tone, with the *fénnid* in old age lamenting his lost youth, and contrasting his present poor condition – with his decision to accept the Christian faith (§41) – to his prime as hunter and warrior.[18] We realize that he is coming towards the end of his life as his head is being washed to prepare him for death.

(c) *DF* §vi 'The fray at Loch Luig'
In this poem of 36 stanzas, beginning *Fuar ar n-aghaidh a Loch Luig* (*DF* I, pp 17–19 [text], pp 114–16 [trans.]), we read of an encounter between the *fian* and the Norsemen (Lochlannaig). Finn is not involved in proceedings as the taboo (*geis*) about his 'Jump' (*léim*) is invoked (§3), in this case over the Norse encampment (*longphort*). The *fian* are refused admission by the Norsemen and so Diarmaid solves the problem:

> Ro ling Diarmaid ó Duibhne· in cladh sin gan comhairle
>   dobadh luthmhar lúth a chos· dúinn gur oslaic in dorus.
>
> Diarmaid O Duibhne leapt that rampart without taking counsel – the agility of his legs was agile indeed – and he opened the door to us.[19]

Fighting ensues. Particular prominence is given to the valour of Diarmaid, Oisín and Oscar,[20] which leads to multiple enemies being beheaded in battle. Finn falls

---

17 Kelly, *A guide to early Irish law*, pp 70–1.   **18** It is reminiscent of a short four-stanza poem from the Book of Leinster, beginning *Bec innocht lúth mo da lua* (*LL* iv, ll 29414–30), put into the mouth of Caílte, and edited by Meyer, 'Cáilte cecinit'. Tension between Saint Patrick and the surviving *fénnidi*, which becomes such a central part of later Fenian tradition, is briefly adverted to in the first verse. Likewise, in the poem beginning *Úathad mé a Temraig a-nocht* (edited by Ó Muirigh, 'Fionn i ndiaidh na ríthe'), a similar elegiac tone is struck with Finn lamenting that he is alone in Tara because nearly all of its famous kings are deceased.   **19** *DF* I, §vi, pp 17, 114.   **20** Traditionally, the name Oscar is etymologized as deriving from

out with Cormac over his *fían*'s slaying of the Lochlannaig who are employed here as the king's rear-guard force, but Cormac's judges side with the *fían* because the Lochlannaig had refused them hospitality.[21]

(d) *DF* §vii 'Caoilte's mischief-making'
This composition contains 36 stanzas, and begins *Maidhim in mhaidin fa ghlonn* (*DF* I, pp 19–21 [text], pp 116–18 [trans.]). Finn is in fetters in Cormac's house and Caílte places himself there in a menial role, disguised as a candle-bearer (§7), in order to help effect his release. As part of his mischief-making (§§14–15), he swaps Cormac's wife with another lady, and substitutes his own sword for that of the king's, symbolically emasculating him in the process. As we have seen in other sources, in order to attain his goals Caílte must capture many pairs of animals, in this case along with a wild man (*geilt*), in order to ransom Finn.[22]

(e) *DF* §xiii 'The headless phantoms'
This is a poem of 44 stanzas, beginning *Áonach so a Moigh Eala in rí* (*DF* I, pp 28–30 [text], pp 127–30 [trans.]). It is based on the earlier metrical 'Finn and the phantoms' beginning *Oenach indiu luid in rí*, preserved in the Book of Leinster,[23] and should be read in conjunction with it (see above p. 131). There are significant inconsistencies in the composition: the poet calls himself Gúaire Dall but says it is not his original name (§§1–2); he speaks of hunting with Caílte (§13) and frequently references Caílte in the third person throughout the poem; yet the poet names himself as Caílte in the final verse:

> Is missi Cáoilte cróidhe· deis na láoch go lánghloine
>   mor shirim amoigh sa mach· nocha a ffaicim an t-áonach.
>
> I am Caoilte the beloved, left behind the faultless heroes: greatly I miss it out and out that I no longer see the Fair.[24]

The lay treats of a number of common Fenian themes; for example, the king's liberality towards Finn is stressed and Finn's reciprocal generosity is also

---

os 'deer' + *-car* [< *caraid* 'love']. However, Arbuthnot, 'On the name Oscar', has shed fresh light on this tradition highlighting (pp 72–3) how Oscar's name was later understood as originating from an injury received and was resolved as *og* 'testicle' + *-scar* [< *scaraid* 'separate']. Interestingly, Arbuthnot also draws attention (p. 73) to Oscar adopting the name of the warrior, Dolb Scóinne, who first affronted him in battle by taking his knife from his hand. This renaming works in two ways: first, Dolb Scóinne is graphically similar to the phrase *dolb scéine* 'the mystery of the knife'; second, the name Oscar can also be etymologized as deriving from *og* 'blade' + *-scar* [< *scaraid* 'separate'], providing a neat resolution of both story and etymology.   **21** See Christiansen, *The Vikings and the Viking wars*, pp 93–4.   **22** For further discussion of Caílte and the animals, see above p. 98, esp. n. 19.   **23** Stokes, 'Find and the phantoms' (= Ní Shéaghdha, *Agallamh na seanórach*, i, pp 173–82; Ó Síocháin, 'Translating *Find and the phantoms* into Modern Irish'). See Nagy, 'Shamanic aspects of the *bruidhean* tale', 306–9.   **24** *DF* I, §xiii, pp 30, 130.

highlighted. The false nature of the hospitality offered by the phantoms is evident from the demonic nature of their singing (§§28–30), from their slaying of the horses of the *fían*, and from their cooking and presenting of them as sustenance to the assembled host. This type of tale, a hostile encounter in an Otherworld abode, becomes very popular in later *fíanaigecht* literature under the title *bruidhean*.[25]

(f) *DF* §xiv 'The enchanted stag'
As its title suggests, this poem of 33 stanzas, beginning *Fuaramar seilg iar samhain* (*DF* I, pp 30–32 [text], pp 130–2 [trans.]), is primarily concerned with hunting. It begins with the killing of Balor's wondrous pig echoing the killing of the famous *mucc slánga* 'pig of healing' in the *Acallam*.[26] The poem then turns its focus on the Otherworld figure, Donn mac Fionnlaoich; when he angers a magical queen, she turns him into a stag (§14). Finn is cryptically warned about the nature of the stag they hunt. Nevertheless, he and his *fían* depart from Almha and pursue him with Finn's hounds – Gaillinn, Sceolang, and Bran – and it is the un-named reciter of the lay (presumably Oisín or Caílte) who eventually kills this enchanted animal.

(g) *DF* §xvi 'The shield of Fionn'
This poetic lay of 63 stanzas, begins *Uchán a sgíeth mo ríogh réil* (*DF* I, pp 34–8 [text], pp 134–9 [trans.]).[27] It commences with a run-through of Finn's many good qualities and special skills. We then hear of the making of a special shield, at Manannán's behest, from a poisonous tree; several workmen are lost in its production. After being made famous by Manannán's martial exploits, the shield passes through many hands at home and abroad. Eventually, Manannán reclaims it in Armenia. It subsequently comes into Cumall's possession (§39) and later is inherited by Finn; it is involved in a battle-roll of famous Fenian encounters with its new wielder until eventually it is destroyed by fire (§60). The poem ends with an invocation of the Christian God and the Virgin Mary.

(h) *DF* §xxxiii 'The sleep-song for Diarmaid'
This poem of 15 stanzas, beginning *Codail begán begán beg* (*DF* I, p. 84 [text], pp 197–8 [trans.]), is recited by an un-named lover, presumably Gráinne, to Diarmaid ua Duibhne. A list of couples who have eloped previously is given (§§4–7), the pursuit of this pair by famous *fénnidi*, including a running Caílte, (§10) is mentioned, while the fact that nature – in many different animal forms – cannot sleep, though Diarmaid can, concludes the lay in beautiful evocative verse:

25 For discussion, see Bruford, *Gaelic folk-tales and mediaeval romances*, pp 115–22; Ó Cróinín, 'Bruíonta na féinne'.   **26** Stokes, 'Acallamh', ll 2217–305 (= O'Grady, 'Agallamh', i, pp 143–5, ii, pp 157–60; Dooley and Roe, *Tales*, pp 68–71); see Murray, 'Editing *Acallam na senórach*: a test case'.   **27** See discussion in Flahive, 'The shield of Fionn'.

> Ní codail in lach lán· maith a lathor re degh-snámh
> ní dhéin súan no sáime ann· ina hadbhaidh ní chodhlann.
> Anocht ní chodail in gerg· os fráochaibh anfaidh imaird
> binn foghar a gotha gloin· eidir srothaibh ní chodail.

The duck of numerous brood sleepeth not, she is well prepared for good swimming: she maketh neither rest nor slumber there, in her lair she does not sleep.

Tonight the grouse(?) sleepeth not up in the stormy heaths of the height: sweet is the sound of her clear cry: between the streamlets she does not sleep.[28]

(i) *DF* §xxxviii 'The naming of Dún Gáire'
This is a poem of 40 stanzas, beginning *A Lorcáin mheic Luighdheach láin* (ed. and trans. *DF* II, pp 20–31), that relates how Dún Gáire 'The Fort of Cries' got its name from the three cries given by the Doghead invaders, under their king Cliabhach (§14), after they had treacherously killed 300 *fénnidi* – led by Dubh mac Duinn – in their sleep (§12). Their deaths are avenged by the *fían*-warrior, Cáol Cródha (here identified with Mac Lughach), who beheads Cliabhach in the process (§22). These events occur while Finn is wooing Dubh's daughter, Daolach, who later dies tragically by drowning (§28). At the end of the poem, Caol is said to die alongside Saint Patrick (§39).

(j) *DF* §xlii 'The standing stones of Ireland'
This long poem of 114 stanzas, beginning *A lía Thulcha Tuaithe shuas* (ed. and trans. *DF* II, pp 66–99), is composed of two distinct parts. The first forty-eight verses are addressed to the stone of Tulach Thuaithe and concern the conception, birth and rearing of the famous *fénnid*, Mac Lughach. From §49 to the end, multiple stones are listed and the famous members of the *fían* buried underneath them – including Oscar (§88), Diarmaid (§111) and Finn (§112) – are named. The major *fénnidi* not mentioned as being buried under such stones are Oisín and Caílte; presumably, the tradition that they survive as revenants into the era of Saint Patrick was well-established by this time.[29]

(k) *DF* §xlvii 'Caoilte's sword'
In this composition of 59 stanzas, beginning *Iss é súd colg in laoích láin* (ed. and trans. *DF* II, pp 124–41), an un-named poet recites to the king the battle-roll in which Caílte's sword was involved; in an echo of the *Acallam*, the king in question here is Díarmait mac Cerbaill (§2).[30] The owners of the sword are listed

---

28 *DF* I, §xxxiii, pp 84, 198.   **29** See above, Chapter One, p. 31.   **30** See above, Chapter One, pp 42–3.

The early tradition of Fenian lays   137

until it is received by Finn; in a typical act of generosity, he bestows it upon his *fénnidi*. Ailbe, daughter of Cormac, decides that the sword should be given to the winner of the race among the *fían*; unsurprisingly, the sword goes to Caílte but the sheath is won by Finn himself. Ailbe, referred to in §22 as 'the best woman judge in the island of Ireland' (*bainbretiomh ... is fearr a n-inis Eireann*), must adjudicate between them; she awards both sword and sheath to Caílte, and her judgement is later confirmed in the presence of Cormac's famous judge, Fíthel. The last verses (§§53–9) tell of the bad days to come after the era of Finn and the reign of Cormac:

> Mairg táir an aimseir día n-éis
> re a hinnisin re a haisnéis
> budh sladaighe fir domhain
> bradaige mná a gcuileadhoibh.
>
> Reacfaigtear iasg mara móir
> risna Gallaib a gcedóir
> ar ttoigheacht docum tíre
> budh comartha drochríge.

Woe for him who reaches the age after theirs, to speak and tell of it: all men will be robbers and women thieves in store rooms.

The fish of the great sea will be sold to the foreigners immediately they have been brought to land; it will be a sign of evil kingship.[31]

(l) *DF* §xlviii 'The wild rush of the house of Morna'
This is a lay of 39 stanzas, beginning *Deargrúathar cloinne Morna* (ed. and trans. *DF* II, pp 142–53).[32] It is based on the earlier poem beginning *Ligi Guill i mMaig Raigni*, preserved in the Book of Leinster,[33] and should be read in conjunction with it. It is a battle-roll – given by an unnamed reciter (though his three sons are named in §§10 and 34) – concerning a great slaughter inflicted on Clann Baíscne by Clann Morna. It is a formulaic list of encounters and slaughters incorporating a strong *dinnsenchas* element.

(m) *DF* §lii 'Rise Up, Osgar'
This short poem of 6 stanzas, beginning *Eirigh súas a Osgair* (ed. and trans. *DF* II, pp 176–7), is also to be found in the *Acallam* where it is put into the mouth of Finn in the context of Oscar's first battle.[34] In Duanaire Finn, it is apparently

---

31 *DF* II, §xlvii, pp 138–9 [stanzas 54–5].   **32** Reprinted with corrigenda by Ó Murchadha, *Lige Guill*, pp 87–99.   **33** Ibid. (= *LL* iv, ll 28620–964).   **34** Stokes, 'Acallamh', ll 1032–43 (= O'Grady, 'Agallamh',

recited by Oisín – though the line upon which this interpretation is based is also in the *Acallam* poem – as he bestows nine-year-old Oscar with his weaponry, foretelling a glorious martial career for him.

(n) *DF* §liv 'The magic pig'
This is a poem of 28 stanzas, beginning *Domhnach lodmair tar Lúachair* (ed. and trans. *DF* II, pp 184–93). It is purely a hunting lay telling of the pursuit of a magical pig across Kerry.[35] In its presentation, it is reminiscent of the *mucc slánga* episode in the *Acallam*.

ANALYSING THE CORPUS

From the outset it must be noted that all but three of the lays under discussion here (§xiii, §xlviii and §lii) are dated by reference to linguistic criteria solely. Notwithstanding the caveats entered above, these fourteen poems that Murphy assigns to dates between c.1100 and c.1175 form a starting point for the investigation of the early tradition of *laoithe fianaigheachta*. When examined together, they give us some idea about the scope and direction of the early compositions from the corpus. There are some themes that get repeated airing throughout: the elegiac remembrance of an earlier time with its twin joys of hunting and feasting; the wondrous nature of the *fénnidi* and of the animals they hunt; the two sides of Finn's nature, the wonderful and generous contrasted with the deceitful and treacherous; the frequent negative portrayal of women and the instability of society around women; the contrast between the public and private spheres; and the significant symbolism of beheading one's opponent in battle. As we have seen, these themes are also prominent in the early texts of the cycle.[36] Other leitmotifs that come to the fore in the *Acallam* and later compositions are also foreshadowed here including magical encounters in Otherworld hostels; Finn as the absent centrepiece of many narratives; and explicit engagement with the Christian faith frequently incorporating invocations of God and the Virgin Mary.

Two other aspects of these *fianaigecht* lays deserve attention here. First, some of this poetic selection has an obvious ekphrastic element with the great Fenian heroes of the past repeatedly mourned through their deeds with famous weaponry. The creation of these is lovingly detailed, such as the shield of Finn (§xvi), the spear of Cáol Cródha (§xxxviii), and the sword of Caílte (§xlvii).[37] This ekphrastic element is also prominent in later lays in compositions such as 'The crane bag' (§viii), 'Caoilte's urn' (§xvii) and 'The sword of Oscar' (§xx).

---

i, p. 117, ii, p. 127; Dooley and Roe, *Tales*, pp 33–4). **35** The placenames have received detailed scrutiny from Ó Murchadha, 'Kerry place-names', 76–9. **36** See Chapter Six, pp 91–3. **37** For a detailed discussion of the use of ekphrasis in *Togail Troí*, see Miles, *Heroic saga and classical epic*, pp 104–22; on its

The early tradition of Fenian lays

Second, the later *fianaigecht* lay tradition was being composed at the same time as *dán díreach* was flourishing in Gaelic scribal tradition but the bulk of Fenian poetry utilizes looser, less formal metres.[38] This gives this reader the distinct impression – perhaps a mistaken one – that this canon of poetry was both popular and populist, and was directed at the widest audience possible.[39] It is also clear that these early Fenian lays are broadly similar in form, function, presentation and tone to the poems on *fianaigecht* themes – discussed throughout this work – preserved in the Book of Leinster and in the metrical *dinnshenchas*.[40]

CONCLUSIONS

It is clear that *fianaigecht* lays emerged as a significant strand within medieval Fenian literature in the Middle Irish period and that they were cultivated alongside a prose (and prosimetric) tradition that had been dominant within the earlier Finn Cycle. As we have seen, the earliest strand of the tradition is preserved within Duanaire Finn;[41] the piecemeal assembly of this collection may be indicated by the scribal activity of Aodh Ó Dochartaigh who 'ran out of material more than once, before receiving more'.[42] The vibrancy of the later tradition is attested to, not only by the significant number of later texts in Duanaire Finn and The Book of the Dean of Lismore, but by the survival and cultivation of the ballad tradition – often in simplified and modified forms – into the modern era in Ireland and Scotland. Modern scholarship rightly stresses the continuity of this poetic oeuvre from the medieval period and points to the strong element of thematic unity which binds together the earliest and latest strands of this aspect of Fenian tradition.[43]

application to the Fenian lay tradition, see Flahive, '*A chloidhimh chléirchín in chluig* and the concept of the literary cycle'. **38** See Ó hUiginn, 'Duanaire Finn', p. 48; Ní Dhomhnaill, *Duanaireacht*, pp 43–4. **39** However, the earlier linguistic forms embedded in many of the poems composed in the Early Modern Irish era would point towards a prolonged period of literary transmission. **40** This nexus is briefly discussed by Schlüter, *History or fable?*, pp 171–2. **41** The importance of a small group of Fenian lays preserved in Leabhar Ua Maine has recently been investigated in Flahive 'The shield of Fionn', and idem, '*A chloidhimh chléirchín in chluig* and the concept of the literary cycle'. **42** Flahive, *The Fenian Cycle in Irish and Scots-Gaelic literature*, p. 36. **43** See, for example, Meek, '*Duanaire Finn* and Gaelic Scotland'; Ó hUiginn, '*Duanaire Finn*'; Flahive, *The Fenian Cycle in Irish and Scots-Gaelic literature*, Chapter Four.

CHAPTER TWELVE

The portrayal of Finn

There are many aspects of Finn's character and portrayal that resonate with other texts within medieval Irish literary tradition. For example, as we have seen in Chapter Nine, the extant material concerning the childhoods of Finn and Cú Chulainn may be profitably compared and contrasted. Furthermore, the concept of the 'heroic biography' and its application to Irish heroes, as detailed by Tomás Ó Cathasaigh,[1] is 'also applicable to the story of Finn's youth'.[2] Indeed, additional investigation of the complete 'heroic biography' formulation with regard to the early extant Finn material would yet yield further dividends.

THE NAMING OF FINN

One respect in which Finn's biography conforms to the broader international pattern concerns the hero's acquiring of a new name, which may be understood as representing 'a rite of incorporation' into adult society.[3] In *Macgnímrada Finn*, his original name is Demne, later Demne Máel after an illness which rendered him *carrach* 'mangy'; while the element *máel* 'bald' is straightforward, the interpretation of *demne* is problematical.[4] He is renamed Finn (understood as 'fair') twice in the story. First, an unnamed adult hearing of the 'shapely fair youth' (*macaem tuchtach find*) who overcomes a large number of boys on Mag Life says: 'Thus, his name is Demne Find (Demne the Fair)' (*Is ainm do Demne Find amlaid sin*).[5] Second, Finn the poet (Finn Éices) renames Demne after he accidentally tastes the 'salmon of knowledge' which he was cooking for him, conceding that 'verily thou art the Finn' (*is tu in Find co fír*).[6]

There are other sources, however, which point to alternate traditions concerning Finn's renaming. The Fenian episode preserved in the late Middle Irish poem beginning *A Rí Ríchid, réidig dam* contains the following couplet:

---

[1] Ó Cathasaigh, *The heroic biography of Cormac mac Airt*. [2] Nagy, *The wisdom of the outlaw*, p. 233. [3] For terminology and discussion, see van Gennep, *The rites of passage*, pp 62–3. [4] Tentative suggestions regarding the 'meaning' of Demne include deriving it from *deimne* 'firmness, stability', from *daimne* 'little stag', or from *demon* 'demon': see Nagy, *The wisdom of the outlaw*, p. 270. The possible significance of his loss of hair has already been commented upon (see Chapter Nine, p. 119). [5] Meyer, 'Macgnimartha Find', 199 §9 (= Meyer, 'The boyish exploits', 183 §9; Nagy, *The wisdom of the outlaw*, p. 212; CHA §93 p. 196). This translation departs from that of Meyer who renders this line 'Then Demne shall be named Finn'. [6] Meyer, 'Macgnimartha Find', 201 §18 (= Meyer, 'The boyish exploits', 186 §18; Nagy, *The wisdom of the outlaw*, p. 214; CHA §93 p. 198).

> Glasdíc ainm dō ar tús tind,
> meic Morna tucsat fair Find.
>
> Glasdic was his name originally,
> the sons of Morna named him Finn.[7]

The origin and meaning of Glasdic remain unclear though it has been compared with the *glaistig*, a name given in Scottish Gaelic folklore to certain supernatural women who lived in the wilds.[8] In later tradition, it is reinterpreted as Gla(i)s Díge 'Stream of the Dyke'. Thus, in a lay known as 'The boyhood of Fionn', dated by Murphy to *c*.1400,[9] we read:

> Glais Díge in ced-ainm tugadh
> air ó rugadh in úair sin ...
> Tugthar air Giolla in Chúassain.
>
> Glais Dige was the first name given him
> when he was born in that hour ...
> He is named the Lad of the Hollow.[10]

The same doctrine recurs in *Feis tighe Chonáin*: *Glas Dige mo c[h]ēad-ainm 7 Giolla an chuasāin m'ai[n]m 'na dhiaigh sin*,[11] 'Glas Díge my original name, Giolla an Chuasáin my name after that'. In a later version of the tale, it is further said that he was also called Giolla na gCroiceann 'Lad of the Skins' because of the clothing he wore.[12] Though the details differ, the basic outline is the same: Finn displays his prowess or attains gifts, receiving a new name in the process; his original name with its obscure meaning is set aside.[13]

FINN'S PATRONYMIC

From the end of the Old Irish period onwards, Finn's solitary first name is enough to distinguish him and no further identifier is necessary. In earlier sources, however, he is generally called úa Baíscne 'descendant of Baíscne'. Later, he is known as mac Cumaill 'son of Cumall' though the earliest materials do not

---

7 *Fian.* pp 46–7 §2 (= *LL* iii, ll 18019–20). **8** *DF* III, p. 33; Nagy, *The wisdom of the outlaw*, pp 109–10. **9** *DF* III, p. 31. **10** *DF* I, §xv, pp 33, 133. In this poem, it is Conn Cétchathach who names him upon seeing his feats at games against the boys of Ireland at the fair of Taillte. **11** Joynt, *Feis tighe Chonáin*, ll 148–50 (cf. O'Kearney, '*Feis tighe Chonain Chinn-Shleibhe*', 128–9). For further discussion, see Ó Cionnfhaolaidh, '*Feis tighe Chonáin*: a window on the medieval *fiannaigheacht* tradition', pp 18–23. **12** O'Kearney, '*Feis tighe Chonain Chinn-Shleibhe*', 130–1. Giolla na gCroiceann is an independent character in later 'helper tales' in *fianaigecht* tradition (*DF* III, pp 178, 193) who is sometimes equated with Céadach (see *DF* III, pp 177–9 §§I–IX). **13** The presentation of Finn here resembles that of Cú

use this patronymic. Alongside the more common úa Baíscne, the early materials refer to Finn as mac Umaill 'son of Umall'.[14] This can be seen, for example, in the genealogy headed *Genelach Find meic hUmaill*, which may date to as early as the seventh century.[15] Similarly, in a *dinnṡenchas* poem attributed to Máel Muru Othna (†887) beginning *Áth Liac Find, cid diatá*, he is called 'son of big-limbed Umall' (*mac Umaill alt-móir*),[16] with the presence of alliteration confirming the reading.[17]

The earliest extant reference which refers to Finn as 'mac Cumaill' dates to the eleventh century.[18] The suggestion has been made that this patronymic may have emerged from a re-analysis of 'macc Umaill' with 'the transference of the *c* of *mac* to the beginning of the following word'.[19] He is occasionally referred to in other ways. For example, in *Macgnímrada Finn*, he is called Finn mac Gleóir because his mother later slept with Gleór Lámderg, king of the Lamraige,[20] a people associated with various parts of the country.[21] He is also known by his metronymic, Finn mac Muirne, in sources such as the poem beginning *Éuchtach inghen Díarmatta*.[22]

FINN AS *FILI*

The most significant aspect of Finn's portrayal concerns his poetic/prophetic ability, which is a constant from the earliest extant sources.[23] Not only is this function attributed to Finn, he is said to possess it to a very high level.[24] Thus, for example, in the literature Finn repeatedly shows extraordinary aptitude for prophesying the future, which Kenneth Jackson has argued is 'the chief qualification of a *file*'.[25]

Chulainn; see above pp 119–21.   **14** Discussed in Meyer, 'Find mac Umaill'.   **15** *CGH* p. 99 (128b9); Meyer, 'Find mac Umaill'.   **16** *MD* iv, p. 38 l. 32 (= *LL* iii, ll 21796).   **17** *Fian*. p. xxi §IX.   **18** *Fian*. pp xxii–xxiii §§XIV, XVI. These *dinnṡenchas* poems, the first sources to unambiguously record the patronymic mac Cumaill, dated by Meyer to the tenth century may be more safely dated to the eleventh: see *DF* III, p. lx.   **19** *DF* III, p. lxxvi.   **20** Meyer, 'Macgnimartha Find', 198 §4 (= Meyer, 'The boyish exploits', 181 §4; Nagy, *The wisdom of the outlaw*, p. 210; *CHA* §93 p. 195). Fionn mac Gleóire is later used as the name of the leader of the Ulster *fian* in *Tóraigheacht Dhiarmada agus Gráinne* (Ní Shéaghdha, *Tóruigheacht*, ll 417–19). They are presented as two separate Finns, though as uterine brothers, in the *banṡenchas: Tarbga ingen Eochamoin, mathair Fhind m. Gleoir rig Lamraidi Ulad, 7 mathair Find hui Baiscne* (Dobbs, 'The ban-shenchus' (*RC* 48, 178) [= *Fian*. p. xxix §XLVII]).   **21** The Lamraige were variously located in Ulster and Munster (see Hogan, *Onomasticon Goedelicum*, p. 475, s.n. lámraigi; Byrne '*Dercu*: the feminine of *mocu*', 63) and their name is also preserved in the townland and parish of Killamery, barony of Kells, County Kilkenny (see *HDGP* 'Ceall Ghabhann – Cláiríne', s.n. Ceall Lam(h)raighe). Due to the location of events in *Macgnímrada Finn*, Nagy (*The wisdom of the outlaw*, pp 91–3) follows O'Donovan (see Meyer, 'Boyish exploits', 181 n. 5) in locating Gleór and the Lamraige in Munster.   **22** *DF* I, §xviii, pp 45, 149.   **23** See discussion in *EIHM* pp 318–40, Chapter Seventeen: 'The wisdom of Finn'.   **24** In Thurneysen, 'Mittelirische Verslehren', pp 65–6 §137, Finn is named as one of twelve famous poets (cf. *Fian*. p. xxv §XXIX). For discussion of Finn's initial forays as a *fili*, see Nagy, 'Finn's student days'.   **25** Jackson, 'Tradition in early Irish prophecy', 68. The Leabhar Breac notes to *Félire Óengusso*, for example, preserve a prophecy uttered by Finn concerning Saint Findchú of Brí Gobann in north-east Cork: Stokes, 'On the

In the *Triads*, the compilation of which is generally dated to the ninth century, we find the 'three things which privilege a *fili*: knowledge which illuminates, chewing the pith/marrow, spontaneous chanting'.[26] This forms part of a list of threefold qualifications for various professions only preserved in two of the manuscript witnesses; perhaps, therefore, these 'professional triads ... were added to the collection at some later date'.[27] However, the individual parts of the triad on the *fili* are attested earlier. Though these practices have been interpreted as deriving from the pre-Christian past, their late collocation renders this unlikely though some aspects may reflect older ideas about poets.

Exceptionally, Finn is named as a *fili* who possesses the three requirements in narratives that may all predate the insertion of these professional qualifications into the collection of *Triads*. Thus, for example, he acquires *imbas forosnai* in 'Finn and the man in the tree' when he jams his finger in the door covering the entrance to the Otherworld.[28] Similarly, in 'Finn and the jester', Finn divines the identity of the jester's headless body through *teinm laído*;[29] this attribute may also underlie the putting of his thumb into his mouth when looking for enlightenment.[30] Furthermore, in the TCD MS H.3.18 copy of the commentary to *Uraicecht becc*, an Old Irish status tract, Finn is named as a practitioner of *díchetal di chennaib*.[31] Finally, in listing the three poetic skills that Finn learns in *Macgnímrada Finn*, the actual triad is cited.[32]

Finn's poetic and prophetic status, in combination with his functions as a warrior, hunter and leader, separate him from other figures in medieval Irish tradition.[33] Even Lug *samildánach* ('possessing many arts'), with whom Finn is often compared,[34] is not said to be a *fili*: this special status, jealously guarded by the *áes dána*, belongs to Finn and is both a sign, and a cause, of his liminality. His function as a *fili*, allied to his already liminal position in society as a *fénnid*, marks him off as a unique individual, particularly as he personifies all the traits that are seen to privilege a poet. In later sources, when Finn is portrayed as the *rígfénnid* of Cormac mac Airt, his high-status position is seen as a counterweight to that of the king himself with *Tochmarc Ailbe* telling us that 'any one of the men of Ireland who was outlawed by the king would be in the house of Finn, until they should be reconciled with Cormac'.[35]

calendar of Oengus', pp clxxii–iii. **26** Meyer, *The triads of Ireland*, p. 16, §123: *Tréde neimthigedar filid: immas forosna, teinm læda, dichetal di chennaib*. **27** Carey, 'The three things required of a poet', 43. **28** As noted above, Chapter Five, p. 79, it is striking that this text is given as an illustration of the acquisition of *imbas forosnai* that qualifies a master *fili*. **29** See above, Chapter Six, pp 90–1. **30** For the significance of fingers, see Nagy, *The wisdom of the outlaw*, pp 130–1. **31** *CIH* iii, pp 1105.35–1106.11 at p. 1106.9. **32** Meyer, 'Macgnimartha Find', 201 §19: *Ro fogluim-sium in treide nemtigius filid .i. teinm laega ocus imus forosna ocus dicedul dicennaib*. **33** Nagy, 'Shamanic aspects of the *bruidhean* tale', advances arguments which would see Finn as a shamanic figure, and which seeks to interpret some Fenian tales as reflecting shamanistic practices. **34** See below, pp 149–50. **35** Thurneysen, 'Tochmarc Ailbe', 254 §1:

THE AGES OF FINN

Medieval Irish literature contains multiple presentations of Finn at all ages and stages in his career. Most significantly for a hero, however, not only do we get examples of the precociousness of Finn as a young boy and *gilla*, we also meet with him as an old man, frequently embittered by life. In Finn's appearances as *gilla*, we see him once more as a liminal figure awaiting adult status, a status he does not attain in many stories, as if in a sense his heroic career is an extension of his boyhood deeds.[36] Similar to his position as a *fili*, his role serves to keep him on the margins and to distance him from mainstream society. Ironically, this enforced separation allows him to better serve this society as a *fénnid*, and later as leader of Cormac's household troop.

There are quite a few notable presentations of Finn as an old man, most of which foreground negative and poisonous aspects of his character. Most famously, his refusal to give a drink of water from his hands to Diarmaid in *Tóraigheacht Dhiarmada agus Ghráinne*, thus allowing him to die, shows how vengeful the older Finn can be. So enraged is his grandson, Oscar, at his behaviour that he threatens him with death at this point, only to be restrained by his father Oisín.[37] Similarly, in stories concerning his death, Finn is often presented as an old and enfeebled character with his desire for a hero's death to be the last swansong of a long and illustrious martial career.[38] Exceptionally in *Tochmarc Ailbe*, Finn is given a positive aging portrayal, treating Ailbe with deference and respect: he reaps the benefits of such treatment with Ailbe bearing him three sons, and his hair turning yellow.[39]

Thus, the conflict between youth and age, which forms an important part of *fíanaigecht* narratives, also plays a significant role in the presentation of Finn's character. Not only is he frequently portrayed as malicious in his old age in juxtaposition to the more positive presentations of him in his youth, his negative actions in stories such as *Tóraigheacht Dhiarmada agus Ghráinne* are implicitly contrasted unfavourably with the nobility of younger characters.[40] Nevertheless, I would argue that it is this more rounded presentation of the hero, one that is not universally positive, which works in Finn's favour by rendering him a more complex and interesting character.

---

cec æn tra do feraib Eirenn no·bid for dimfeirg on ri, is a tig Find no·bidis, comdis sidhaighthi fri Cormac: see above, Chapter Eight, p. 112 n. 37. We also see Finn in the role of negotiatior and arbitrator in a brief text edited by Meyer, 'Mitteilungen aus irischen Handschriften: Ailelb und Glangrēssach' and by Hull, 'How Finn made peace'. **36** For detailed discussion of Finn's role as *gilla*, see Nagy, *The wisdom of the outlaw*, pp 124–63. **37** Ní Shéaghdha, *Tóruigheacht*, ll 1667–84. **38** Discussed above in Chapter Ten. **39** For details, see above, Chapter Eight. **40** Ó Cathasaigh, 'Tóraíocht', p. 44.

FINN AND GWYNN

In many of the early narratives which have been considered thus far, we see Finn regularly presented as possessing remarkable abilities and powers, particularly with regard to his roles as a fighter and seer. This has prompted some scholars to see in Finn a reflex of an earlier Celtic god, *Windos. This putative descent from a very sketchily attested Continental Celtic god has influenced much of the analysis of Finn's presentation.[41] However, as John Carey has noted:

> Find is never portrayed in the tradition as a supernatural being (as distinct from a human being with some supernatural powers); nor – despite the statements of many scholars to the contrary – is there any real evidence for the cult of a god *Windos among the Continental Celts.[42]

Nevertheless, the lack of a clear connection with an earlier Celtic god should not blind us to the numerous parallels which may be drawn between Finn and an Otherworld figure from medieval Welsh tradition, Gwynn ap Nudd.[43] Their names are cognates and, if not descended from an earlier *Windos, may be traced back, as Wagner has suggested, to the Indo-European root *wind- (originally 'knows, finds out'), which is also to be seen in the Old Irish verb of the same meaning, ro-finnadar.[44] In the literature, Gwynn is son of Nudd while Finn is great-grandson of Núadu on his mother's side and is said to be paternally descended from Núadu Necht in early Leinster poetry:[45] Nudd and Núadu are cognates derived from Nōdons, best known as the name of the Romano-British god with a temple dedicated to him at Lydney Park in Gloucestershire.[46] As hunters and warriors, there are many parallels between Gwynn and Finn; however, Gwynn is not presented as having poetic or prophetic function.[47]

Two further points of comparison: Gwynn kidnaps Creiddylad daughter of Llud (< Nudd) Llaw Ereint in *Culhwch ac Olwen*,[48] just as Finn's father, Cumall, kidnaps Muirne granddaughter of Núadu in *Fotha catha Cnucha*.[49] Second, in this episode Gwynn abducts Creiddylad from her husband Gwythyr uab Greiddawl 'Victor son of scorcher', which calls to mind the fact that enemies of

---

41 See, for example, *DF* III, p. lxxxii. **42** Carey, 'Nōdons, Lugus, Windos', p. 109. **43** See Foster, 'Appendix G – Gwynn ap Nudd' (*DF* III, pp 198–204); Nagy, *The wisdom of the outlaw*, p. 236 n. 18. **44** Wagner, 'Old Irish *fír*', 22–3 n. 27. See Sims-Williams, *Irish influence on medieval Welsh literature*, pp 10–11 (and further references cited therein). **45** Corthals, 'The rhymeless "Leinster poems"', 121–2. **46** Discussed in detail in Carey, 'Nodons in Britain and Ireland'; idem, 'Nōdons, Lugus, Windos'. **47** For references, see Carey, 'Nodons in Britain and Ireland', 14–15; idem, 'Nōdons, Lugus, Windos', p. 123 n. 36. **48** Bromwich and Evans, *Culhwch and Olwen*, pp 1–42 at pp 35–6, ll 985–1007 (= Jones and Jones, *The Mabinogion*, pp 95–136 at p. 128; Gantz, *The Mabinogion*, pp 134–76 at p. 168; Davies, *The Mabinogion*, pp 179–213 at p. 207). **49** Hennessy, 'The battle of Cnucha', 88 (= *LU* ll 3167–8; Nagy, *The wisdom of the outlaw*, p. 219).

Finn are traditionally depicted as being burners and/or as having only one eye.⁵⁰ Though one should not overemphasize the connections between Finn and Gwynn, sufficient comparisons may be drawn to suggest that certain materials concerning these figures may derive from a shared Celtic mythological complex.

FINN AND ARTHUR

The Fenian and Arthurian Cycles have often been compared by scholars who place a particular emphasis on the points of similarity between the characters of Finn and Arthur.⁵¹ For example, Proinsias Mac Cana believes that 'the remarkable analogies between his [Finn's] myth and that of king Arthur of Britain are such that both must be presumed to derive from a common insular Celtic tradition',⁵² agreeing with Alfred Nutt's earlier reference to Arthur as 'the Brythonic counterpart of the Goidelic Finn-Mongan'.⁵³ The most basic point of comparison occurs with regard to their roles as warrior-band leaders. As Oliver Padel has noted concerning the presentation of Arthur in *Culhwch ac Olwen*:

> He and his band of warriors are akin to the *fianna*, bands of youths in Ireland who apparently used to roam the countryside, living temporarily or permanently outside normal society. The primary definition of early Irish *fían* perfectly describes Arthur and his followers as seen in this tale: 'a band of roving men whose principal occupations were hunting and war'.⁵⁴

John Carey has drawn my attention to early references to Arthur in European literature that emphasize his role as warrior-band leader and hunter.⁵⁵ This is comparable, for example, to Finn's presentation in the *Acallam* where he assumes the leadership of the *fían* at a young age and (we are told) remains in this position until his death.⁵⁶ Similar to Arthur, his role as a hunter is consistently emphasized in the sources. There are quite a number of stories and ballads in the tradition which focus in great detail on hunting, and on prowess in the hunt.

---

50 Discussed in more detail below, p. 149. The fact, however, that the name Gwythyr is borrowed from Latin may indicate that he is at some remove from any mythological antecedents. **51** Nutt, *The Celtic doctrine of rebirth*, pp 22–9; van Hamel, 'Aspects of Celtic mythology', pp 23–9 (cf. *DF* III, Appendix K, pp 213–17); Rees and Rees, *Celtic heritage*, pp 70–2; Ó hÓgáin, *Fionn mac Cumhaill*, pp 126, 128, 309; Padel, 'The nature of Arthur', 19–24, 30–1. Arthur may appear in *AcS* in the person of Artúir mac Béinne Brit: see Bernhardt-House, 'Horses, hounds and high kings', pp 12, 19–21. The following is much indebted to these earlier studies. **52** Mac Cana, '*Fianaigecht* in the pre-Norman period', p. 83. **53** Nutt, *The Celtic doctrine of rebirth*, p. 23. Later scribes and storytellers became more familiar with Arthurian literature as it was adapted into the Gaelic language; for discussion, see Gillies, 'Arthur in Gaelic tradition' (I–II). **54** Padel, 'The nature of Arthur', 13. **55** The sources in question are the *Otia imperialia* [*c.*1211] (Banks and Binns, *Gervase of Tilbury. Otia imperialia*, pp 336–7, II, 12) and the *Didot Perceval* [*c.*1200] (Bryant, *Merlin and the grail*, p. 171). **56** Stokes, 'Acallamh', ll 1756–67 (= O'Grady, 'Agallamh', i, p. 132, ii, p. 145; Dooley and Roe, *Tales*, pp 54–5).

The portrayal of Finn 147

An element of magic is common to many Arthurian and Finn Cycle tales with descriptions of giants and marvellous animals. For example, when Patrick and his retinue meet with Caílte and the surviving *fían*-warriors at the beginning of the *Acallam*, the description of the ancient warriors is awe-inspiring:

> Ocus atconncatar na cléirigh dá n-indsaighi iat-sum, 7 ro ghabh gráin 7 egla iat roimh na feraibh móra cona conaibh móra leo, uair nír' lucht coimhré na comhaimsire dóibh iatt.[57]
>
> And the clerics saw them coming towards them and hatred and fear of the enormous men with their huge hounds seized them because they were not of that era or time.

Throughout *AcS*, there are references to interactions between giants and the *fían*,[58] though the uniting of Patrick, giants and *fénnidi* may be traced back in written sources as far as Tírechán in the seventh century,[59] and the references in the *Acallam* might derive from Patrician elements in the narrative.[60] Similar marvellous presentations are also present in the Arthurian corpus. In *Breuddwyd Rhonabwy*, to take just one example, Rhonabwy visits the time of Arthur in a dream, and Arthur is indignant that Wales is now protected by such small men when such great men protected it in the past.[61] Both story cycles also have an emphasis on marvellous animals, particularly pigs. Finn and the *fían* are often depicted as hunting magical swine including the one that kills Diarmaid in *Tóraigheacht Dhiarmada agus Ghráinne*,[62] Balor's pig in the lay known as 'The enchanted stag',[63] and the famous *mucc slánga* 'pig of healing' in the *Acallam*.[64] Similarly, *Culhwch ac Olwen* paints a picture of Arthur and his warriors pursuing the magical boar, Twrch Trwyth,[65] across Ireland, Wales and Cornwall until it is driven into the sea.[66]

---

[57] Stokes, 'Acallamh', ll 60–3 (= O'Grady, 'Agallamh', i, p. 95, ii, p. 103; Dooley and Roe, *Tales*, p. 5; Dillon, *Stories from the Acallam*, ll 60–3). Ó Cadhla, 'Gods and heroes', pp 129–30, has pointed out that such presentations of earlier generations as bigger and longer-lived 'is very much in keeping with archaic mythologies' worldwide.   [58] For example, see Stokes, 'Acallamh', ll 1883–934 (= O'Grady, 'Agallamh', i, pp 135–6, ii, pp 148–50; Dooley and Roe, *Tales*, pp 58–9; Dillon, *Stories from the Acallam*, ll 571–614) and Stokes, 'Acallamh', ll 5917–6082 [part. trans. p. 236] (= O'Grady, 'Agallamh', i, pp 210–14, ii, pp 238–42; Dooley and Roe, *Tales*, pp 166–71). See further Roe, '*Acallamh na senórach*: the confluence of lay and clerical oral traditions', pp 334–7.   [59] Bieler, *The Patrician texts*, pp 154–5 §40 (= *CHA* §99 pp 211–12).   [60] On these Patrician elements, see Chapter One, pp 35–6; Dooley, 'The deployment of some hagiographical sources', pp 98–104.   [61] Richards, *Breuddwyt Ronabwy*, pp 6–7 (= Jones and Jones, *The Mabinogion*, pp 137–52 at p. 141; Gantz, *The Mabinogion*, pp 177–91 at p. 182; Davies, *The Mabinogion*, pp 214–26 at p. 217).   [62] Ní Shéaghdha, *Tóruigheacht*, ll 1433–1564.   [63] *DF* I, §xiv, pp 30, 130; see Chapter Eleven, p. 135 §(f).   [64] Stokes, 'Acallamh', ll 2217–305 (= O'Grady, 'Agallamh', i, pp 143–5, ii, pp 157–60; Dooley and Roe, *Tales*, pp 68–71). For *gessa* associated with the killing of a *mucc slánga*, see Joynt, *Feis tighe Chonáin*, ll 1497–507.   [65] Possible connections with the *orc tréith* of Irish tradition are explored by O'Rahilly, *Ireland and Wales*, pp 120–2; Carey, 'A *Túath Dé* miscellany', 32–3, 41–5; Sims-Williams, *Irish influence on medieval Welsh literature*, pp 39–44.   [66] Bromwich and Evans, *Culhwch and*

We have previously seen how the many connections between *dinnṡenchas* and *fíanaigecht* may have contributed to increased written cultivation of the latter;[67] indeed, *AcS* is largely constructed around the *dinnṡenchas* conceit of 'explaining' how famous places came to be so called. Though this onomastic element is far more pronounced in the Finn Cycle, Padel points out that it is not altogether absent from Arthurian literature either. He discusses the explanatory stories bound up with Arthur from *Historia Brittonum* of how Carn Cabal 'Cafall's rockpile/hoof' and Licat Amr 'The eye/source of Amr' came to be so called.[68] There is a further onomastic parallel in these literatures as much of the early material tends to be localized in both cycles. Thus, in Old Irish sources, Finn is presented as being associated with Badamair, Mide and Slíab Bladma among other places,[69] and he is a mainstay of later *dinnṡenchas* narratives; similarly, Arthur is connected to Ercing, Devon, Cornwall and Pictland in the earliest references,[70] and in later folklore he features in a great many toponymic legends.

Although Arthurian tales tend to be localized in this way, Arthur is also presented as a national hero in the earliest written records. In *Historia Brittonum*, we see him portrayed as leading the native resistance to the invading Saxons.[71] Similar presentation is not a feature of the earliest Fenian tales but this gradually changes under the influence of the synthetic historians from the tenth century onwards.[72] This is reflected in this period in the written sources by Finn's association with king Cormac mac Airt. This national dimension had obviously become standard dogma by the time of the composition of the *Acallam*; therein, Finn and his *fían* defend Ireland from multiple incursions from outside, primarily by the Lochlannaig 'Norsemen' who are presented as the national enemy.[73]

Part of the attraction for audiences of these cycles of stories is the rounded presentation of the central characters. Although there are many formulaic laudatory depictions of Arthur and Finn, the respective literatures do not shy away from showing us the more destructive side of their characters. Thus, the positive portrayal of Finn in *AcS* is counterbalanced by the negative presentation

---

Olwen, pp 37–41 (= Jones and Jones, *The Mabinogion*, pp 131–5; Gantz, *The Mabinogion*, pp 170–5; Davies, *The Mabinogion*, pp 209–12). Cf. Ford, 'A highly important pig', esp. 294–5. In *Culhwch ac Olwen*, Arthur's hunting party also pursue a second wondrous pig, Yskithyrwyn Penn Beid 'White-Tusk, Chief of Boars', across the landscape (see Bromwich and Evans, *Culhwch and Olwen*, p. 36). **67** Chapter Two, p. 154. **68** Padel, 'The nature of Arthur', 2–4. **69** See above, Chapters Five and Six. **70** Padel, 'The nature of Arthur', 3–6. **71** For references, see ibid., 2. **72** See above, Chapter Two, p. 55. **73** For references to Lochlann and the Lochlannaig, see Stokes, 'Acallamh', ll 1248, 3131–67, 4556, 6792–6 [trans. p. 254], 6919–7013 (= O'Grady, 'Agallamh', i, pp 121, 163–4, 187, […], 218–19, ii, pp 131, 182–3, 211, […], 247–9; Dooley and Roe, *Tales*, pp 39, 95–6, 128, 190, 194–7). The term *Gallgoídel* 'Irish Viking' is also used: Stokes, 'Acallamh', l. 7951 (= O'Grady, 'Agallamh', i, p. 232, ii, p. 263; Dooley and Roe, *Tales*, p. 222). The role of the Vikings in medieval Gaelic literature has been discussed by Christiansen, *The Vikings and the Viking wars* (with particular reference to the Finn Cycle on pp 2–38 and to the Ossianic ballads on pp 39–76); Mac Cana, 'The influence of the Vikings'; and Ní Mhaonaigh, 'Friend and foe'.

of him as a spiteful old man in *Tóraigheacht Dhiarmada agus Ghráinne*. Similarly, we may contrast the image of Arthur as a just ruler and loyal friend in *Culhwch ac Olwen*[74] with his role in *Vita Cadoci* where he sees a princess being abducted and, rather than going immediately to her aid, wishes to abduct her for himself.[75]

Traditionally, the central point of contrast in modern scholarship between Finn and Arthur has been that, in origin, Finn is perceived as fictional and Arthur as historical. Though Finn is named in the annals and genealogies, it is universally held that he was a fictional character and that it was the medieval synthetic historians who found a place for him in the historical record. Recently, the position of an 'historical' Arthur has been challenged by Oliver Padel,[76] who suggests that similar processes may have been at work in this case and argues that since it is not considered necessary to hypothesize a historical figure behind the cycle of folklore and literature centred on Finn, that there may be no need to postulate one behind the tales focused on Arthur.[77] Comparisons between Finn and Arthur lie at the heart of Padel's arguments. If the case that he makes becomes generally accepted, it will serve to strengthen the affinities which may be noted between both figures with the removal of what was traditionally seen as the greatest contrast between them, their ultimate origins.

FINN AND LUG

There have been many comparisons drawn between the characters of Finn and Lug in medieval Irish tradition. These similarities have been explicated most fully by Gerard Murphy who argues that comprehending the nature of the relationship between Finn and Lug allows us to better understand the 'original pattern' of the Finn Cycle. He believes that Finn 'was originally a mythological figure possessing some kinship with the god Lugh'.[78] As part of this analysis, comparisons are drawn between the inveterate opponents of Finn and Lug, frequently presented as 'one-eyed burners': Balor in the case of Lug, and Goll 'one-eyed' (whose original name was Áed 'fire'), along with Aillén (the burner of Tara), in the case of Finn.[79] As noted above (pp 145–6), these comparisons are rendered even more striking when one considers that the Otherworld figure of medieval Welsh tradition with whom we have already compared Finn, Gwynn ap Nudd, abducts Creiddylad daughter of Llud Llaw Ereint in *Culhwch ac Olwen* from an enemy appropriately named Gwythyr uab Greiddawl 'Victor son of scorcher'.

---

74 For reference to editions and translations, see above n. 48. **75** Wade-Evans, *Vita sanctorum*, p. 26. See discussion in Padel, 'The nature of Arthur', 7–8. **76** For references to earlier scholarship on the subject, see Padel, 'The nature of Arthur', 1 nn. 1–2. **77** Ibid., 30. **78** Murphy, *Ossianic lore*, p. 8. **79** Ibid., pp 8–9; *DF* III, pp lxx–lxxvii; *EIHM* pp 277–8.

Such an interpretation of the nature of the Finn–Lug connection has found favour with other scholars. For example, Proinsias Mac Cana sees Fothad Canainne (along with Áed, Balor and Goll) as one of the forms of the opponent of the hero, whom he sees as epitomized by Finn and Lug.[80] Similarly, Tomás Ó Cathasaigh agrees with much that Murphy has to say on the nature of their relationship; however, he enters the following caveat:

> But whatever about the origins of the extant traditions about Lug and Finn, there is one important difference between them which is not taken into account in Murphy's analysis, and that is that Lug is a divine hero, whereas Finn is not: Lug is a hero among the gods, and lives on in a *síd* after the coming of man to Ireland, whereas Finn dies, and when he is dead he is dead.[81]

Thus, though both may be said to have divine origins ultimately, according to Ó Cathasaigh's reading of the evidence it is only Lug who may be considered a divine hero in Irish tradition.

Another significant point of comparison between Finn and Lug occurs in two texts that have been tentatively dated to the fourteenth century, *Tóraigheacht Dhiarmada agus Ghráinne* and *Oidheadh Chloinne Tuireann*.[82] As mentioned above, in the *Tóraigheacht*, Finn refuses to give a drink from his hands to Diarmaid after he has been mortally wounded by the magic boar of Beann Ghulban; his treachery ensures that Diarmaid dies subsequently. In *Oidheadh Chloinne Tuireann*, Lug refuses to give the badly injured sons of Tuireann the pig skin of the king of Greece that can heal all wounds and illnesses; the irony is that it is the sons of Tuireann who obtained this pig skin for Lug in partial compensation for their killing of his father.[83] They die thereafter, as does their father of a broken heart. In these stories (which are both very late), Lug and Finn display similar vituperative sides to their personalities, showing that revenge is more important to them than fair play and honour.

CONCLUSIONS

The analysis presented above shows that different approaches to analysing the character of Finn are beneficial in elucidating the varying ways in which he is

---

80 Mac Cana, '*Fianaigecht* in the pre-Norman period', p. 79. **81** Ó Cathasaigh, '*Cath Maige Tuired* as exemplary myth', p. 13. **82** For the dating of the *Tóraigheacht*, see above, Chapter Seven, pp 95–6. With regard to *Oidheadh Chloinne Tuireann*, see Breatnach, '*Oidheadh Chloinne Tuireann agus Cath Maige Tuired*', 43–5. **83** Ua Ceallaigh, *Trí truagha na scéaluidheachta*, pp 5–41 at pp 40–1 (= O'Curry, 'The fate of the children of Tuireann', pp 157–227 at pp 224–7; translation is reprinted in Cross and Slover, *Ancient Irish tales*, pp 49–81 at pp 80–1).

The portrayal of Finn

presented in the literature. Comparisons drawn with Arthur, Gwynn, and Lug foreground some of Finn's most important traits and highlight comparanda that are of assistance in obtaining a fuller understanding of how he functions in many Fenian narratives. The roles Finn occupies in these stories – hunter, *fían*-leader, *fili*, advisor – and the various stages of his life that are presented to us – as child, as *gilla*, in his prime and in old age – all serve to render the character of Finn more nuanced and more interesting. His acquisition of a new name, so intimately bound up with his attainment of poetic and prophetic function, is a central part of his evolution from the wildernesses of his childhood to his role as the leader of the *fíana*. And yet the journey which brings him thus far remains forever truncated; with a couple of notable exceptions – particularly his important societal role as leader of the *fían* of Ireland under the king of Tara – he is fated to repeat in narrative format the life of the outsider, never evolving beyond the role attained while still a *gilla*. Nevertheless, within this static picture the dominance of Finn's personality waxes and wanes in the tales, sometimes central, sometimes sidelined, but never forgotten even when occupying a marginal role in a particular account. Only a character of complexity and depth could fully sustain a cycle named in his honour.

CHAPTER THIRTEEN

Fothad Canainne

Fothad Canainne, also known as Fothad Canann,[1] is presented in medieval Irish literature as one of three brothers all called Fothad ('na trí Fothaid'),[2] the others being Fothad Airgtech and Fothad Cairptech.[3] They also have alternate names: Caíndía 'fair god' (Fothad Canainne), Óendía 'singular god' (Fothad Airgtech) and Tréndía 'strong god' (Fothad Cairptech). We saw in Chapter Six the role that Fothad Airgtech plays in an early *fianaigecht* story from Ulster. However, it is his brother, Fothad Canainne, whose presentation is most intimately bound up with that of Finn mac Cumaill.[4]

INTRODUCTION

Though it is clear that traditions concerning the two *fian*-leaders, Finn and Fothad, were intertwined from a very early period, it would seem that they were originally separate. This was implicitly recognized by Proinsias Mac Cana who argued that 'from the early seventh century onwards … the Fionn cycle was in the ascendant as a comprehensive expression of *fianaigecht*, expanding and diversifying and assimilating to itself the traditions of the other *fiana* and their leaders'.[5] Likewise, Peter McQuillan asserts that associations between Finn and Fothad 'must go back to the earlier stage of relative parity between the two'.[6] Nevertheless, although scholarship recognizes Fothad Canainne as 'a figure still trailing behind him the remnants of a complex mythology',[7] it is primarily as a character within the Finn Cycle that he is analysed rather than as the hero of his own narrative cycle, minor and fragmentary though that may have been.

---

[1] He is said to be named after his dog, Canann, in Arbuthnot, *Cóir anmann*, i, pp 106, 143 §116 (cf. pp 178, 185 §6): *Fothad Canund .i. Canand ainm na con bai oga. Is uadh ro hainmnaigead*, 'Fothad Canann, i.e. Canann was the name of the dog that he had. He was named after it'. [2] For details, see *Fian*. pp 4–7; *LL* iv, ll 25010–46; Byrne '*Dercu*: the feminine of *mocu*', 62–3. O'Rahilly (*EIHM* p. 10) interprets the evidence as pointing towards 'a mythical Fothad … split up into three brothers'. He also argues (n. 3) that Fothad may be the name of the ancestor deity of the Uaithne (located on the borders of counties Limerick and Tipperary) and that it might 'be cognate with *Votādīnī* (O[ld] W[elsh] *Guotodin*), the name of a British tribe near the Firth of Forth'. [3] Fothad Airgtech might be translated as 'Fothad of silver', while Fothad Cairptech probably means 'Fothad of chariots'. [4] Some of this material has been discussed previously in Ó Muirigh, 'Rangú litríocht mheánaoiseach na Gaeilge', pp 708–11. [5] Mac Cana, '*Fianaigecht* in the pre-Norman period', p. 83. [6] McQuillan, 'Finn, Fothad, and *fian*', 4. [7] Mac Cana, '*Fianaigecht* in the pre-Norman period', p. 78.

TRADITIONS CONCERNING FOTHAD (1): FOTHAD'S DEATH

There is a poem of 49 quatrains concerning Fothad's death that is almost completely independent of a Finn Cycle context.[8] This composition, titled *Reicne Fothaid Chanainne*, probably dates to the eighth or ninth century.[9] It stands alone in the sole manuscript to preserve it though separate prose narratives have survived which serve to contextualize the events delineated in the verse.[10] The central conceit of the poem is that it is recited by Fothad's spirit to the unnamed wife of Ailill Flann Becc telling her that death will prevent him from keeping his appointment with her.

> A ben, náchamaicille! nī friot atá mo menmo:
> atā mo menma collēic isind imairiuc oc Féic.
>
> Atā mo corpān crūäch i taobh Letrach dā mbrūäch,
> atā mo cenn cen nighe eitir fiena for garbhslighe.

Hush, woman, do not speak to me! My thoughts are not with thee. My thoughts are still in the encounter at Féic.

My bloody corpse lies by the side of the Slope of two Brinks, my head all unwashed is among warrior-bands in fierce slaughter.[11]

In her study of the *Reicne*, Jacqueline Borsje has made a schematic survey of the poem which usefully guides us through its structure:[12]

§§1–7 constitute a lament for Fothad's death;
§§8–19 are a lament for the death of his men;
§20 is a lament for the present situation;
§§21–2 concern the battle and mutual slayings of Fothad and Ailill;
§23 is a warning to the woman not to leave without Fothad's treasures;
§§24–40 contain a description of the treasures;
§§41–5 constitute a further warning to the woman to beware the Morrígain and Fothad's imminent departure is noted;
§§46–7 is a request for memorials, i.e. to remember the *Reicne* and to put a stone on Fothad's grave;
§§48–9 contain the final farewell.

---

8 *Fian.* pp 10–17. **9** Hull, 'The Helgi lay and Irish literature', pp 271–3, has highlighted parallels between the *Reicne* and the Old Norse 'second lay' of the killer of Helgi. Dronke, 'Learned lyric and popular ballad', p. 184, acknowledges the important analogies between these sources which he would see as 'drawing on a popular tradition both more extensive and more ancient than has yet been realized'. **10** For comments on the gap between the poem's composition and the lateness of the manuscript, see Hull, '*Reicne Fothaid Canainne*', 29. **11** *Fian.* pp 10–11 §§1–2. The prose versions are united in saying that the *Reicne* is recited by Fothad's severed head rather than by his spirit. **12** Borsje, 'The "terror of the night" and the

Though Kuno Meyer placed this poem first in his book, *Fianaigecht*, it only contains two brief references to Finn and Caílte. In quatrain 27, Caílte's brooch is mentioned in passing while in quatrain 38, Finn's possession of mantic abilities is touched upon: *iar n-ól fíona, ba mesc linn, / is ann foillsighti do Find* ('after a banquet of wine, – 'twas an intoxicating drink, – 'tis then it was revealed to Find').[13] There is no further context for these references to Finn and Caílte in the poem;[14] however, it serves as an early example of Finn being cited in traditions concerning Fothad.

There is additional material concerning the death of Fothad Canainne that provides further indications that the early traditions concerning him were independent of stories concerning Finn and his *fían*. First, there is the separate prose narrative which contextualizes *Reicne Fothaid Chanainne*, and which was printed by Meyer as an introduction to the poem;[15] part of this tradition is also preserved in *Cóir anmann*.[16] From the titles provided by the medieval tale-lists, it is clear that this story was known as *Aithed mná Ailella maic Eógain la Fothad Canainne*.[17] It would seem unlikely that this composition should be dated to earlier than the tenth century. However, there is an earlier and simpler untitled version of this *aithed*, which, for the sake of convenience, will be referred to as 'The death of Fothad Canainne'; it is probably to be dated to the first half of the eighth century.[18] Thus, it is older than the sole surviving copy of *Reicne Fothaid Chanainne*. This narrative, which may be a fore-runner to the poem or, perhaps, may be the original prose introduction to it, contains no mention of Finn or his *fían*. Therein, we read about the attempts of Fothad, leader of the *fían* of Connacht, to woo the wife of Ailill mac Eochain, leader of the *fían* of Munster. The story tells of her willingness to come to him provided she receives her brideprice (*tinnscra*), of her going to tryst with him subsequently, and of Ailill's killing of Fothad. The tale concludes with Fothad's head, not his spirit, singing the first verse of the *Reicne* to Ailill's wife.[19]

Joseph Nagy has analysed the significance of this talking head, one of many famous examples in Irish tradition, highlighting 'the contrast between an active, heroic past informed by life among fellow *féinnidi* and a present shaped … by a conflict over a woman and marked by a living death'.[20] The one-sided nature of the interaction between dead head and living woman is exemplified by the

Morrígain', p. 73. **13** *Fian*. pp 14–15 §27; 16–17 §38. **14** Geraldine Parsons has suggested to me, however, that the citing of Art (mac Cuinn), father of Cormac, as king in quatrain 37 might also serve as a contextualizing reference. **15** *Fian*. pp 4–9. **16** Arbuthnot, *Cóir anmann*, ii, pp 59–60, 132–3, §§223–8 (= Stokes, 'Cóir anmann', 376 §220). **17** Mac Cana, *The learned tales*, pp 46, 57: *A. mná Ailella maic Eógain re Fothud Canann / A. mna Oilella maic Eogain re Fothud Canann* (List A); *A. mna Oililla maic Eogain la Fothadh Canann / A. mna Oilella maic Eogain ri Fothadh Canann / Aithed mna Ailella maic Eucchain la Fathadh Canand* (List B). **18** Hull, 'The death of Fothath Cananne'. **19** Ibid., 401. **20** Nagy, *Conversing with angels and ancients*, pp 299–303 at p. 300.

opening line, which also functions as the *dúnad, A ben, náchamaicille* 'Hush, woman, do not speak to me!'.²¹ The next line is just as unambiguously dismissive; in this opening verse, therefore, the head intends to ignore anything the woman might say before she has a chance to utter it.

There is one aspect of the poem that on first reading does not chime with the rest of the composition; this is the allusion to the Christian God in quatrain 48: *serc bethu cé is miri, / ingi adradh Rígh nimhi*, 'Save (for) the worship of Heaven's King, love of this world is folly'.²² However, Nagy takes this utterance from Fothad as modelled 'along the lines of the Christian scripting of the dialogue between saint and miraculously recovered hero from the past', thus placing it squarely within the mainstream of Irish literary tradition;²³ similar to Cú Chulainn in *Síaburcharpat Con Culainn*, now that he is dead, Fothad is aware of the realities of the beyond and the importance of the promised afterlife.²⁴ Furthermore, Borsje suggests in her analysis of the phrase *aidc[h]e úath* ('terror of night')²⁵ that it would take on added significance 'if the author of *Reicne Fothaid Canainne* was acquainted with the Bible [as] the demonic nature of the terror of the night is obvious from Psalm 90'.²⁶ Her arguments demonstrate that the presentation of the supernatural beings in the *Reicne*, though grounded in medieval Irish culture, may have been influenced in part by Jewish and Biblical demonic traditions.

TRADITIONS CONCERNING FOTHAD (2): OTHER SOURCES

The poem beginning *Eól dam i ndairib dréchta* attributed to Flann mac Maíl Máedóc (†977) includes the following lines referring to various famous *fiana*:

> Fīanna Find, fāth cen timme,
> hūi Bāiscne brecctais rinne
> fianna Foilnge, forom nglē,
> fianna Fothaid Canainne.²⁷

The *fiana* of Finn úa Baíscne who used to spatter spear-points (with blood), a subject matter without fear, the *fiana* of Foilnge, a course of battle (?), the *fiana* of Fothad Canainne.

There is nothing in this verse to suggest that the Finn Cycle had enveloped and subsumed the Fothad Canainne material at this stage.

---

21 *Fian.* pp 10–11 §1. Hull, 'The death of Fothath Cananne', 401, 403, cites this line as *A ben nacham·aic i-lle* and translates as 'O woman, do not entreat me (to come) hither!'. **22** *Fian.* pp 16–17 §48. **23** Nagy, *Conversing with angels and ancients*, p. 302. **24** See Ó Béarra, 'The Otherworld realm of *Tír scáith*'. **25** *Fian.* pp 12–13 §23. **26** Borsje, 'The "terror of the night" and the Morrígain', p. 81. **27** *Fian.* p. xv (= Meyer,

The Middle Irish poem beginning *A Mór Maigne Moigi Siúil* contains a list of deaths of famous heroes. Therein, alongside references to Cú Chulainn and Mongán among others, Fothad gets equal prominence in a verse with Finn:

> Nách cúala in ngním ngalann ngann,
> Fothad Canann (clú nád binn)
> ocus in rígféinnid ríam
> dárb ainm toísech na Fían Finn?

> Have you not heard of the ill-famed strange act of violence concerning Fothad Canann, nor of the royal warrior in the past whose name was Finn, leader of the Fíana?[28]

There is no indication here that Fothad is a minor character in a story-cycle focused on Finn; rather the parity of treatment serves to endorse the view of Ann Dooley and Harry Roe that he is 'a figure who is equally well represented [with Finn] in the literature of the tenth century'.[29]

In the *dinnśenchas* of Carraic Lethdeirg, Fothad is named as the abductor of Lethderg, daughter of Conchobur mac Nessa and wife of Tromda mac Calatruim. Lethderg falls in love with Fothad in a dream and he arrives with a number of companions to take her with him, killing her husband in the process. In the poetic version, he is said to depart not only with Lethderg, but also with Tromda's head.[30]

The title of a now-lost tale, *Serc Caillige Bérre do Fothud Chanainne*, mentioned in the medieval Irish tale-lists, would also seem to point to a wider cultivation of Fothad narratives at the time, a cultivation that may not necessarily have been bound up with Finn.[31] However, even here there are connections with the Fenian Cycle as the Caillech Bérre is elsewhere referred to as Finn's mother or as the mother of his son, Fénnid,[32] as well as being named as Fothad's wife.[33] It is

'Mitteilungen aus irischen Handschriften: *Do chomramaib Laigen inso sís*', 119 §35). **28** Murphy, *Early Irish lyrics*, p. 90 §9 (= *Fian*. pp 44–5 §9). **29** Dooley and Roe, *Tales*, p. xvi. **30** *MD* iv, pp 120–3; Stokes, 'The prose tales in the Rennes dindśenchas', §92 (*RC* 16, 43–4). McQuillan, 'Finn, Fothad, and *fian*', 3, has suggested that this short piece of *senchas* might be taken as referring to Medb Lethderg, 'the Leinster sovereignty figure par excellence' but, as John Carey points out to me, she is usually presented as the daughter of Conán of Cúalu. **31** Mac Cana, *The learned tales*, pp 48, 58: *Serc Caillige Berre do Fothud Chanand / Searc Caille Berra do Fothad Canand* (List A); *Searc Cailligi Berre do Focha Canainde / Serc Chaillighi Bérre do Fothad Canainne / Serc Caillige Berrae do Fothad Canoinne* (List B). There is another lost narrative from this period named in Tale-list A only, *Longes Fothaid / Londes Fothaid* 'The exile of Fothad' (Mac Cana, *The learned tales*, p. 43), which might also have been connected with Fothad Canainne; lack of supporting evidence renders this conjectural, however. **32** Hull, 'The old woman or nun of Beare', 176 (cf. Meyer, *Aislinge Meic Con Glinne*, p. 210); many of these and subsequent references are from Nagy, *The wisdom of the outlaw*, p. 265 n. 13. **33** Dobbs, 'The ban-shenchus' [*RC* 47, 302; *RC* 48, 176, 211] and Dillon, 'Laud Misc. 610', 73. Fuindche ingen Náir, the wife of Lugaid Mac Con, is also named as the

possible that these materials are bound up with the association of *fíanaigecht* with Corcu Loígde which acts as an important intersection point between the traditions connected to Finn and Fothad.³⁴

FOTHAD CANAINNE AND *FÍANAIGECHT*

Despite the arguments presented above for analysing this early material primarily in the context of the survival of independent traditions concerning Fothad Canainne, there is no doubt that it does have important thematic links with the Finn Cycle. By way of illustration, we may instance the following: Fothad and Finn are *fían*-leaders; neither is able to maintain a lasting relationship with a member of the opposite sex though Finn loses the women instead of his life; they abduct women; both are decapitated and their heads continue to communicate after being severed from their bodies.³⁵ Fundamental similarities such as these must have accommodated the wholesale intertwining of the two traditions in the early medieval period with the subsequent downgrading of the distinct narrative cycle associated with Fothad Canainne. There is no later separate cultivation, outside of the *fíanaigecht* genre, of literature pertaining to Fothad; modern scholarship and folklore are united in seeing him as a character of the Fenian Cycle.³⁶

The earliest text to connect Fothad with Finn is a genealogy headed *Genelach Find meic hUmaill*:³⁷

> Trī meic Nuadat: Gnáthaltach senathair na trī Fothad, et Baīscne senathair Find 7 Fergus Fairrce senathair rīgraide Lagen.³⁸
>
> Three sons of Núadu: Gnáthaltach grandfather of the three Fothaid, Baíscne grandfather of Finn and Fergus Fairrce grandfather of the kings of the Laigin.

This early source explicitly connects 'na trí Fothaid' with Finn; however, we must be aware that there are alternate early genealogies recorded for Fothad Canainne and his brothers.³⁹

---

mother of the Fothads in the *banšenchas* (Dobbs, 'The ban-shenchus' [*RC* 48, 176, 211]) and in the prose introduction to *Reicne Fothaid Chanainne* (*Fian.* pp 4–5). **34** See above, Chapter Six, pp 88–9; Ó Muirigh, 'Fionn, fian agus Corca Laoidhe'. **35** The proclamations of Fothad's head are analysed in detail by Nagy, *Conversing with angels and ancients*, pp 299–303. **36** The sole exception of which I am aware is a lone marginal acephalous verse at the top of Leabhar Breac (p. 115), which is said to be recited by Fothad Canainne's spirit ('Spir*ut* fath*aid* chana*nd* c*ecinit*') concerning the torments of hell (see Wright, *The Irish tradition in Old English literature*, p. 140 n. 128). This is consonant with the mention in the *Reicne* of his torture in the afterlife (*Fian.* pp 16–17 §48). **37** See above, Chapter Six, pp 85–6. **38** *CGH* p. 99 (128b9); *senathair* might also be translated as 'ancestor' here. **39** *EIHM* pp 10–11. See McQuillan, 'Finn,

The earliest explicit *fianaigecht* reference to Finn and Fothad Canainne together is in *Bruiden Átha Í*, which probably dates to the late eighth century and where the causes of the enmity between the two are explained. Therein, as we have seen above, Finn's killing of Cuirrech leads him to attempt to make peace with the slain man's half-brother, Fothad, by organizing an ale-feast in his honour. Fothad is under a taboo only to drink ale in the company of severed heads. In seeking to fulfil this condition, Finn decapitates Fothad's sister, Téite, which serves only to increase the hostility between the two; consequently, Fothad Canainne is presented as Finn's opponent in the earliest stratum of the Fenian Cycle.[40]

Repeated references to Fothad Canainne in opposition to Finn in the *Acallam* clearly delineate his primary role within *fianaigecht* at the end of the Middle Irish period.[41] His death in the battle of Clárach is alluded to at the very opening of the tale.[42] His enmity towards Finn (who desires peace with him) is mentioned in a poem narrated by Finn concerning Fenian battles,[43] while in another poem recited to Oisín, Caílte refers to the occasion when Fothad deceived the *fían* (*ó rus-brég Fathad in Féind*).[44] A great battle in Leinster between Finn, Fothad and their followers is noted,[45] and the location of a further contention with Fothad Canainne is also remarked upon.[46] Thus, his role is consistently portrayed in the early Finn Cycle and in the *Acallam* as that of an inveterate foe of Finn.

CONCLUSIONS

As we have seen, the close relationship between the narrative traditions associated with Finn and Fothad led to the eventual merging of these materials under the banner of *fianaigecht* and the extinguishing of any residual independent cultivation of stories and events associated with Fothad Canainne.[47] Such considerations underlie Proinsias Mac Cana's assertion that:

Fothad, and *fían*', 1–2, where it is shown that the genealogical connections of the Fothaid with Corcu Loígde and Dál nAraide are paralleled by Finn's associations with these population groups (see above, Chapter Six, pp 86–9, for further details).   **40** For further information concerning this narrative, see Chapter Five, pp 74–6.   **41** In other roughly contemporary sources, Finn is married to Fothad's daughter who is alternatively called Smirgat (Dobbs, 'The ban-shenchus' [*RC* 48, 178]; O'Grady, 'Teasmolad Corbmaic', i, p. 91, ii, p. 98 [= Meyer, *Cath Finntrága*, p. 74]) and Smirnat (Dobbs, 'The ban-shenchus' (*RC* 47, 301–2, 327; 48, 214) [= *Fian*. p. xxix §§XLVI–VII]).   **42** Stokes, 'Acallamh', ll 99–100 (= O'Grady, 'Agallamh', i, p. 96; Dooley and Roe, *Tales*, p. 6; Dillon, *Stories from the Acallam*, ll 102–5).   **43** Stokes, 'Acallamh', ll 1135–6, 1143–4 (= O'Grady, 'Agallamh', i, p. 118; Dooley and Roe, *Tales*, p. 36).   **44** Stokes, 'Acallamh', l. 2494 (= O'Grady, 'Agallamh', i, p. 149, ii, p. 165 [text and translation corrupt]; Dooley and Roe, *Tales*, p. 77).   **45** Stokes, 'Acallamh', ll 3395–9 (= O'Grady, 'Agallamh', i, p. 169, ii, p. 189; Dooley and Roe, *Tales*, pp 102–3).   **46** Stokes, 'Acallamh', ll 7581–3 (= O'Grady, 'Agallamh', i, p. 230, ii, p. 261).   **47** However, there seems to have been some lingering autonomous development of narratives associated with 'na trí Fothaid'.

the fact that Fothad Canainne is evidently one of the forms (together with Goll, Aed, and Balor) assumed by the constant opponent of the hero represented by Fionn and Lug, there cannot be any doubt about the close interrelationship between the principal leaders of *fiana* on the mythico-ideological level.[48]

This is a bold claim and is at a far remove from seeing Fothad as the central figure of his own body of tales which were later incorporated into the Finn Cycle. T.F. O'Rahilly has gone even further, suggesting that Fothad was merely 'a double of Finn's enemy, Goll';[49] the foregoing analysis would tend to undermine this hypothesis.

In later *fianaigecht*, we find one Fatha Canann mentioned as a member of Finn's *fian*. He would appear to represent a reworking of the character of Fothad Canainne, similar to the process whereby Aillén the burner in the *Acallam* reappears in a friendlier guise in 'The chase of Síd na mBan Finn'.[50] The earliest reference to Fatha Canann seems to be in the lay concerning the battle of Cronnmhóin, which may date to the thirteenth or fourteenth century,[51] and he also plays a significant role in the later *Bruidhean chaorthainn*.[52] In this transformed way, the figure of Fothad survived within subsequent *fianaigecht* sources, albeit in a form far removed from his original character.

48 Mac Cana, '*Fianaigecht* in the pre-Norman period', p. 79. **49** *EIHM* p. 11 n. 3. **50** See above, Chapter Ten, pp 127–8, and *DF* III, pp 197–8. **51** *DF* I, §iv, pp 10–14, 106–10 at pp 11, 107, verses 12, 19; for the date, see *DF* III, p. 13. For further references to Fatha Canann, see Ó Cadhlaigh, *An fhiannuidheacht*, p. 500, s.nn. 'Fatha Canann', 'Fatha Chonáin'; Ó hÓgáin, *Myth, legend and romance*, p. 233, s.n. 'Fothadh Canainne'. **52** Mac Piarais, *Bruidhean chaorthainn* (cf. Campbell, *Leabhar na feinne*, pp 86–8).

CHAPTER FOURTEEN

Later literary developments of the early *fianaigecht* corpus

Acallam na senórach stands as a cultural high-water mark within Gaelic literary tradition and yet, as we have seen, there is no evidence for the cultivation of a large corpus of *fianaigecht* literature in the decades and centuries before its composition. Although the formation of long narratives (such as the *Acallam*) was a feature of Irish-language literature from the late Old Irish period onwards, with the creation of texts such as *Táin bó Cúailnge* and *Togail bruidne Da Derga* and the influence of translations and adaptations of Classical compositions, nevertheless there is nothing in the earlier Finn Cycle corpus to hint at the richness and breadth of the tradition that is so evident in the *Acallam*. Factors contributing to the emergence of the Finn Cycle from the sidelines into the mainstream have been outlined in Chapter Two; prominent among these were the intertwining of *fianaigecht* with the ever-expanding literary genre of *dinnšenchas* alongside what must have been a sustained and vibrant oral cultivation of material from the Fenian Cycle. This sets the context for our analysis of the literary development of the corpus from its earliest written attestation to the beginning of the thirteenth century.

SCOPE AND FORM

The most readily apparent difference between the late and early materials within our window of study is the extent of the narratives created. Similar to tales across the entire spectrum of early medieval Irish literature, *fianaigecht* texts that date to the Old Irish period (few and all as they are) tend to be concise tracts – mainly in prose – incorporating brief and pithy verses, frequently mantic in nature. The style of these stories tends towards understatement, with plotlines delivered in a tight and succinct manner. Tales such as those located around the river Suir, *Scél asa mberar combad hé Finn mac Cumaill Mongán*, and 'Finn and the jester' conform to this pattern, and give us brief glimpses of a rich and varied narrative tradition associated with various parts of the country. Character development is practically non-existent though some important characteristics of Finn are highlighted, characteristics which are repeated across the tradition.

However, there are other sources that do not conform to this broader pattern. Exceptions include 'The quarrel between Finn and Oisín', a poem of sixteen quatrains prefaced by a short prose introduction, and lengthier poems such as *Reicne Fothaid Chanainne* which contains forty-nine quatrains, though (as we have seen) this composition emerged within the tradition concerning Fothad Canainne that eventually merged with Finn Cycle materials under the banner of *fíanaigecht*. The metres of these poems are very mixed and such compositions are generally written in a 'freer type of syllabic verse which was current in the Old Irish and Middle Irish periods',[1] and represent a further strand of early Fenian tradition.

STYLE AND PRESENTATION

From the Middle Irish period onwards, written Fenian traditions in both prose and poetry increase. The prose texts with an enhanced poetic element – the traditional prosimetrum format – expand in size, becoming more verbose, resulting in tales such as *Úath Beinne Étair* and *Tesmolta Cormaic 7 aided Finn*, and texts of significant length such as *Macgnímrada Finn* and *Tochmarc Ailbe*. At the same time, *fíanaigecht* was adding a specific type of poetic text to its written corpus, the medieval Irish narrative poem, with the early examples from the cycle possibly among the oldest in the genre, if we accept the dating arguments advanced by John Carey.[2] By the time of the scripting of the Book of Leinster in the second half of the twelfth century, long narrative poems such as those beginning *Oenach indiu luid in rí* (see above p. 134) and *Dám thrír táncatar ille* were an established part of the cycle,[3] while some metrical *dinnṡenchas* texts – many containing a *fíanaigecht* element – also fall under this rubric.[4] The cultivation of this new poetic genre might well be bound up with contemporary developments concerning the promotion of *senchas*, and connected with the ongoing professional jostling between *filid* and *baird* in the Middle Irish period. The emergence of the long narrative poem as a medium of presentation, within and without *fíanaigecht*, is a significant literary development in medieval Irish literary culture and it is noteworthy to see the expanding Finn Cycle in the vanguard of such a change.[5]

---

1 Ó Cuív, 'Some developments in Irish metrics', 273. **2** See above, Chapter Eleven, pp 130–1. **3** Texts edited from the Book of Leinster by Stokes, 'Find and the phantoms' and Stern, 'Eine ossianische Ballade aus dem XII. Jahrhundert'; see *LL* iv, ll 29089–300, 29301–92 (cf. *ZCP* 3, 433–4). **4** We may instance here, for example, the poem beginning *Almu Lagen, les na fían* (*MD* ii, pp 72–7). **5** For a detailed study of this topic, see Clancy, 'Before the ballad: Gaelic narrative verse before 1200'. Interestingly, in his discussion, the author (p. 118) 'excluded verse narratives of *fíannaigecht* because the relationship between this genre and narrative verse may be thought to be differently complex'.

It is clear that a very broad range of Fenian materials underpins the growing literary cultivation of *fianaigecht* in the late Middle Irish period. This becomes abundantly clear with the creation of *Acallam na senórach*, which in a way straddles the boundaries between the two dominant genres. Though the *Acallam* is categorized primarily as a prosimetric text, nevertheless it incorporates within it aspects of the long narrative poem tradition, utilizing poetic compositions that were created independently of the frame text, and which were later re-employed in its construction. Such an ambitious project instituted by the author of the *Acallam* allowed for the creation of something new, yet something which drew extensively on existing written and oral Fenian traditions, and on the extant styles and formats of its literary cultivation. Consequently, we might argue that the vitality of the Finn Cycle from the late Middle Irish period onwards came about partly because of a fusion in its forms of presentation, and from its ability to adapt, change and broaden its cultural relevance.

CONTENTS AND SUBJECT MATTERS

The contents and subject matters of the pre-Norman *fianaigecht* corpus are remarkably consistent across a diverse range of materials that seem to have originated in different parts of the country. As discussed earlier, the earliest sources emphasize Finn's doomed relationships with women who are presented as inherently treacherous; his mantic abilities are consistently alluded to; and issues such as severed heads, hunting and cooking, and the conflict between youth and age are recurrent themes.[6] The exponential growth of *fianaigecht*, particularly in the later Middle Irish period, expands the range of subject matters addressed in the literature. Nevertheless, this development remains centred upon a limited number of specific themes, particularly focused on the issue of remembrance:[7] the poetic and prose texts from this era reveal layer upon layer of additional incidents, happenings, and events, the majority of them invoking the heyday of Finn, and with many of them based implicitly around the premise – made explicit in the *Acallam* – that the glory days of the *fian* have gone, never to return. Consequently, all story is history; all the noble deeds are projected onto an imperfectly remembered past; and all heroic achievements belong to people of a different time and of a greater era.

DEVELOPMENTS AND CONCLUSIONS

The later ballads, romances and adventures capture this spirit of the idyllic days of the *fian*. They are frequently set in a land of '*Es war einmal* / Once upon a

---

[6] See Chapter Six, pp 91–3. [7] See Schlüter, '"For the entertainment of lords and commons of later times"'.

time', when giants stalked the land and when there were few limits on magic, on heroic attainments, and on the creation of 'a land where the strange is always familiar and the familiar often tinged with strangeness, where things are rarely what they seem and nothing ever really is but what is not'.[8] Consequently, the literature is moving towards adventure and romance, partially under the influence of foreign models; we part with 'an inheritance of tragic fables, for the sake of vanities, wonders, and splendours among which character and the tragic motives lost their pre-eminent interest and their old authority over poets and audience'.[9] As students of the genre, we are unsurprised to discover that the Finn Cycle not only adapted to these changes but was in a position to do so.

By the beginning of the Early Modern Irish period, the existence of *Acallam na senórach* alongside a growing corpus of Fenian lays, meant that literary cultivation of Finn Cycle materials was in a very strong position. Later developments including the dramatic expansion of the Fenian ballad tradition,[10] and the cultivation of new *fíanaigecht* adventures and romances, are therefore consonant with the position won for the genre within Gaelic literary culture from the thirteenth century onwards.[11] In contradistinction to the difficulty in accounting for the emergence of the *Acallam* from fragmentarily documented beginnings, there is no such problem in explaining the growth of *fíanaigecht* in the post-*Acallam* era; by the Early Modern Irish period, the genre of literature focused on Finn and his *fían* had moved to centre stage in the Irish literary canon.

---

8 Ó Coileáin, 'Place and placename', 46. **9** Ker, *Epic and romance*, p. 34. **10** The strength of the later ballad tradition in Scotland is particularly noteworthy: see Meek, 'The Gaelic ballads of Scotland: creativity and adaptation'. For fluidity in the use therein of toponyms across Ireland and Scotland, see idem, 'Place-names and literature: evidence from the Gaelic ballads'. **11** The best discussions of these topics are those by Murphy, *Ossianic lore*; Bruford, *Gaelic folk-tales and mediaeval romances*; and Flahive, *The Fenian Cycle in Irish and Scots-Gaelic literature*, Chapter Five. The breadth and richness of this literature is evident, for example, from the collection of Finn Cycle translations available in Lady Gregory's *Gods and fighting men*, pp 117–324. Mention should also be made here of the Ossianic phenomenon of the eighteenth century when James Macpherson published adaptations of Fenian lays and romances which were claimed as translations of archaic Gaelic materials. An Ossianic craze swept across Europe and provided the impetus for the collection of much later Finn Cycle material, as well as contributing to the early growth of Celtic Studies on the continent. For texts and discussion, see Gaskill, *The poems of Ossian*; idem (ed.), *Ossian revisited*; Flahive, *The Fenian Cycle in Irish and Scots-Gaelic literature*, Chapter Seven.

Bibliography

Almqvist, B., S. Ó Catháin and P. Ó Héalaí (eds), *The heroic process: form, function and fantasy in folk epic* (Dublin, 1987). The Fenian essays from this collection were also printed with the same pagination in *Béaloideas*, 54–5 (1986–7), and separately as *Fiannaíocht: essays on the Fenian tradition of Ireland and Scotland* (Baile Átha Cliath, 1987).

Alter, R., *The art of Biblical narrative* (New York, 1981).

Anderson, E.R. and V. Norouzalibeik, 'Father-son combat: an Indo-European typescene and its variations', *Journal of Indo-European Studies*, 36 (2008), 269–332.

Arbuthnot, S., *Cóir anmann: a late Middle Irish treatise on personal names*, 2 vols, Irish Texts Society 59–60 (London, 2005–6).

— 'On the name Oscar and two little-known episodes involving the *fían*', *Cambrian Medieval Celtic Studies*, 51 (Summer, 2006), 67–81.

— 'Finn, Ferchess and the *rincne*: versions compared' in Arbuthnot and Parsons (eds), *The Gaelic Finn tradition*, pp 62–80.

Arbuthnot, S. and G. Parsons (eds), *The Gaelic Finn tradition* (Dublin, 2012).

Arnold, M., *Poems* (London, 1853).

Atkinson, R., *The Book of Leinster, sometime called the Book of Glendalough*, autotype facsimile with introduction, analysis of contents, and index (Dublin, 1880).

— *The passions and the homilies from Leabhar Breac*, Todd Lecture Series 2 (Dublin, 1882).

Banks, S.E. and J.W. Binns, *Gervase of Tilbury. Otia imperialia: recreation for an emperor*, Oxford Medieval Texts (Oxford, 2002).

Baumgarten, R., 'Placenames, etymology and the structure of *fianaigecht*' in Almqvist, Ó Catháin and Ó Héalaí (eds), *Fiannaíocht*, pp 1–24.

— (ed.), *Newsletter of the School of Celtic Studies*, 9 (Dublin, 1996).

Bernhardt-House, P.A., 'Horses, hounds and high kings: a shared Arthurian tradition across the Irish Sea' in J.F. Nagy (ed.), *Myth in Celtic literatures: CSANA Yearbook 6* (Dublin, 2007), pp 11–21.

Best, R.I., *Bibliography of Irish philology and of printed Irish literature to 1912* (Dublin, 1913; 2nd repr. [with augmented indexes] Dublin, 1992).

— 'The settling of the manor of Tara', *Ériu*, 4 (1920), 121–72.

Best, R.I. and O. Bergin, *Lebor na Huidre: The Book of the Dun Cow* (Dublin, 1929).

Best, R.I., O. Bergin, M.A. O'Brien and A. O'Sullivan, *The Book of Leinster formerly Lebar na Núachongbála*, 6 vols (Dublin, 1954–83).

Bieler, L., *The Patrician texts in the Book of Armagh*, Scriptores Latini Hiberniae 10 (Dublin, 1979).

Binchy, D.A., 'Bretha crólige', *Ériu*, 12 (1938), 1–77.

— *Críth gablach*, Mediaeval and Modern Irish Series 11 (Dublin, 1941).

— 'The saga of Fergus mac Léti', *Ériu*, 16 (1952), 33–48.
— 'The Old-Irish table of penitential commutations', *Ériu*, 19 (1962), 47–72.
— *Scéla Cano meic Gartnáin*, Mediaeval and Modern Irish Series 18 (Dublin, 1963).
— *Corpus iuris Hibernici*, 6 vols (Dublin, 1978).
Borsje, J., 'The "terror of the night" and the Morrígain: shifting faces of the supernatural' in M. Ó Flaithearta (ed.), *Proceedings of the Seventh Symposium of Societas Celtologica Nordica*, Studia Celtica Upsaliensia 6 (Uppsala, 2007), pp 71–98.
Bosley, K., *The Kalevala: an epic poem after oral tradition by Elias Lönnrot* (Oxford, 1989).
— *The Kanteletar: lyrics and ballads after the oral tradition by Elias Lönnrot*, Oxford World's Classics (Oxford, 1992).
Bostock, J.K., *A handbook on Old High German literature*, 2nd ed. revised by K.C. King and D.R. McLintock (Oxford, 1976).
Bourke, A., S. Kilfeather, M. Luddy, M. Mac Curtain, G. Meaney, M. Ní Dhonnchadha, M. O'Dowd and C. Wills (eds), *The Field Day anthology of Irish writing IV: Irish women's writing and traditions* (Cork, 2002).
Boyd, M. (ed.), *Ollam: studies in Gaelic and related traditions in honor of Tomás Ó Cathasaigh* (Madison/Teaneck, 2016).
Boyle, E., 'Allegory, the *áes dána* and the liberal arts in Medieval Irish literature' in D. Hayden and P. Russell (eds), *Grammatica, gramadach and gramadeg. Vernacular grammar and grammarians in medieval Ireland and Wales* (Amsterdam, 2016), pp 11–34.
Boyle, E. and D. Hayden (eds), *Authorities and adaptations: the reworking and transmission of textual sources in medieval Ireland* (Dublin, 2014).
Bracken, D. and D. Ó Riain-Raedel (eds), *Ireland and Europe in the twelfth century: reform and renewal* (Dublin, 2006).
Braune, W. (ed.), *Althochdeutsches Lesebuch* (Halle, 1902).
Breatnach, C., '*Oidheadh Chloinne Tuireann* agus *Cath Maige Tuired*: dhá shampla de mhiotas eiseamláireach', *Éigse*, 32 (2000), 35–46.
— 'The transmission and text of *Tóruigheacht Dhiarmada agus Ghráinne*: a re-appraisal' in Arbuthnot and Parsons (eds), *The Gaelic Finn tradition*, pp 139–50.
Breatnach, L., 'The caldron of poesy', *Ériu*, 32 (1981), 45–93.
— *Uraicecht na ríar: the poetic grades in early Irish law* (Dublin, 1987).
— 'Law and literature in early medieval Ireland', *L'irlanda e gli irlandesi nell'alto medioevo: Spoleto, 16–21 aprile 2009*, Atti delle Settimane 57 (Spoleto, 2010), pp 215–38.
Breatnach, P.A., Review of J.F. Nagy, *The wisdom of the outlaw: the boyhood deeds of Finn in Gaelic narrative tradition*, *Éigse*, 24 (1990), 155–67.
Breatnach, R.A., 'Tóraigheacht Dhiarmada agus Ghráinne' in Dillon (ed.), *Irish sagas*, pp 135–47.
Broderick, G., 'Manx stories and reminiscences of Ned Beg Hom Ruy (introduction and texts)', *Zeitschrift für celtische Philologie*, 38 (1981), 113–78.
— 'Manx stories and reminiscences of Ned Beg Hom Ruy (translation and notes)', *Zeitschrift für celtische Philologie*, 39 (1982), 117–94.

— 'Boddagh yn Cooat Laaghagh: a Manx version of a Fenian tale', *Béaloideas*, 51 (1983), 1–10.
— 'Fin as Oshin', *Celtica*, 21 (1990), 51–60.
— 'Fíanaigecht in Manx tradition', *Scottish Gaelic Studies*, 30 (2016), 191–241.
Bromwich, R., 'Some remarks on the Celtic sources of "Tristan"', *Transactions of the Honourable Society of Cymmrodorion* (1953), 32–60.
— 'The *Tristan* of the Welsh' in R. Bromwich, A.O.H. Jarman and B.F. Roberts (eds), *The Arthur of the Welsh: the Arthurian legend in medieval Welsh literature* (Cardiff, 1991), pp 209–28.
Bromwich, R. and D.S. Evans, *Culhwch and Olwen: an edition and study of the oldest Arthurian tale* (Cardiff, 1992).
Brown, A.C.L., 'The Grail and the English *Sir Perceval*', *Modern Philology*, 16 (1918–19), 553–68; 17 (1919–20), 361–82; 18 (1920–1), 201–28, 661–73; 22 (1924–5), 79–96, 113–32.
Bruford, A., *Gaelic folk-tales and mediaeval romances* (published as *Béaloideas* 34 [1966]).
— 'Oral and literary Fenian tales' in Almqvist, Ó Catháin and Ó Héalaí (eds), *Fiannaíocht*, pp 25–56.
Bryant, N., *Merlin and the Grail; Joseph of Arimathea, Merlin, Perceval. The trilogy of prose romances attributed to Robert de Boron* (Woodbridge/Rochester, 2001).
Burrow, J.A., *Medieval writers and their work* (Oxford, 1982; revised OPUS edition, n.d.).
Byrne, C.J., M. Harry and P. Ó Siadhail (eds), *Celtic languages and Celtic peoples: proceedings of the Second North American Conference of Celtic Studies* (Halifax, Nova Scotia, 1992).
Byrne, F.J. '*Dercu*: the feminine of *mocu*', *Éigse*, 28 (1994–5), 42–70.
— 'The Viking age' in D. Ó Cróinín (ed.), *A new history of Ireland, i: prehistoric and early Ireland* (Oxford, 2005), pp 609–34.
Campbell, J.F., *Leabhar na feinne: heroic Gaelic ballads collected in Scotland, chiefly from 1512 to 1871* (London, 1872; repr. Shannon, 1972).
Carey, J., 'The name "Tuatha Dé Danann"', *Éigse*, 18, ii (1981), 291–4.
— 'Nodons in Britain and Ireland', *Zeitschrift für celtische Philologie*, 40 (1984), 1–22.
— 'Scél Tuáin meic Chairill', *Ériu*, 35 (1984), 94–111.
— 'Suibne Geilt and Tuán mac Cairill', *Éigse*, 20 (1984), 93–105.
— 'Time, space, and the Otherworld', *Proceedings of the Harvard Celtic Colloquium*, 7 (1987), 1–27.
— 'The two laws in Dubthach's judgement', *Cambridge Medieval Celtic Studies*, 19 (1990), 1–18.
— 'A *Túath Dé* miscellany', *The Bulletin of the Board of Celtic Studies*, 39 (1992), 24–45.
— 'The testimony of the dead', *Éigse*, 26 (1992), 1–12.
— 'An edition of the pseudo-historical prologue to the *Senchas már*', *Ériu*, 45 (1994), 1–32.
— 'On the interrelationships of some *Cín Dromma Snechtai* texts', *Ériu*, 46 (1995), 71–92.
— 'Obscure styles in medieval Ireland', *Mediaevalia*, 19 (1996), 23–39.

— 'The three things required of a poet', *Ériu*, 48 (1997), 41–58.
— 'Nōdons, Lugus, Windos' in C.M. Ternes and H. Zinser (eds), *Dieux des Celtes / Goetter der Kelten / Gods of the Celts* (Luxembourg, 2002), pp 99–126.
— (ed.), *Duanaire Finn: reassessments*, Irish Texts Society, Subsidiary Series 13 (London, 2003).
— 'Remarks on dating' in Carey (ed.), *Duanaire Finn: reassessments*, pp 1–18.
— 'Two notes on names', *Éigse*, 35 (2005), 116–24.
— *Ireland and the Grail* (Aberystwyth, 2007).
— 'Dán doiléir atá curtha i leith Chormaic mhic Cuileannáin' in S. Ó Coileáin, L.P. Ó Murchú and P. Riggs (eds), *Séimhfhear suairc: aistí in ómós don Ollamh Breandán Ó Conchúir* (An Daingean, 2013), pp 39–45.
— '*Acallam na senórach*: a conversation between worlds' in Doyle and Murray (eds), *In dialogue with the Agallamh*, pp 76–89.
— 'The death of Diarmaid: Pessinus to Ben Bulben?' in S. Arbuthnot, S. Ní Mhurchú and G. Parsons (eds), *Proceedings of the Second International Finn Cycle Conference* (forthcoming).
Carney, J., 'Two poems from Acallam na senórach' in J. Carney and D. Greene (eds), *Celtic studies: essays in memory of Angus Matheson* (London, 1968), pp 22–32.
— 'Three Old Irish accentual poems', *Ériu*, 22 (1971), 23–80.
Chadbourne, K., 'The beagle's cry: dogs in the Finn ballads and tales', *Proceedings of the Harvard Celtic Colloquium*, 16–17 (1996–7), 1–14.
— 'The voices of hounds: heroic dogs and men in the Finn ballads and tales' in J.F. Nagy (ed.), *Heroic poets and poetic heroes in Celtic tradition. A Festschrift for Patrick K. Ford: CSANA Yearbook 3–4* (Dublin, 2005), pp 28–41.
Chadwick, N.K., 'Imbas forosnai', *Scottish Gaelic Studies*, 4:2 (1935), 97–135.
An Chraoibhín: *see* D. Hyde.
Christiansen, R.T., *The Vikings and the Viking wars in Irish and Gaelic tradition* (Oslo, 1931).
Clancy, T.O., 'Fools and adultery in some Early Irish texts', *Ériu*, 44 (1993), 105–24.
— 'Before the ballad: Gaelic narrative verse before 1200' in C. Ó Baoill and N.R. McGuire (eds), *Caindel Alban. Fèill-sgrìobhainn do Dhòmhnall E. Meek* (Aberdeen, 2008), pp 115–36 (= *Scottish Gaelic Studies*, 24).
Clinton, J.W., *The tragedy of Sohrab and Rostam: from the Persian national epic, the Shahname of Abol-Qasem Ferdowsi*, Publications on the Near East (Seattle/London; rev. ed. 1996).
Clover, C., 'The long prose form', *Arkiv för Nordisk Filologi*, 101 (1986), 10–39.
Comyn, D., *Mac-ghníomhartha Fhinn: The youthful exploits of Fionn* (Dublin, 1881).
Connon, A., 'Plotting *Acallam na senórach*: the physical context of the "Mayo" sequence' in Sheehan, Findon and Follett (eds), *Gablánach in scélaigecht*, pp 69–102.
— 'The Roscommon *locus* of *Acallam na senórach* and some thoughts as to *tempus* and *persona*' in Doyle and Murray (eds), *In dialogue with the Agallamh*, pp 21–59.
Cormier, R.J., 'Open contrast: Tristan and Diarmaid', *Speculum*, 51, no. 4 (1976), 589–601.

Corthals, J., 'The rhymeless "Leinster poems"', *Celtica*, 21 (1990), 111–25.
— 'Die Trennung von Finn und Gráinne', *Zeitschrift für celtische Philologie*, 49–50 (1997), 71–91.
— 'Ailbe zoekt een Man', *Kelten*, 4 (1999), 4–5.
— 'Ailbe's speech to Cithruad (*Tochmarc Ailbe*)', *Éigse*, 34 (2004), 1–9.
Cross, T.P., 'A note on "Sohrab" and "Rustum" in Ireland', *Journal of Celtic Studies*, 1 (1949–50), 176–82.
Cross, T.P. and C.H. Slover, *Ancient Irish tales* (New York, 1936; repr. 1996).
Curteis, E., 'Age and origin of the Fenian tales', *Journal of the Ivernian Society*, 1 (1908–9), 159–68.
Dagenais, J., *The ethics of reading in manuscript culture: glossing the Libro de buen amor* (Princeton, 1994).
d'Arbois de Jubainville, H. (avec la collaboration de G. Dottin, M. Grammont, L. Duvau, et F. Lot), *L'épopée celtique en Irlande*, Cours de littérature celtique, vol. 5 (Paris, 1892).
Davies, S., *The Mabinogion* (Oxford, 2007).
de Vries, J., 'Das Motiv des Vater-Sohn-Kampfes im Hildebrandslied' (mit einer Nachschrift des Verfassers) in K. Hauck (ed.), *Zur germanisch-deutschen Heldensage. Sechzehn Aufsätze zum neuen Forschungsstand* (Bad Homburg, 1961), pp 248–73 (repr. from *Germanisch-Romanische Monatsschrift*, 3 (1953), 257–74).
— 'Le conte irlandais Aided óenfir Aífe et le thème du combat du père et du fils dans quelques traditions indo-européennes' in K. Hauck (ed.), *Zur germanisch-deutschen Heldensage. Sechzehn Aufsätze zum neuen Forschungsstand* (Bad Homburg, 1961), pp 273–84 (repr. from *Ogam*, 9 (1957), 122–38).
Dillon, M., 'Nominal predicates in Irish', *Zeitschrift für celtische Philologie*, 16 (1927), 313–56; 17 (1928), 307–46; 19 (1933), 153–4.
— 'Stories from the law tracts', *Ériu*, 11 (1930), 42–65.
Early Irish literature (Chicago, 1948; repr. Dublin, 1994).
— (ed.), *Irish sagas* (Dublin, 1959; repr. Cork, 1968).
— 'Laud Misc. 610', *Celtica*, 5 (1960), 64–76.
— *Lebor na cert*, Irish Texts Society 46 (Dublin, 1962).
— *Stories from the Acallam*, Mediaeval and Modern Irish Series 23 (Dublin, 1970; repr. 1984).
> The six excerpts printed here correspond to the standard editions as follows: [1] Stokes, 'Acallamh', ll 1–120; O'Grady, 'Agallamh', i, 94–6. [2] Stokes, 'Acallamh', ll 329–53; O'Grady, 'Agallamh', i, 101–2. [3] Stokes, 'Acallamh', ll 354–468; O'Grady, 'Agallamh', i, 102–4. [4] Stokes, 'Acallamh', ll 718–871; O'Grady, 'Agallamh', i, 110–13. [5] Stokes, 'Acallamh', ll 949–1002; O'Grady, 'Agallamh', i, 115–16. [6] Stokes, 'Acallamh', ll 1868–1934; O'Grady, 'Agallamh', i, 135–6. Furthermore, the Introduction is a reprint of Gerard Murphy's essay on the *Acallam* first published in *Irish sagas*.

Dillon, M., C. Mooney and P. de Brún, *Catalogue of Irish manuscripts in the Franciscan library, Killiney* (Dublin, 1969).
Dobbs, M., 'The ban-shenchus', *Revue celtique*, 47 (1930), 283–339; *Revue celtique*, 48 (1931), 163–233; *Revue celtique*, 49 (1932), 437–89.

Donahue, A., 'The *Acallam na senórach*: a medieval instruction manual', *Proceedings of the Harvard Celtic Colloquium*, 24–5 (2004–5), 206–14.

Dooley, A., 'From: Acallam na senórach (The colloquy of the ancients)' in Bourke et al. (eds), *The Field Day anthology of Irish writing IV*, pp 228–33.

— 'The date and purpose of *Acallam na senórach*', *Éigse*, 34 (2004), 97–126.

— 'The deployment of some hagiographical sources in *Acallam na senórach*' in Arbuthnot and Parsons (eds), *The Gaelic Finn tradition*, pp 97–110.

— 'The European context of *Acallam na senórach*' in Doyle and Murray (eds), *In dialogue with the Agallamh*, pp 60–75.

— 'Pagan beliefs and Christian redress in *Acallam na senórach*' in J. Borsje, A. Dooley, S. Mac Mathúna and G. Toner (eds), *Celtic cosmology: perspectives from Ireland and Scotland* (Toronto, 2014), pp 249–67.

Dooley, A. and H. Roe, *Tales of the elders of Ireland: a new translation of Acallam na senórach*, Oxford World's Classics (Oxford, 1999).

Dorson, R.M., 'Introduction' in F.J. Oinas (ed.), *Heroic epic and saga: an introduction to the world's great folk epics* (Bloomington/London, 1978), pp 1–6.

Doyle, A. and K. Murray (eds), *In dialogue with the Agallamh: essays in honour of Seán Ó Coileáin* (Dublin, 2014).

Dronke, P., 'Learned lyric and popular ballad in the early Middle Ages' in idem, *The medieval poet and his world*, Storia a Letteratura 164 (Rome, 1984), pp 167–207 (originally published in *Studi Medievali*, 3rd series, 17 (1976), 1–40).

Enright, M.J., 'Fires of knowledge: a theory of warband education in medieval Ireland and Homeric Greece' in P. Ní Chatháin and M. Richter (eds), *Irland und Europa im früheren Mittelalter: Texte und Überlieferung / Ireland and Europe in the early Middle Ages: texts and transmission* (Dublin, 2002), pp 342–67.

Eska, C.M., *Cáin lánamna: an Old Irish tract on marriage and divorce law* (Leiden/Boston, 2010).

Eson, L., 'Riddling and wooing in the medieval Irish text *Tochmarc Ailbe*', *Études celtiques*, 40 (2014), 101–15.

Etchingham, C., *Church organization in Ireland AD 600 to 1000* (Maynooth, 1999).

Findon, J., 'A woman's words: Emer versus Cú Chulainn in *Aided óenfir Aífe*' in J.P. Mallory and G. Stockman (eds), *Ulidia: proceedings of the First International Conference on the Ulster Cycle of Tales* (Belfast, 1994), pp 139–48.

— *A woman's words: Emer and female speech in the Ulster Cycle* (Toronto, 1997).

FitzPatrick, E., '*Formaoil na fiann*: hunting preserves and assembly places in Gaelic Ireland', *Proceedings of the Harvard Celtic Colloquium*, 32 (2012), 95–118.

Flahive, J., 'Revisiting the Reeves *Agallamh*' in Doyle and Murray (eds), *In dialogue with the Agallamh*, pp 164–84.

— 'The shield of Fionn: the poem *Uchán a sciath mo rígh réigh* in Leabhar Ua Maine' in J. Carey, K. Murray and C. Ó Dochartaigh (eds), *Sacred histories: a Festschrift for Máire Herbert* (Dublin, 2015), pp 139–60.

— *The Fenian Cycle in Irish and Scots-Gaelic literature*, Cork Studies in Celtic Literatures 1 (Cork, 2017).

— 'A chloidhimh chléirchín in chluig and the concept of the literary cycle in mediaeval Ireland' in S. Arbuthnot, S. Ní Mhurchú and G. Parsons (eds), *Proceedings of the Second International Finn Cycle Conference* (forthcoming).

Flanagan, M.T., 'John de Courcy, the first Ulster plantation and Irish church men' in B. Smith (ed.), *Britain 900–1300: insular responses to medieval European change* (Cambridge, 1999), pp 154–78.

— *The transformation of the Irish church in the twelfth century*, Studies in Celtic History 29 (Woodbridge, 2010).

Foley, J.M., *Immanent art: from structure to meaning in traditional oral epic* (Bloomington and Indianapolis, 1991).

Ford, P., 'The well of Nechtan and "La gloire lumineuse"' in G.J. Larson, C.S. Littleton and J. Puhvel (eds), *Myth in Indo-European antiquity* (Berkeley/Los Angeles/London, 1974), pp 67–74.

— 'A highly important pig' in A.T.E. Matonis and D.F. Melia (eds), *Celtic language, Celtic culture: a Festschrift for Eric P. Hamp* (Van Nuys, CA, 1990), pp 292–304.

Foster, I., 'Appendix G – Gwynn ap Nudd' in Murphy, *Duanaire Finn: the book of the lays of Fionn*, part 3, pp 198–204.

Frazer, J.G., *Apollodorus: the library*, 2 vols, Loeb Classical Library 121–2 (Cambridge/London, 1921).

Frye, N., *Anatomy of criticism: four essays* (Princeton, 1957).

Fulton, H. (ed.), *Medieval Celtic literature and society* (Dublin, 2005).

Gantz, J., *The Mabinogion* (London/New York, 1976).

— *Early Irish myths and sagas* (London/New York, 1981).

Gaskill, H. (ed.), *Ossian revisited* (Edinburgh, 1991).

— *The poems of Ossian and related works: James Macpherson*, with an introduction by F. Stafford (Edinburgh, 1996).

Gay, D.E., 'The creation of the *Kalevala*, 1833–1849', *Jahrbuch für Volksliedforschung*, 42 (1997), 63 77.

Gillies, W., 'Arthur in Gaelic tradition. Part I: folktales and ballads', *Cambridge Medieval Celtic Studies*, 2 (Winter, 1981), 47–72.

— 'Arthur in Gaelic tradition. Part II: romances and learned lore', *Cambridge Medieval Celtic Studies*, 3 (Summer, 1982), 41–75.

— 'Heroes and ancestors' in Almqvist, Ó Catháin and Ó Héalaí (eds), *Fiannaíocht*, pp 57–73.

Gray, E.A., '*Cath Maige Tuired*: myth and structure', *Éigse*, 18 (1981), 183–209; 19 (1982–3), 1–35, 230–62.

— *Cath Maige Tuired*, Irish Texts Society 52 (London, 1982).

Greene, D., *Fingal Rónáin and other stories*, Mediaeval and Modern Irish Series 16 (Dublin, 1955).

Gregory, A., *Gods and fighting men* (London, 1904); repr. as part of *Lady Gregory's complete Irish mythology* (London, 1994), pp 1–324.

Gwynn, E.J., *The metrical dindshenchas*, 5 vols, Todd Lecture Series 8–12 (Dublin, 1906–35; repr. 1991).

— 'Varia III, 3: "Finn and the man in the tree"', *Ériu*, 11 (1932), 152–3.
Hamp, E., 'Goídil, Féni, Gŵynedd', *Proceedings of the Harvard Celtic Colloquium*, 12 (1992), 43–50.
— '*Fian*¹', *Studia Celtica Japonica*, 8 (1996), 87–95.
Hancock, W.N., T. O'Mahony, A.G. Richey and R. Atkinson, *Ancient laws of Ireland*, 6 vols (Dublin, 1865–1901).
Hapgood, I.F., *The epic songs of Russia* (New York, 1886).
Harmon, M., *The dialogue of the ancients of Ireland: a new translation of* Acallam na senórach (Dublin, 2009); reprint of idem, *The colloquy of the old men* (Dublin, 2001), with a Foreword by S. Ó Coileáin.
Hatto, A.T., 'On the excellence of the "Hildebrandslied": a comparative study in dynamics', *Modern Language Review*, 68 (1973), 820–38.
Hennessy, W.M., 'The battle of Cnucha', *Revue celtique*, 2 (1873), 86–93.
Herbert, M., 'Múineadh na fiannaíochta' in P. Ó Fiannachta (ed.), *An Ghaeilge á múineadh: Léachtaí Cholm Cille* 9 (Má Nuad, 1978), pp 44–57.
— 'Celtic heroine? The archaeology of the Deirdre story' in T. O'Brien Johnson and D. Cairnes (eds), *Gender in Irish writing* (Philadelphia, 1991), pp 13–22.
— 'The universe of male and female: a reading of the Deirdre story' in Byrne, Harry and Ó Siadhail (eds), *Celtic languages and Celtic peoples*, pp 53–64.
Hibbard, L.A., *Medieval romance in England: a study of the sources and analogues of the non-cyclic metrical romances* (Oxford, 1924; new ed., New York, 1960).
Hogan, E., *Onomasticon Goedelicum locorum et tribuum Hiberniae et Scotiae: an index, with identifications, to the Gaelic names of places and tribes* (Dublin/London, 1910).
Hollo, K., '"Finn and the man in the tree" as verbal icon' in Arbuthnot and Parsons (eds), *The Gaelic Finn tradition*, pp 50–61.
Honko, L. (ed.), *Religion, myth, and folklore in the world's epics: the Kalevala and its predecessors* (Berlin/New York, 1990).
— 'The Kalevala: the processual view' in idem (ed.), *Religion, myth, and folklore in the world's epics*, pp 181–229.
— 'The Kalevala as performance' in idem (ed.), *The Kalevala and the world's traditional epics* (Helsinki, 2002), pp 13–25.
Hull, E., 'The Helgi lay and Irish literature' in R.S. Loomis (ed.), *Medieval studies in memory of Gertrude Schoepperle Loomis* (Paris/New York, 1927), pp 265–75.
Hull, V., 'An incomplete version of the *Imram Brain* and four stories concerning Mongan', *Zeitschrift für celtische Philologie*, 18 (1930), 409–19.
— 'How Finn made peace between Sodelb and Glangressach', *Zeitschrift für celtische Philologie*, 18 (1930), 422–4.
— 'The old woman or nun of Beare', *Zeitschrift für celtische Philologie*, 19 (1933), 174–6.
— 'The death of Fothath Cananne', *Zeitschrift für celtische Philologie*, 20 (1936), 400–4.
— 'Two tales about Find', *Speculum*, 16 (1941), 322–33.
— 'The quarrel between Finn and Oisin', *Modern Language Notes*, 57:6 (June, 1942), 434–6.
— '*Reicne Fothaid Canainne*', *Modern Language Notes*, 58:1 (January, 1943), 29–31.
— *Longes mac nUislenn: the exile of the sons of Uisliu* (New York, 1949).

— 'A rhetoric in *Finn and the man in the tree*', *Zeitschrift für celtische Philologie*, 30 (1967), 17–20.
— 'Apgitir chrábaid: the alphabet of piety', *Celtica*, 8 (1968), 44–89.
Hyde, D., 'The Reeves manuscript of the Agallamh na senórach', *Revue celtique*, 38 (1920), 289–95.
— (An Chraoibhín), 'An Agallamh bheag', *Lia Fáil*, 1 (1924), 79–107.
— (An Chraoibhín), 'Báirne mór', *Béaloideas*, 3 (1931–2), 187–95.
Innes, S., 'Fionn and Ailbhe's riddles between Ireland and Scotland' in Boyd (ed.), *Ollam*, pp 271–85.
Jackson, K., 'Tradition in Early Irish prophecy', *Man*, 34 (1934), 67–70.
— *The international popular tale and early Welsh tradition* (Cardiff, 1961).
— *Aislinge Meic Con Glinne* (Dublin, 1990).
Johnston, E., *Literacy and identity in early medieval Ireland*, Studies in Celtic History 33 (Woodbridge, 2013).
Jones, G. and T. Jones, *The Mabinogion*, Everyman's Library 97 (London/New York, 1949).
Joynt, M., *Feis tighe Chonáin*, Mediaeval and Modern Irish Series 7 (Dublin, 1936).
Kaivola-Bregenhøj, A., *Riddles: perspectives on the use, function and change in a folklore genre*, Studia Fennica Folkloristica 10 (Helsinki, 2001).
Kaukonen, V., 'The Kalevala as epic' in Honko (ed.), *Religion, myth, and folklore in the world's epics*, pp 157–79.
Kelly, F., *A guide to early Irish law* (Dublin, 1988).
Ker, W.P., *Epic and romance: essays on medieval literature* (New York, 1897; 2nd rev. ed. 1908, repr. 1957).
Khaleghi-Motlagh, D., A. Khatibi and M. Omidsakar, *Abul'l-Qasem Ferdowsi. The Shahnameh (The book of kings)*, Persian Text Series, 8 vols [plus 4 vols of notes] (New York, 1988–2008).
Kinsella, T., *The Tain* (Dolmen, 1969).
Knott, E., 'Why Mongán was deprived of noble issue', *Ériu*, 8 (1916), 155–60.
— *Togail bruidne Da Derga*, Mediaeval and Modern Irish Series 8 (Dublin, 1936).
Koch, J., 'Ériu, Alba, and Letha: when was a language ancestral to Gaelic first spoken in Ireland?', *Emania*, 9 (1991), 17–27.
Koch, J. and J. Carey, *The Celtic heroic age: literary sources for ancient Celtic Europe and early Ireland and Wales* (Aberystwyth, 4th ed. 2003).
Krappe, A.H.,[1] 'Diarmuid and Grainne', *Folklore*, 47 (1936), 347–61.
Kühns, J.S., 'An edition and translation of the *Agallamh bheag* from the Book of Lismore', unpublished MPhil. thesis (University of Glasgow, 2006).
— 'Some observations on the *Acallam bec*' in Arbuthnot and Parsons (eds), *The Gaelic Finn tradition*, pp 122–38.
Kuusi, M., 'Epic cycles as the basis for the Kalevala' in Honko (ed.), *Religion, myth, and folklore in the world's epics*, pp 133–55.

---

[1] The article in *Folklore* mistakenly gives his surname as Krapple.

Kuusi, M., K. Bosley and M. Branch, *Finnish folk poetry epic: an anthology in English and Finnish* (Helsinki, 1977).
Lehmann, R., *Fled Dúin na nGéd*, Mediaeval and Modern Irish Series 21 (Dublin, 1964).
Lloyd, J.H., O.J. Bergin and G. Schoepperle, 'The reproach of Diarmaid', *Revue celtique*, 33 (1912), 41–57.
— 'The death of Diarmaid', *Revue celtique*, 33 (1912), 157–79.
Macalister, R.A.S., *Lebor gabála Érenn: the book of the taking of Ireland*, 5 vols, Irish Texts Society 34–5, 39, 41, 44 (Dublin and London, 1938–56); vol. 6 'Index of Names', compiled by P. Ó Riain, Irish Texts Society 63 (London, 2009).
Mac Cana, P., 'The influence of the Vikings on Celtic literature' in B. Ó Cuív (ed.), *The impact of the Scandinavian invasions on the Celtic-speaking peoples. Introductory papers read at plenary sessions of the International Congress of Celtic Studies held in Dublin, 6–10 July 1959* (Dublin, 1962), pp 78–118.
— 'Irish literary tradition' in B. Ó Cuív (ed.), *A view of the Irish language* (Dublin, 1969), pp 35–46.
— *The learned tales of medieval Ireland* (Dublin, 1980).
— '*Fianaigecht* in the pre-Norman period' in Almqvist, Ó Catháin and Ó Héalaí (eds), *Fiannaíocht*, pp 75–99.
— 'Notes on the combination of prose and verse in Early Irish narrative' in S.N. Tranter and H.L.C. Tristram (eds), *Early Irish literature: media and communication / Mündlichkeit und Schriftlichkeit in der frühen irischen Literatur*, ScriptOralia 10 (Tübingen, 1989), pp 125–47.
— 'Narrative openers and progress markers in Irish' in K.A. Klar, E.E. Sweetser and C. Thomas (eds), *A Celtic florilegium: studies in memory of Brendan O'Hehir*, Celtic Studies Publications 2 (Cambridge, MA, 1996), pp 104–20.
— 'Prosimetrum in insular Celtic literature' in J. Harris and K. Reichl (eds), *Prosimetrum: cross-cultural perspectives on narrative in prose and verse* (Cambridge, MA, 1997), pp 99–130.
McCone, K., 'Werewolves, cyclopes, *díberga*, and *fíanna*: juvenile delinquency in early Ireland', *Cambridge Medieval Celtic Studies*, 12 (Winter, 1986), 1–22.
— 'Dubthach maccu Lugair and a matter of life and death in the pseudo-historical prologue to the *Senchas már*', *Peritia*, 5 (1986), 1–35.
— 'Hund, Wolf, und Krieger bei den Indogermanen' in W. Meid (ed.), *Studien zum indogermanischen Wortschatz* (Innsbruck, 1987), pp 101–54.
— *Pagan past and Christian present in early Irish literature*, Maynooth Monographs 3 (Maynooth, 1990).
— 'Cúlra Ind-Eorpach na féinne' in Ó Fiannachta (ed.), *An fhiannaíocht*, pp 7–29.
— *Echtrae Chonnlai and the beginnings of vernacular narrative writing in Ireland*, Maynooth Medieval Irish Texts 1 (Maynooth, 2000).
— 'The Celtic and Indo-European origins of the *fían*' in Arbuthnot and Parsons (eds), *The Gaelic Finn tradition*, pp 14–30.
— 'The death of Aífe's only son and the heroic biography' in Boyd (ed.), *Ollam*, pp 3–17.

Mac Craith, M. and P. Ó Héalaí (eds), *Diasa díograise: aistí i gcuimhne ar Mháirtín Ó Briain* (Indreabhán, 2009).
Mac Eoin, G., Review of *Zeitschrift für celtische Philologie* 27 (Heft 3/4), *Studia Hibernica*, 1 (1961), 259–61.
McLeod, N., 'The lord of slaughter' in P. O'Neill (ed.), *The land beneath the sea: essays in honour of Anders Ahlqvist's contribution to Celtic studies in Australia*, Sydney Series in Celtic Studies 14 (Sydney, 2013), pp 101–14.
McLeod, W., A. Burnyeat, D.U. Stiùbhart, T.O. Clancy and R. Ó Maolalaigh (eds), *Bile ós chrannaibh: a Festschrift for William Gillies* (Pertshire, 2010).
Mac Mathúna, S., *Immram Brain: Bran's journey to the Land of Women* (Tübingen, 1985).
— 'An fhilíocht a leagtar ar Ghearóid Iarla i Leabhar Fhear Maí: iontaofa nó bréagach' in McLeod et al. (eds), *Bile ós chrannaibh*, pp 245–70.
MacNeill, E., *Duanaire Finn: the book of the lays of Fionn*, part 1, Irish Texts Society 7 (London, 1908; repr. 1996).
— 'Ancient Irish law: the law of status or franchise', *Proceedings of the Royal Irish Academy*, 36C (1923), 265–316.
— 'De origine Scoticae linguae', *Ériu*, 11 (1932), 112–29.
Mac Niocaill, G., 'Duanaire Ghearóid Iarla', *Studia Hibernica*, 3 (1963), 7–59.
Mac Piarais, P., *Bruidhean chaorthainn* (Baile Átha Cliath, 1924).
McQuillan, P., 'Finn, Fothad, and *fian*: some early associations', *Proceedings of the Harvard Celtic Colloquium*, 8 (1988), 1–10.
Magoun, F.P., *The Kalevala, or, poems of the Kalevala district, compiled by Elias Lönnrot* (Cambridge Mass., 1963; repr. 1985).
Meek, D.E., 'Development and degeneration in Gaelic ballad texts' in Almqvist, Ó Catháin and Ó Héalaí (eds), *Fiannaíocht*, pp 131–60.
— 'The banners of the *fian* in Gaelic ballad tradition', *Cambridge Medieval Celtic Studies*, 11 (1986), 29–69.
— 'The Scots-Gaelic scribes of late medieval Pertshire: an overview of the orthography and contents of the Book of the Dean of Lismore' in J.D. McClure and M. Spiller (eds), *Bryght lanterns: essays on the language and literature of medieval and renaissance Scotland* (Aberdeen, 1989), pp 387–404.
— 'The death of Diarmaid in Scottish and Irish tradition', *Celtica*, 20 (1990), 335–61.
— 'The Gaelic ballads of Scotland: creativity and adaptation' in Gaskill (ed.), *Ossian revisited*, pp 19–48.
— 'Place-names and literature: evidence from the Gaelic ballads' in S. Taylor (ed.), *The uses of place-names* (Edinburgh, 1998), pp 147–68.
— '*Duanaire Finn* and Gaelic Scotland' in Carey (ed.), *Duanaire Finn: reassessments*, pp 19–38.
Melia, D., 'Parallel versions of "The boyhood deeds of Cuchulainn"' in J.J. Duggan (ed.), *Oral literature: seven essays* (New York, 1975), pp 25–40.
— 'What are you talking about? *Tochmarc Ailbe* and courtship flytings' in A. Ahlqvist and P. O'Neill (eds), *Celts and their culture at home and abroad: a Festschrift for Malcolm Broun*, Sydney Series in Celtic Studies 15 (Sydney, 2013), pp 197–211.

Meyer, K., 'Macgnimartha Find', *Revue celtique*, 5 (1881–3), 195–204 (corrigenda: *Archiv für celtische Lexicographie* 1, 482).
— 'Anecdota from the Stowe MS no. 992', *Revue celtique*, 6 (1883–5), 173–86.
— *Cath Finntrága, or the battle of Ventry*, Anecdota Oxoniensia (Oxford, 1885).
— 'The wooing of Emer', *Archaeological Review*, 1 (1888), 68–75, 150–5, 231–5, 298–307.
— 'Uath Beinne Etair: "The hiding of the hill of Howth". An episode of the pursuit of Diarmait and Grainne', *Revue celtique*, 11 (1890), 125–34.
— 'The oldest version of Tochmarc Emire', *Revue celtique*, 11 (1890), 433–57.
— *Aislinge Meic Con Glinne: The vision of MacConglinne. A Middle-Irish wonder tale* (London, 1892).
— 'Scél Baili binnbérlaig', *Revue celtique*, 13 (1892), 220–27.
— 'Two tales about Finn', *Revue celtique*, 14 (1893), 241–9.
— *The voyage of Bran son of Febal to the Land of the Living*, Grimm Library no. 4 (London, 1895; repr. Llanerch, 1994).
— 'Finn and Grainne', *Zeitschrift für celtische Philologie*, 1 (1897), 458–61.
— 'The death of Finn mac Cumaill', *Zeitschrift für celtische Philologie*, 1 (1897), 462–5.
— 'Finn and the man in the tree', *Revue celtique*, 25 (1904), 344–9.
— 'Cáilte cecinit', *Ériu*, 1 (1904), 72–3.
— 'The death of Conla', *Ériu*, 1 (1904), 113–21.
— 'The boyish exploits of Finn', *Ériu*, 1 (1904), 180–90.
— *The triads of Ireland*, Todd Lecture Series 13 (Dublin, 1906).
— *The instructions of king Cormac mac Airt*, Todd Lecture Series 15 (Dublin, 1910).
— *Fianaigecht: being a collection of hitherto inedited Irish poems and tales relating to Finn and his fiana*, Todd Lecture Series 16 (Dublin, 1910; 2nd repr. Dublin, 1993).
— 'Find mac Umaill', *Revue celtique*, 32 (1911), 391–5.
— 'Mitteilungen aus irischen Handschriften: Cath Sléphe Cāin inso', *Zeitschrift für celtische Philologie*, 8 (1912), 105.
— 'Mitteilungen aus irischen Handschriften: Do chomramaib Laigen inso sís', *Zeitschrift für celtische Philologie*, 8 (1912), 117–19.
— 'Mitteilungen aus irischen Handschriften: Finns Stammbaum und die Fiana', *Zeitschrift für celtische Philologie*, 8 (1912), 560–61.
— 'Sanas Cormaic: an Old-Irish glossary' in O.J. Bergin, R.I. Best, Kuno Meyer and J.G. O'Keeffe (eds), *Anecdota from Irish manuscripts*, iv (Halle/Dublin, 1912; repr. Felinfach, 1994), pp 1–128.
— 'Mitteilungen aus irischen Handschriften: Ailelb und Glangrēssach', *Zeitschrift für celtische Philologie*, 12 (1918), 374–5.
— 'Der irische Totengott und die Toteninsel', *Sitzungsberichte der preussischen Akademie der Wissenschaften*, 32 (1919), 537–46.
Miles, B., *Heroic saga and classical epic in medieval Ireland*, Studies in Celtic History 30 (Cambridge/New York, 2011).

Miller, D., 'Defining and expanding the Indo-European *Vater-Sohnes-Kampf* theme', *The Journal of Indo-European Studies*, 22 (1994), 307–27.

— 'Cú Chulainn and Il'ya of Murom: two heroes, and some variations on a theme' in S. Mac Mathúna and M. Fomin (eds), *Parallels between Celtic and Slavic: proceedings of the First International Colloquium of Societas Celto-Slavica* (Coleraine, 2006), pp 175–84.

Miller, J., 'The role of the female warrior in Early Irish literature: the case of *Tochmarc Emire*', unpublished PhD thesis (University College Cork, 2011).

Mills, K., 'Sorrow and conversion in *Acallam na senórach*', *Éigse*, 38 (2013), 1–19.

Moody, T.W., F.X. Martin, F.J. Byrne, W.E. Vaughan et al., *The new history of Ireland*, 9 vols [under the auspices of the Royal Irish Academy] (Oxford, 1976–2005).

Murphy, D., *The annals of Clonmacnoise being annals of Ireland from the earliest period to A.D. 1408* (Dublin, 1896).

Murphy, G., *Duanaire Finn: the book of the lays of Fionn*, part 2, Irish Texts Society 28 (London, 1933; repr. 1991).

— *Duanaire Finn: the book of the lays of Fionn*, part 3, Irish Texts Society 43 (Dublin, 1953; repr. 1986).

— *The Ossianic lore and romantic tales of medieval Ireland*, Irish Life and Culture vol. 11 (Cork, 1955; revised ed. 1971).

— *Early Irish lyrics: eighth to twelfth century* (Oxford, 1956; repr. Dublin, 1998).

— '*Acallam na senórach*' in Dillon (ed.), *Irish sagas*, pp 119–34 (repr. as 'Introduction' to Dillon, *Stories from the Acallam*, pp xiii–xxv).

— 'Irish storytelling after the coming of the Normans' in B. Ó Cuív (ed.), *Seven centuries of Irish learning, 1000–1700* (Dublin, 1961; repr. Cork, 1971), pp 62–74.

Murray, K., 'The role of the *cuilebad* in *Immram Snédgusa 7 Maic Riagla*' in J. Wooding (ed.), *The otherworld voyage in early Irish literature* (Dublin, 2000), pp 187–93

— 'A Middle Irish tract on *cró* and *díbad*' in A.P. Smyth (ed.), *Seanchas: essays in early and medieval archaeology, history and literature in honour of Francis J. Byrne* (Dublin, 2000), 251–60.

— 'The finding of the *Táin*', *Cambrian Medieval Celtic Studies*, 41 (Summer, 2001), 17–23.

— 'A reading from *Scéla Moshauluim*', *Zeitschrift für celtische Philologie*, 53 (2003), 198–201.

— 'The Fenian Cycle' in S. Duffy (ed.), *Medieval Ireland: an encyclopedia* (New York, 2005), pp 166–7.

— 'Some thoughts on *Baile binnbérlach mac Búain*' in Wiley (ed.), *Essays on the early Irish king tales*, pp 84–90.

— (C. Ó Muirigh), 'Fionn, fian agus Corca Laoidhe', *Journal of the Cork Historical and Archaeological Society*, 113 (2008), 24–7.

— (C. Ó Muirigh), 'Fionn i ndiaidh na ríthe: Úathad mé a Temraig a-nocht' in E. Mac Cárthaigh and J. Uhlich (eds), *Féilscríbhinn do Chathal Ó hÁinle* (Conamara, 2012), pp 769–86.

— 'Interpreting the evidence: problems with dating the early *fianaigecht* corpus' in Arbuthnot and Parsons (eds), *The Gaelic Finn tradition*, pp 31–49.

— (C. Ó Muirigh), 'Rangú litríocht mheánaoiseach na Gaeilge' in S. Ó Coileáin, L.P. Ó Murchú and P. Riggs (eds), *Séimhfhear suairc: aistí in ómós don Ollamh Breandán Ó Conchúir* (An Daingean, 2013), pp 705–11.

— 'The reworking of Old Irish narrative texts in the Middle Irish period: contexts and motivations' in Boyle and Hayden (eds), *Authorities and adaptations*, pp 291–306.

— 'The treatment of placenames in the early *fíanaigecht* corpus' in E. Purcell, P. MacCotter, J. Nyhan and J. Sheehan (eds), *Clerics, kings and vikings: essays on medieval Ireland in honour of Donnchadh Ó Corráin* (Dublin, 2015), pp 452–7.

— 'Genre construction: the creation of the *dinnshenchas*', *Journal of Literary Onomastics*, 6 (2017), 11–21.

— 'Editing *Acallam na senórach*: a test case' in S. Arbuthnot, S. Ní Mhurchú and G. Parsons (eds), *Proceedings of the Second International Finn Cycle Conference* (forthcoming).

— *The early Fenian corpus* (forthcoming).

Nagy, J.F., 'Intervention and disruption in the myths of Finn and Sigurd', *Ériu*, 31 (1980), 123–31.

— 'Demne Mael', *Celtica*, 14 (1981), 8–14.

— 'Shamanic aspects of the *bruidhean* tale', *History of Religions*, 20:4 (1981), 302–22.

— 'Liminality and knowledge in Irish tradition', *Studia Celtica*, 16–17 (1981–2), 135–43.

— 'Heroic destinies in the *macgnímrada* of Finn and Cú Chulainn', *Zeitschrift für celtische Philologie*, 40 (1984), 23–39.

— *The wisdom of the outlaw: the boyhood deeds of Finn in Gaelic narrative tradition* (Berkeley and Los Angeles, 1985).

— 'Fenian heroes and their rites of passage' in Almqvist, Ó Catháin and Ó Héalaí (eds), *Fiannaíocht*, pp 161–82.

— 'The sign of the outlaw: multiformity in Fenian narrative' in J.M. Foley (ed.), *Comparative research on oral traditions: a memorial for Milman Parry* (Columbus, 1987), pp 465–95.

— 'Compositional concerns in the *Acallam na senórach*' in Ó Corráin, Breatnach and McCone (eds), *Sages, saints and storytellers*, pp 149–58.

— 'Oral tradition in the *Acallam na senórach*' in W.F.H. Nicolaisen (ed.), *Oral tradition in the Middle Ages* (Binghamton, 1995), pp 77–95.

— *Conversing with angels and ancients: literary myths of medieval Ireland* (Dublin, 1997).

— 'Observations on the Ossianesque in medieval Irish literature and modern Irish folklore', *Journal of American Folklore*, 114, no. 454 (2001), 436–46.

— 'Life in the fast lane: the *Acallam na senórach*' in Fulton (ed.), *Medieval Celtic literature and society*, pp 117–31.

— '*Acallam na senórach*, "a tri-cycle"?' in Wiley (ed.), *Essays on the early Irish king tales*, pp 68–83.

— 'Tristanic, Fenian, and lovers' leaps' in Mac Craith and Ó Héalaí (eds), *Diasa díograise*, pp 157–72.

— 'Finn and the Fenian tradition' in J.M. Wright (ed.), *A companion to Irish literature*, vol. 1 (Wiley-Blackwell, 2010), pp 27–38.

— 'Fenian female food and other health and beauty secrets' in McLeod et al. (eds), *Bile ós chrannaibh*, pp 307–14.
— *Mercantile myth in medieval Celtic traditions*, H.M. Chadwick Memorial Lectures 20 (Cambridge, 2011).
— 'Keeping the *Acallam* together' in Arbuthnot and Parsons (eds), *The Gaelic Finn tradition*, pp 111–21.
— 'Oral tradition and performance in medieval Ireland' in K. Reichl (ed.), *Medieval oral literature* (Berlin, 2012), pp 279–93.
— 'Some strands and strains in *Acallam na senórach*' in Doyle and Murray (eds), *In dialogue with the Agallamh*, pp 90–108.
— 'The Celtic love-triangle revisited' in L. Breatnach, R. Ó hUiginn, D. McManus and K. Simms (eds), *An XIV Comhdháil Idirnáisiúnta sa Léann Ceilteach, Maigh Nuad 2011: imeachtaí / Proceedings of the XIV International Congress of Celtic Studies, Maynooth 2011* (Dublin, 2015), pp 221–44.
— 'Finn's student days' in Boyd (ed.), *Ollam*, pp 237–41.
New Webster's encyclopedic dictionary of the English language (New York, 1997 edition).
Ní Bhrolcháin, M., *An introduction to early Irish literature* (Dublin, 2009).
Nic Cárthaigh, E., 'Surviving the flood: revenants and antediluvian lore in medieval Irish texts' in K. Cawsey and J. Harris (eds), *Transmission and transformation in the Middle Ages* (Dublin, 2007), pp 40–64.
Ní Chonghaile, N., and H.L.C. Tristram, 'Die mittleirischen Sagenlisten zwischen Mündlichkeit und Schriftlichkeit' in H.L.C. Tristram (ed.), *Deutsche, Kelten und Iren: 150 Jahre deutsche Keltologie. Gearóid Mac Eoin zum 60. Geburtstag gewidmet* (Hamburg, 1990), pp 249–68.
Ní Dhomhnaill, C., *Duanaireacht* (Baile Átha Cliath, 1975).
Ní Dhonnchadha, M., 'The semantics of *banscál*', *Éigse*, 31 (1999), 31–5.
— 'Creidne the she-warrior' in Bourke et al. (eds), *The Field Day anthology of Irish writing IV*, pp 179–80.
— 'From: Tochmarc Ailbe (The wooing of Ailbe)' in Bourke et al. (eds), *The Field Day anthology of Irish writing IV*, pp 206–10.
Ní Mhaonaigh, M., 'Friend and foe: Vikings in ninth- and tenth-century Irish literature' in H.B. Clarke, M. Ní Mhaonaigh and R. Ó Floinn (eds), *Ireland and Scandinavia in the early Viking Age* (Dublin, 1998), pp 381–402.
— 'Classical compositions in medieval Ireland: the literary context' in K. Murray (ed.), *Translations from Classical literature: Imtheachta Æniasa and Stair Ercuil ocus a Bás*, Irish Texts Society, Subsidiary Series 17 (London, 2006), pp 1–19.
— 'Pagans and holy men: literary manifestations of twelfth-century reform' in Bracken and Ó Riain-Raedel (eds), *Ireland and Europe in the twelfth century*, pp 143–61.
— 'Poetic authority in Middle Irish narrative: a case study' in Boyle and Hayden (eds), *Authorities and adaptations*, pp 263–89.
Ní Mhurchú, S., '*Agallamh Oisín agus Phádraig*: the growth of an Ossianic lay' in S. Zimmer (ed.), *Kelten am Rhein: Akten des dreizehnten Internationalen Kelologie-*

kongresses / Proceedings of the Thirteenth International Congress of Celtic Studies, 23. bis 27. Juli 2007 in Bonn. Zweiter Teil. Philologie, Sprachen und Literaturen, Beihefte der Bonner Jahrbücher 58 (Mainz am Rhein, 2009), pp 175–80.

— 'Agallamh Oisín agus Phádraig: composition and transmission' in Arbuthnot and Parsons (eds), *The Gaelic Finn tradition*, pp 195–208.

— 'An tAgallamh nua: athleagan déanach d'Agallamh na seanórach' in Doyle and Murray (eds), *In dialogue with the Agallamh*, pp 185–217.

Ní Shéaghdha, N., *Agallamh na seanórach*, 3 vols, Leabhair ó Láimhsgríbhnibh 7, 10, 15 (Dublin, 1942–5); repr. in one volume (with a new introduction) by the Irish Texts Society (London, 2014).

— *Tóruigheacht Dhiarmada agus Ghráinne*, Irish Texts Society 48 (London, 1967).

Ní Uigín, N., 'Goll mac Morna: laoch Connachtach na fiannaíochta agus ceist an chúigeachais' in Mac Craith and Ó Héalaí (eds), *Diasa díograise*, pp 237–55.

Ní Úrdail, M., *The scribe in eighteenth- and nineteenth-century Ireland: motivations and milieu*, Studien und Texte zur Keltologie 3 (Münster, 2000).

Norman, F., 'Hildebrand and Hadubrand', *German Life and Letters*, 11, iv (1958), 325–34 (repr. in idem, *Three essays on the Hildebrandslied* [London, 1973], pp 33–49).

Nuner, R.D., 'The verbal system of the Agallamh na senórach', *Zeitschrift für celtische Philologie*, 27 (1959), 230–309.

Nutt, A., 'The Aryan expulsion-and-return formula', *Folk-Lore Record*, 4 (1881), 1–44.

— 'Problems of heroic legend' in J. Jacobs and A. Nutt (eds), *The International Folklore Congress, 1891: papers and transactions* (London, 1892), pp 113–34.

— *The Celtic doctrine of rebirth*, vol. 2 of *The voyage of Bran* (ed. K. Meyer), Grimm Library no. 6 (London, 1895; repr. Llanerch, 1994).

— *Ossian and the Ossianic literature*, Popular Studies in Mythology, Romance and Folklore, no. 3 (London, 1899; 2nd ed., 1910).

Ó Béarra, F., 'The Otherworld realm of *Tír scáith*' in G. Hemprich (ed.), *Festgabe für Hildegard L.C. Tristram: überreicht von Studenten, Kollegen und Freunden des ehemaligen Faches Keltologie der Albert-Ludwigs-Universität in Freiburg* (Berlin, 2009), pp 81–100.

Ó Briain, M., 'Some material on Oisín in the Land of Youth' in Ó Corráin, Breatnach and McCone (eds), *Sages, saints and storytellers*, pp 181–99.

— 'Oisín's biography: conception and birth' in H.L.C. Tristram (ed.), *Text und Zeittiefe* (Tübingen, 1994), pp 455–86.

— 'The conception and birth of Fionn mac Cumhaill's canine cousin' in A. Ahlqvist, G.W. Banks, R. Latvio, H. Nyberg and T. Sjöblom (eds), *Celtica Helsingiensia: proceedings from a symposium on Celtic Studies*, Societas Scientarum Fennica, Commentationes Humanarum Litterarum 107 (Helsinki, 1996), pp 179–202.

— 'Seanchas agus oileamhain Oisín mhic Fhinn', unpublished PhD thesis (University College Galway, 2000).

— 'Duanaire Finn XXII: Goll and the champion's portion' in Carey (ed.), *Duanaire Finn: reassessments*, pp 51–78.

— 'Ginealach "Geinealach Oisín"' in D. Ó Baoill, D. Ó hAodha and N. Ó Muraíle (eds), *Saltair saíochta, sanasaíochta agus seanchais: a Festschrift for Gearóid Mac Eoin* (Dublin, 2013), pp 261–73.

O'Brien, M.A., *Corpus genealogiarum Hiberniae* 1 (Dublin, 1962; repr. 1976).

Ó Cadhla, S., 'Gods and heroes: approaching the *Acallam* as ethnography' in Doyle and Murray (eds), *In dialogue with the Agallamh*, pp 125–43.

Ó Cadhlaigh, C., *An fhiannuidheacht* (Baile Átha Cliath, 1936; 6ú cló, 1947).

Ó Cathasaigh, T., *The heroic biography of Cormac mac Airt* (Dublin, 1977).

— '*Cath Maige Tuired* as exemplary myth' in P. de Brún, S. Ó Coileáin and P. Ó Riain (eds), *Folia Gadelica* (Cork, 1983), 1–19.

— 'The eponym of Cnogba', *Éigse*, 23 (1989), 27–38.

— 'Mythology in *Táin bó Cúailnge*' in H.L.C. Tristram (ed.), *Studien zur Táin bó Cúailnge*, ScriptOralia 52 (Tübingen, 1993), pp 114–32.

— 'Tóraíocht Dhiarmada agus Ghráinne' in Ó Fiannachta (ed.), *An fhiannaíocht*, pp 30–46.

Ó Cionnfhaolaidh, C., '*Feis tighe Chonáin*: a window on the medieval *fiannaigheacht* tradition', unpublished MA thesis (University College Cork, 2016).

Ó Coileáin, S., 'The structure of a literary cycle', *Ériu*, 25 (1974), 88–125.

— 'Oral or literary? Some strands of the argument', *Studia Hibernica*, 17–18 (1977–8), 7–35.

— 'Irish literature' in J.R. Strayer (ed.), *Dictionary of the Middle Ages*, vol. 6 (New York, 1985), pp 521–33.

— 'Place and placename in *fianaigheacht*', *Studia Hibernica*, 27 (1993), 45–60 (repr. in Doyle and Murray (eds), *In dialogue with the Agallamh*, pp 6–20).

— 'The setting of *Géisid cúan*' in J. Carey, M. Herbert and K. Murray (eds), *Cín Chille Cúile: texts, saints and places. Essays in honour of Pádraig Ó Riain* (Aberystwyth, 2004), pp 234–48 (repr. in Doyle and Murray (eds), *In dialogue with the Agallamh*, pp 218–30).

O'Connell, J., '"*Airem muinntari Finn*" and "*Anmonna oesa fedma Find*": manuscripts, scribes and texts', unpublished MA thesis (University College Cork, 2012).

O'Connor, F., *A short history of Irish literature: a backward look* (New York, 1967).

O'Connor, R., *The destruction of Da Derga's hostel: kingship and narrative artistry in a mediaeval Irish saga* (Oxford, 2013).

Ó Corráin, D., 'Nationality and kingship in pre-Norman Ireland' in T.W. Moody (ed.), *Historical Studies*, 9 (Belfast, 1978), pp 1–35.

— 'Cad d'imigh ar lámhscríbhinní na hÉireann?' in R. Ó hUiginn (ed.), *Oidhreacht na lámhscríbhinní: Léachtaí Cholm Cille* 34 (Má Nuad, 2004), pp 7–27.

Ó Corráin, D., L. Breatnach and K. McCone (eds), *Sages, saints and storytellers: Celtic Studies in honour of Professor James Carney* (Maynooth, 1989).

Ó Cróinín, B., 'Bruíonta na féinne' in S. Ó Coileáin, L. Ó Múrchú and P. Riggs (eds), *Séimhfhear suairc: sistí in ómós don Ollamh Breandán Ó Conchúir* (An Daingean, 2013), pp 480–501.

Ó Cróinín, D., *Early medieval Ireland, 400–1200* (London/New York, 1995).

Ó Cuív, B., 'Some developments in Irish metrics', *Éigse*, 12, iv (1968), 273–90.
— 'Miscellanea 2: Agallamh Fhinn agus Ailbhe', *Celtica*, 18 (1986), 111–15.
— *Catalogue of Irish language manuscripts in the Bodleian Library at Oxford and Oxford College Libraries*, 2 vols (Dublin, 2001–3).
O'Curry, E., *Lectures on the manuscript materials of ancient Irish history* (Dublin, 1861; repr. 1995).
— 'The fate of the children of Tuireann', *Atlantis*, 4 (1863), 157–240 (repr. in *Gaelic Journal*, 2 [1884]).
— *On the manners and customs of the ancient Irish*, with an introduction, apppendixes, etc. by W.K. Sullivan, 3 vols (London/New York/Dublin, 1873).
O Daly, M., 'Úar in lathe do Lum Laine' in J. Carney and D. Greene (eds), *Celtic Studies: essays in memory of Angus Matheson* (London, 1968), pp 99–108.
— *Cath Maige Mucrama: the battle of Mag Mucrama*, Irish Texts Society 50 (London, 1975).
O'Donovan, J., *Annála ríoghachta Éireann: annals of the kingdom of Ireland by the Four Masters*, 7 vols (Dublin, 1848–51; 2nd ed. 1856; facs. repr. with introduction and appendix by K. Nicholls, Dublin, 1990).
— '*Mac-gnimartha Finn mac Cumaill*: the boyish exploits of Finn mac Cumhaill', *Transactions of the Ossianic Society*, 4 (1859), 281–304.
— (trans.), *Sanas Chormaic: Cormac's glossary*, ed. W. Stokes (Calcutta, 1868).
Ó Duilearga, S., *Leabhar Sheáin Í Chonaill: sgéalta agus seanchas ó Íbh Ráthach* (Baile Átha Cliath, 1948; 3rd ed., Scríbhinní Béaloidis / Folklore Studies 3, 1977).
Ó Fiannachta, P., 'The development of the debate between Pádraig and Oisín' in Almqvist, Ó Catháin and Ó Héalaí (eds), *Fiannaíocht*, pp 183–205.
— (ed.), *An fhiannaíocht: Léachtaí Cholm Cille* 25 (Má Nuad, 1995).
O'Grady, S.H., *Tóruigheacht Dhiarmuda agus Ghráinne. The pursuit of Diarmuid and Grainne*, Society for the Preservation of the Irish Language, 2 parts (Dublin, 1880–1; repr. of *Transactions of the Ossianic Society*, 3 [Dublin, 1857], 40–211]).
— 'Teasmolad Corbmaic úi Cuinn ocus [Aighed] Finn meic Cumhaill sunn', *Silva Gadelica*, 2 vols (London, 1892), i, pp 89–92 [edition]; ii, pp 96–9 [translation].
— 'Airem muintiri Finn', *Silva Gadelica*, 2 vols (London, 1892), i, pp 92–3 [edition]; ii, pp 99–101 [translation].
— 'Agallamh na senórach', *Silva Gadelica*, 2 vols (London, 1892), i, pp 94–233 [edition]; ii, pp 101–265 [translation].
O'Grady, S.H. and R. Flower, *Catalogue of Irish manuscripts in the British Library (formerly British Museum)*, 2 vols (London, 1926; repr. Dublin, 1992).
Ó Háinle, C., '"Scéala Catha Cronnmhóna": anailís liteartha ar laoi in *Duanaire Finn*' in Mac Craith and Ó Héalaí (eds), *Diasa díograise*, pp 329–54.
Ó hAodha, D., 'The first Middle Irish metrical tract' in H.L.C. Tristram (ed.), *Metrik und Medienwechsel / Metrics and media* (Tübingen, 1991), pp 207–44.
Ó hÓgáin, D., *An file: staidéar ar osnádúrthacht na filíochta sa traidisiún Gaelach* (Baile Átha Cliath, 1982).
— *Fionn mac Cumhaill: images of the Gaelic hero* (Dublin, 1988).

— 'Fionn féin: pearsa agus idéal' in Ó Fiannachta (ed.), *An fhiannaíocht*, pp 144–64.
— *Myth, legend and romance: an encyclopaedia of Irish folk tradition* (New York, 1991).
Ó hUiginn, R., 'The background and development of *Táin bó Cúailnge*' in J.P. Mallory (ed.), *Aspects of the Táin* (Belfast, 1992), pp 29–67.
— 'Duanaire Finn' in Ó Fiannachta (ed.), *An fhiannaíocht*, pp 47–68.
— '*Tóruigheacht Dhiarmada agus Ghráinne*', *Maynooth University Record* (2000), 159–62.
— 'Rúraíocht agus rómánsaíocht: ceisteanna faoi fhorás an traidisiúin', *Éigse*, 32 (2000), 77–87.
— '*Duanaire Finn*: patron and text' in Carey (ed.), *Duanaire Finn: reassessments*, pp 79–106.
— 'Growth and development in the late Ulster Cycle: the case of *Táin bó Flidais*' in J.F. Nagy (ed.), *Memory and the modern in Celtic literatures: CSANA Yearbook* 5 (Dublin, 2006), pp. 143–161.
— 'Somhairle Mac Domhnaill agus *Duanaire Finn*' in P. Breatnach, C. Breatnach and M. Ní Urdail (eds), *Léann lámhscríbhinní Lobháin: the Louvain manuscript heritage*, Éigse: Foilseachán 1 (Dublin, 2007), pp 42–53.
— 'Captain Somhairle and his books revisited' in P. Ó Macháin (ed.), *The Book of the O'Conor Don: essays on an Irish manuscript* (Dublin, 2010), pp 88–102.
— '*Fiannaigheacht*, family, faith and fatherland' in Arbuthnot and Parsons (eds), *The Gaelic Finn tradition*, pp 151–62.
— *Marriage, law and Tochmarc Emire*, E.C. Quiggin Memorial Lectures 15 (Cambridge, 2013).
Oinas, F.J., 'Russian byliny' in idem (ed.), *Heroic epic and saga: an introduction to the world's great folk epics* (Bloomington/London, 1978), pp 236–56.
— *Studies in Finnic folklore: homage to the Kalevala* (Helsinki, 1985).
O'Kearney, N., '*Feis tighe Chonain Chinn-Shleibhe*; or the festivities at the house of Conan of Ceann-Sleibhe in the county of Clare', *Transactions of the Ossianic Society*, 2 (1855), 118–215.
O'Keeffe, J.G., *Buile Suibhne (The frenzy of Suibhne) being the adventures of Suibhne Geilt*, Irish Texts Society 12 (London, 1913).
Ó Macháin, P., 'Aonghus Ó Callanáin, Leabhar Leasa Móir agus an *Agallamh bheag*' in Doyle and Murray (eds), *In dialogue with the Agallamh*, pp 144–63.
Ó Máille, T., 'Contributions to the history of the verbs of existence in Irish', *Ériu*, 6 (1912), 1–102.
Ó Muirgheasa, É., 'An dóigh a chuaidh Fionn i dtreis', *Béaloideas*, 1 (1927–8), 405–10.
Ó Muirigh, C.: see K. Murray.
Ó Muraíle, N., 'Agallamh na seanórach' in Ó Fiannachta (ed.), *An fhiannaíocht*, pp 96–127.
Ó Murchadha, D., 'Early history and settlements of the Laígis' in P.G. Lane and W. Nolan (eds), *Laois: history and society. Interdisciplinary essays on the history of an Irish county* (Geography Publications, 1999), pp 35–62.
— 'Kerry place-names in two twelfth-century poems', *Journal of the Kerry Archaeological and Historical Society*, 8 [series 2] (2008), 74–86.

— *Lige Guill: the grave of Goll. A Fenian poem from the Book of Leinster*, Irish Texts Society 62 (London, 2009).

Ó Néill, P.P., 'The date and authorship of *Apgitir chrábaid*: some internal evidence' in P. Ní Chatháin and M. Richter (eds), *Irland und die Christenheit: Bibelstudien und Mission / Ireland and Christendom: the Bible and the missions* (Stuttgart, 1987), pp 203–15.

O'Rahilly, C., *Ireland and Wales: their historical and literary relations* (London, 1924).

— *Táin bó Cúailnge: recension 1* (Dublin, 1976).

O'Rahilly, T.F., *A miscellany of Irish proverbs* (Dublin, 1922).

— *Early Irish history and mythology* (Dublin, 1946; repr. 1999).

Ó Riain, P., 'Boundary association in early Irish society', *Studia Celtica*, 7 (1972), 12–29.

— *Cath Almaine*, Mediaeval and Modern Irish Series 25 (Dublin, 1978).

— *Corpus genealogiarum sanctorum Hiberniae* (Dublin, 1985).

Ó Riain, P., D. Ó Murchadha and K. Murray, *Historical dictionary of Gaelic placenames / Foclóir stairiúil áitainmneacha na Gaeilge* (London, 2003–present [ongoing]).

Ó Síocháin, T., 'Translating *Find and the phantoms* into Modern Irish' in T. Birkett and K. March-Lyons (eds), *From eald to new: translating early medieval poetry for the 21st century* (Woodbridge, 2017), pp 122–47.

Ó Siochfhradha, P.: *see* An Seabhac.

Owen, M.E., 'Royal propaganda: stories from the law-texts' in T.M. Charles-Edwards, M.E. Owen and P. Russell (eds), *The Welsh king and his court* (Cardiff, 2000), pp 224–54.

Padel, O.J., 'The Cornish background of the Tristan stories', *Cambridge Medieval Celtic Studies*, 1 (Summer, 1981), 53–81.

— 'The nature of Arthur', *Cambrian Medieval Celtic Studies*, 27 (Summer, 1994), 1–31.

Parsons, G., '*Acallam na senórach* as prosimetrum', *Proceedings of the Harvard Celtic Colloquium*, 24 (2004), 86–100.

— 'The structure of *Acallam na senórach*', *Cambrian Medieval Celtic Studies*, 55 (Summer, 2008), 11–39.

— Review of J. Carey, *Duanaire Finn: reassessments*, *Cambrian Medieval Celtic Studies*, 55 (Summer, 2008), 70–72.

— 'Whitley Stokes, Standish Hayes O'Grady and *Acallam na senórach*' in E. Boyle and P. Russell (eds), *The tripartite life of Whitley Stokes (1830–1909)* (Dublin, 2011), pp 185–95.

— 'Breaking the cycle? Accounts of the death of Finn' in Arbuthnot and Parsons (eds), *The Gaelic Finn tradition*, pp 81–96.

— 'The narrative voice in *Acallam na senórach*' in Doyle and Murray (eds), *In dialogue with the Agallamh*, pp 109–24.

— 'Revisiting Almu in Middle Irish texts' in Boyle and Hayden (eds), *Authorities and adaptations*, pp 211–31.

Pennington, W., 'The little colloquy', *Philological Quarterly*, 9, ii (April, 1930), 97–110.

Pentikäinen, J.Y., *Kalevala mythology*, expanded edition, translated and edited by R. Poom (Bloomington and Indianapolis, 1999).
Poppe, E., *Of cycles and other critical matters. Some issues in medieval Irish literary history and criticism*, E.C. Quiggin Memorial Lectures 9 (Cambridge, 2008).
Potter, M.A., *Sohrab and Rustum: the epic theme of a combat between father and son. A study of its genesis and use in literature and popular tradition* (London, 1902).
Qiu, F., 'Narratives in early Irish law: a typological study' in A. Ahlqvist and P. O'Neill (eds), *Medieval Irish law: text and context*, Sydney Series in Celtic Studies 12 (Sydney, 2013), pp 111–41.
Quin, E.G. (general editor), *Dictionary of the Irish language, based mainly on Old and Middle Irish materials*, compact edition (Dublin, 1983).
Radner, J., 'The hag of Beare: the folklore of a sovereignty goddess', *Tennessee Folklore Society Bulletin*, 40 (1974), 75–81.
— '"Fury destroys the world": historical strategy in Ireland's Ulster epic', *Mankind Quarterly*, 23 (1982), 41–60.
Ranero, A.M., '"That is what Scáthach did not teach me": *Aided óenfir Aife* and an episode from the *Mahābhārata*', *Proceedings of the Harvard Celtic Colloquium*, 17 (1997), 244–55.
— 'An old Indo-European motif revisited: the mortal combat between father and son' in K. Jones-Bley, A. della Volpe, M.R. Dexter and M.E. Huld (eds), *Proceedings of the Ninth Annual UCLA Indo-European Conference*, The Journal of Indo-European Studies Monograph Series 28 (Washington, 1998), pp 123–39.
Rees, A. and B. Rees, *Celtic heritage: ancient tradition in Ireland and Wales* (London, 1961).
Richards, M., *Breudwyt Ronabwy: allan o'r Llyfr Coch o Hergest* (Cardiff, 1948).
Roe, H., '*Acallamh na senórach*: the confluence of lay and clerical oral traditions' in Byrne, Harry and Ó Siadhail (eds), *Celtic languages and Celtic peoples*, pp 331–46.
— 'The *Acallam*: the Church's eventual acceptance of the cultural inheritance of pagan Ireland' in Sheehan, Findon and Follett (eds), *Gablánach in scélaigecht*, pp 103–15.
Ross, N., *Heroic poetry from the Book of the Dean of Lismore* (Edinburgh, 1939).
Russell, P., 'Poets, power and possessions in medieval Ireland: some stories from *Sanas Cormaic*' in J.F. Eska (ed.), *Law, literature and society: CSANA Yearbook* 7 (Dublin, 2008), pp 9–45.
Schoepperle, G., *Tristan and Isolt: a study of the sources of the romance*, Ottendorfer Memorial Series of Germanic Monographs 3–4, 2 vols (Frankfurt / London, 1913).
Schlüter, D., '"For the entertainment of lords and commons of later times": past and remembrance in *Acallam na senórach*', *Celtica*, 26 (2010), 146–60.
— *History or fable? The Book of Leinster as a document of cultural memory in twelfth-century Ireland* (Münster, 2010).
Scott, R.D., *The thumb of knowledge in legends of Finn, Sigurd and Taliesin: studies in Celtic and French literature* (New York, 1930).
Seabhac, an [P. Ó Siochfhradha], *Laoithe na féinne* (Áth Cliath, 1941).

Severs, J.B. (general ed.), *A manual of the writings in Middle English 1050–1500*, vol. 1 (New Haven, 1967).
Shapur Shahbazi, A., *Ferdowsi: a critical biography* (Harvard, 1991).
Sharpe, R., 'Hiberno-Latin *laicus*, Irish *láech* and the devil's men', *Ériu*, 30 (1979), 75–92.
Sheehan, S., J. Findon and W. Follett (eds), *Gablánach in scélaigecht: Celtic Studies in honour of Ann Dooley* (Dublin, 2013).
Siikala, A.-L., 'Transformations in the Kalevala epic' in eadem and S. Vakimo (eds), *Songs beyond the Kalevala* (Helsinki, 1994), pp 15–38.
Sims-Williams, P., *Irish influence on medieval Welsh literature* (Oxford, 2010).
Sjoestedt, M.-L. (trans. M. Dillon), *Gods and heroes of the Celts* (Methuen, 1949; repr. Dublin, 1994).
Slotkin, E., 'Medieval Irish scribes and fixed texts', *Éigse*, 17 (1978–9), 437–50.
Smith, P.J., *Three historical poems ascribed to Gilla Cóemáin: a critical edition of an eleventh-century Irish scholar* (Münster, 2007).
Sommerfelt, A., 'Le système verbal dans Cath Catharda', *Revue celtique*, 36 (1916), 24–62, 295–334; *Revue celtique*, 37 (1917–19), 230–46, 353–7; *Revue celtique*, 38 (1920–1), 25–47; *Revue celtique*, 40 (1923), 157–69.
Stacey, R.C., 'Law and literature in medieval Ireland and Wales' in Fulton (ed.), *Medieval Celtic literature and society*, pp 65–82.
— 'Learning and law in medieval Ireland' in F. Edmonds and P. Russell (eds), *Tome: studies in medieval Celtic history and law in honour of Thomas Charles-Edwards*, Studies in Celtic History 31 (Woodbridge, 2011), pp 135–44.
Stern, L.C., 'Le manuscrit irlandais de Leide', *Revue celtique*, 13 (1892), 1–31.
— 'Fiannshruth', *Zeitschrift für celtische Philologie*, 1 (1897), 471–3.
— 'Eine ossianische Ballade aus dem XII. Jahrhundert' in K. Meyer, L.C. Stern, R. Thurneysen, F. Sommer, W. Foy, A. Leskien, K. Brugmann and E. Windisch (eds), *Festschrift Whitley Stokes zum siebzigsten Geburtstage am 28. Februar 1900 gewidmet* (Leipzig, 1900), pp 7–19.
— 'Die Bekehrung der Fianna', *Zeitschrift für celtische Philologie*, 5 (1905), 179–83.
Stewart, A. and Stewart, D., *Cochruinneacha taoghta de shaothair nam bard Gaëleach: a choice collection of the works of the Highland bards*, Collected in the Highlands and Isles by Alexander and Donald Stewart (Duneidin, 1804).
Stokes, W., *Three Irish glossaries* (London and Edinburgh, 1862).
— 'On the calendar of Oengus', *The Transactions of the Royal Irish Academy*, 1 (1880), 1–32, i–ccclii.
— 'Find and the phantoms', *Revue celtique*, 7 (1886), 289–307.
— *The tripartite Life of Patrick*, Rolls Series, 2 vols (London, 1887).
— 'The Irish ordeals, Cormac's adventure in the Land of Promise, and the decision as to Cormac's sword' in W. Stokes and E. Windisch (eds), *Irische Texte* iii, 1 (Leipzig, 1891), pp 183–229.
— 'The borama', *Revue celtique*, 13 (1892), 32–124.
— 'The prose tales in the Rennes dindśenchas', *Revue celtique*, 15 (1894), 272–336, 418–84; *Revue celtique*, 16 (1895), 31–83, 135–67, 269–312.

— 'The annals of Tigernach', *Revue celtique*, 16 (1895), 374–419; *Revue celtique*, 17 (1896), 6–33, 119–263, 337–420; *Revue celtique*, 18 (1897), 9–59, 150–97, 267–303 [repr. 2 vols (Felinfach, 1993)].

— 'Cóir anmann' in W. Stokes and E. Windisch (eds), *Irische Texte* iii, 2 (Leipzig, 1897), pp 285–444.

— 'The Bodleian Amra Choluimb Chille', *Revue celtique*, 20 (1899), 31–55, 132–83, 248–89, 400–437 (corrigenda in *Revue celtique*, 21 (1900), 133–6).

— 'O'Mulconry's glossary' in W. Stokes and K. Meyer (eds), *Archiv für celtische Lexikographie* 1 (Halle/London/Paris, 1900), pp 232–324, 473–81, 629.

— 'Acallamh na senórach' in W. Stokes and E. Windisch (eds), *Irische Texte* iv, 1 (Leipzig, 1900), 1–438.

— 'On the deaths of some Irish heroes', *Revue celtique*, 23 (1902), 303–48, 438.

— 'The colloquy of the two sages', *Revue celtique*, 26 (1905), 4–64 (repr. as a separate volume Paris, 1905).

Thanisch, E., 'What the Butlers saw: *Acallam na senórach* and its marginalia in the Book of the White Earl', *Aiste*, 4 (2014), 35–57.

Theuerkauf, M.-L., 'The Celtic dragon slayer: a literary analysis of *Tochmarc Emire* in connection with *Tristan et Iseut*', unpublished PhD thesis (University College Cork, 2014).

Thompson, S., *The folktale* (New York, 1946; repr. Berkeley/Los Angeles/London, 1977).

— *Motif index of folk literature: a classification of narrative elements in folktales, ballads, myths, fables, mediaeval romances, exempla, fabliaux, jest-books, and local legends*, 6 vols (revised ed., Copenhagen, 1955–8).

Thurneysen, R., 'Mittelirische Verslehren' in W. Stokes and E. Windisch (eds), *Irische Texte* iii, 1 (Leipzig, 1891), pp 1–182.

— *Die irische Helden- und Königsage bis zum siebzehnten Jahrhundert* (Halle, 1921).

— 'Tochmarc Ailbe: "Das Werben um Ailbe"', *Zeitschrift für celtische Philologie*, 13 (1921), 251–82, 297–8 (corrigenda).

— *Die Bürgschaft im irischen Recht*, Aus den Abhandlungen der Preussischen Akademie der Wissenschaften, Jahrgang 1928. Phil.-Hist. Klasse. Nr. 2 (Berlin, 1928).

— 'Zu Verslehre II', *Zeitschrift für celtische Philologie*, 17 (1928), 263–75.

Tolkien, J.R.R. 'Beowulf: the monsters and the critics', *Proceedings of the British Academy*, 22 (1936), 245–95; repr. in his *The monsters and the critics and other essays*, ed. C. Tolkien (London, 2006), pp 5–48.

Toner, G., 'Reconstructing the earliest Irish tale lists', *Éigse*, 32 (2000), 88–120.

— 'Authority, verse and the transmission of *senchas*', *Ériu*, 55 (2005), 59–84.

Tristram, H.L.C., 'Early modes of Insular expression' in Ó Corráin, Breatnach and McCone (eds), *Sages, saints and storytellers*, pp 427–48.

Ua Ceallaigh, S., *Trí truagha na scéaluidheachta: Oidhe chlainne Tuireann, Oidhe chlainne Lir, Oidhe chlainne Uisnigh* (Baile Átha Cliath, 1927).

Uhlich, J., *Die Morphologie der komponierten Personennamen des Altirischen*, Beiträge zu Sprachwissenschaften, Band 1 (Witterschlick / Bonn, 1993).

van Gennep, A., *The rites of passage*, trans. M.B. Vizedom and G.L. Caffee with an Introduction by S.T. Kimball (Chicago, 1960).
van Hamel, A.G., *Compert Con Culainn and other stories*, Mediaeval and Modern Irish Series 3 (Dublin, 1933).
—— 'Aspects of Celtic mythology', *Proceedings of the British Academy*, 20 (1934), 207–48 (repr. separately in 1934 with pagination, pp 3–44).
Velasco Lopez, M. del Henar, 'Adonis y el jabalí', *Perfiles de Grecia y Roma: actas del XII Congreso Español de Estudios Clásicos* (2009), 657–64.
Wade-Evans, A.W., *Vitae sanctorum Britanniae et genealogiae* (Cardiff, 1944).
Wagner, H., 'Old Irish *fír* "truth, oath"', *Zeitschrift für celtische Philologie*, 31 (1970), 1–45, 57–8, 146.
White, N., *Compert Mongáin and three other early Mongán tales*, Maynooth Medieval Irish Texts 5 (Maynooth, 2006).
Wiley, D. (ed.), *Essays on the early Irish king tales* (Dublin, 2008).
Williams, M., *Ireland's immortals: a history of the gods of Irish myth* (Princeton and Oxford, 2016).
Wright, C. *The Irish tradition in Old English literature*, Cambridge Studies in Anglo-Saxon England 6 (Cambridge, 1993).
Zimmer, H., 'Keltische Beiträge III. Weitere nordgermanische Einflüsse in der ältesten Ueberlieferung der irischen Heldensage', *Zeitschrift für deutsches Alterthum und deutsche Litteratur*, 35 (1891), 1–172.
—— 'Ossin und Oskar. Ein weiteres Zeugnis für den Ursprung der irisch-gälischen Finn (– Ossian–) Sage in der Vikingerzeit', *Zeitschrift für deutsches Alterthum und deutsche Litteratur*, 35 (1891), 252–5.

Index

Acallam na senórach, 21–50, 52, 56, 59, 72, 75, 78–9, 85, 89, 93, 97, 106, 119, 122, 127–8, 135–8, 146–9, 159–60, 162–3
   and Church reform agenda, 37–8, 47
   as epic, 23–4
   date of composition of, 24–8
   death of Cuirrech Lifi noted in, 75
   death of Finn noted in, 127n.
   flexibility of time in, 42
   harmonisation of different viewpoints in, 31
   importance of baptism in, 37
   importance of writing and remembering in, 33
   literacy in, 33, 41
   music in, 32, 34, 39–40
   mythological elements in, 39
   Patrician elements in, 35
   payment of clerics in, 38
   position of the arts in, 33
   references to Fothad Canainne in, 158
   role of the revenants in, 31
   sanctity of marriage in, 36–7
   significance of memory in, 33, 41
   tears in the tale, 40
Adarca Iuchna, 126
Adonis, 102–4
Áed mac Fidga, 78–9
Áed mac Muiredaig, 26, 28, 32, 36, 38, 42
Áed Rinn mac Rónáin, 132–3
Áengus mac Echdach Fáebardeirg, 36
áes dána, 33–4, 38, 52, 143
áes síde, 32–3, 36–7, 39
Agallamh bheag, 21n., 25n., 38n.
Agallamh na seanórach (Reeves version), 21n.
Agallamh Oisín agus Phádraig, 21–2n.

Aghagower, Co. Mayo, 26, 29–30, 35
Aiclech mac Dubdrenn, 90, 124–6 (also called Aiclech mac Duibrenn), 127
Aided Finn, 89, 126–7
Aided óenfir Aífe, 65, 67, 69, 71
Aífe, 37
Aífe Derg, 26
Ailbe, daughter of Cormac mac Airt, 73, 100, 105–16, 137, 144
Ailill Flann Becc, 91, 153
Ailill mac Eochain, 154
Ailill mac Máta, 102
Aill in Bruic, Co. Kerry, 127
Aillén mac Eogabáil, 37
Aillén mac Midna, 39–40, 78, 122, 128, 149, 159
   grave of, 78n.
   killing of, 78n.
   later form, Máillén mac Midhna, 128n.
Aillenn, daughter of Bodb Derg, 29, 32, 36, 38
Áine, daughter of Eogabál, 37
aire échta, 60
Áirem muintire Finn, 63, 121
Aithed Gráinne la Diarmaid, 96, 99
Aithed mná Ailella maic Eógain la Fothad Canainne, 154
Almu/Almha (Hill of Allen), Co. Kildare, 19, 85, 94, 135
Amra Coluim Chille, 98, 113
Anglo-Normans, 52
Anglo-Saxon England, 66, 68
Annals of Tigernach, 125
Aodh Ó Dochartaigh, 130, 139
Aonghus, 95, 99, 102–3
Apgitir chrábaid, 58
Aphrodite, goddess of love, 102
Arabic, 69

Index

Arbuthnot, S., 88
Ard Caille, Co. Cork, 127
Ares, god of war, 102
Arjuna, 65–6
Armagh, 27
Armenia, 135
Armenian, 65
Arnold, M., 65
Art mac Cuinn, 154n.
Arthur, King, 146–9, 151
as aithe cach ndelg as sou (maxim), 72
Assaroe, Co. Donegal, 38
Áth Brea, 124–5, 127–8
athgabál, 79n.
Athy, Co. Kildare, 75n.
Attis, myth of, 102n.

Babhruvāhana, 65–6
Badamair, 74–5, 80, 148
Baile binnbérlach mac Búain, 100
ba(i)rd, 55–6, 161
Baíscne, 157
Balor, 149–50, 159
    wondrous pig of, 135, 147
banfénnid(i), 62–3, 117
banṡenchas, the, 142, 156
    prose, 85
baptism, 38
    as part of Church reform agenda, 37
    of Caílte, 32
    theological discussion concerning, 38
Barrow, river, 75
Baumgarten, R., 53–4, 82
Beann Ghulban, Co. Sligo, 28, 95, 150
Bear peninsula, Co. Cork, 87n.
Beóla Brogaige, 127
Beowulf, 41n., 72
Bible, the, 155
    Book of Genesis, 44n.
Binchy, D.A., 60
Blaí Derg, 21n.
Bodb Derg, 29, 32, 42
Bodbmall, 117

bóroime, 85
Borsje, J., 153, 155
Bostock, J.K., 66
Boyne, river, 89–90, 124–7, 129
Bran, 93n., 135
Breatnach, C., 100–1
Breóthigern, 87
Bretha crólige, 60
Breuddwyd Rhonabwy, 147
Brí Gobann, Co. Cork, 142n.
bride-price (*coibche / tinnscra*), 36, 59,
    107, 109, 133, 154
Brigid, Saint, 27–8
Briody, M., 12, 44n., 46n., 104n.
Broccán, 33, 41
Bromwich, R., 103
Brug(h) na Bóinne, Co. Meath, 90, 95, 99
Bruiden Átha Í, 74–7, 80, 89, 91, 93, 158
bruidhean, 135
Bruidhean chaorthainn, 159
Búanann: see Scáthach (Búanann)
Buchet the hospitaller, 72n.
Buckley, S., 108n.
Buile Ṡuibne, 33
Buttimer, N., 112
bylina, 65

Caillech Bérre, 156
    as sovereignty goddess, 89
Caílte mac Rónáin, 20n., 21–22, 31–3,
    35–8, 41–2, 72, 75–7, 84, 87–8,
    133–8, 147, 154, 158
    and the animals, 76, 98n., 134n.
    called Scilti Scawntroet in Welsh
        literature, 88n.
    epithet as *coslúath*, 88
cáin Cormaic, 75n.
Caíndía (alternate name for Fothad
    Canainne), 152
Cairpre the *fénnid*, 90–1
Cairpre Lifechair, 85n., 91
Caittil Finn: see Kvetil Hvíte
'Caldron of poesy, the', 81

Cáma, 35
Campbells, earls of Argyll, 105n.
Canann, 152n.
Cáol Cródha, 136
Carey, J., 12, 34n., 42, 80–81, 92, 101n., 104, 106n., 109n., 121, 131, 145–6, 161
Carmun, Co. Kildare, 20n.
Carn Cabal, 148
Carn Finnachaid, 39
Cas Corach, 32, 34, 43
Castleknock, Co. Dublin
  battle of, 117–18
Cath Cnucha, 118n.
Cath Maige Tuired, 67n.
Cathair Dúin Iascaig (Cahir, Co. Tipperary), 74, 80, 84
Cathaír Már, 72n.
Cathal Croibderg, 26–7, 29
Cathub the druid, 109
Céadach, 141n.
Celtic
  god *Windos*, 145
  heritage of Ireland, 40
  love triangle, 102
  mythological complex, 146
  pantheon, 105
  warbands, 62
Celtic Studies, 103, 163
Ces Ulad, 112
chanson de geste, 70
'Chase of Síd na mBan Finn, the', 127, 159
Christ's crucifixion, 80–81
Christiansen, R.T., 55
Church, 35, 48–9
  antipathy towards *fían*, 53
  depiction of *fían*, 63
  manuscripts of, 34
  politics, 22
  reform movement, 29, 34, 37–8, 47
  role in marginalization of *fíanaigecht*, 57
Cíarraige, 88n.
Cináed úa hArtacáin, 89–90, 124
Cistercians, 27
Cithrúad the druid, 106, 108
Clann Baíscne, 40, 137
Clann Morna, 42n., 137
Clann Riocaird, Co. Galway, 95–6
Clann Tomaltaig, 26
Clárach, battle of, 158
Cliabhach, 136
coibche: see bride-price
Cóir anmann, 154
Collectanea of Tírechán, 35, 88
Colum Cille, Saint, 27–8
Comar (near Clonard), Co. Meath
  battle of, 91
Conán of Cúalu, 156n.
Conán the *fénnid*, 132
Conchobur mac Nessa, 63, 98, 107–12, 156
Conn Cétchathach, 39–40, 90, 141
Connacht, 28, 30, 111
  king(s) of, 29, 32, 36, 38
Connlae, 37, 65, 67–70
Connon, A., 25, 27, 30, 34–5
Corcu Loígde, 88–9, 93, 157
Cormac mac Airt, 34, 55, 73, 89, 91, 98–100, 106–7, 109–12, 115, 124, 126, 133–4, 137, 143–4, 148, 154
  standing army of, 19
Cormac mac Cuilennáin, 81
Cornwall, 103, 147–8
corrbolg, 118
Creiddylad, daughter of Llud Llaw Ereint, 102n., 145, 149
Creidne, 62, 121
Crimall, 30
Críth gablach, 59
Cross, T.P., 66, 70
Cruithin, 86, 93
Cú Chulainn, 37, 62, 65, 67–70, 98, 108, 114, 119–21, 140–41, 155–6
cuire (derived from PIE *$korjos$*), 62
Cuirrech Lifi, 74–5, 93, 158
Cuirrech Lifi (Curragh of Kildare), 75n., 76

Cúldub, 79
Culhwch ac Olwen, 145–7, 149
Cumall mac Trénmóir, 39–40, 85, 86n., 117–18, 135, 141, 145
Cybele (Phrygian mother-goddess), 102n.
Cycle of Historical Tales (Cycles of the Kings), 19

Dagenais, J., 101
Dáire, 118
Dáire mac Dedaid, 85
Dál nAraide, 86, 93, 157
Daolach, daughter of Dubh mac Duinn, 136
David, King, 72n.
de Courcy family, 27
Déisi, 74, 84, 93
Demne (Finn's original name), 119, 140
    meaning of name, 140n.
Derc Corra, 80, 92
    and attainment of knowledge, 81
Derdriu, 107–9, 111–15
Devil, the, 38, 57
Devon, 148
Di chethairslicht athgabálae, 59–60
Di šuidigud tellaig Temra, 114–15
dían airšeng, 76
Dían Cécht, 67n.
Diarmaid ua Duibhne, 28, 41, 75–6, 92, 95–105, 110–11, 133, 135–6, 144, 150
    his *ball seirce*, 104
Díarmait mac Cerbaill, 37, 41–3, 136
díberg, 53, 58
díberg(ach), 58–60
    accepting *votum mali*, 57
    wearing *signa diabolica*, 57
díchetal di chennaib, 143
Dichuil, 35
díguin, 79n.
Dillon, M., 25
dinnšenchas, 20, 54, 75, 137, 148, 160
    metrical, 76, 139, 142, 161

of Carmun, 20
of Carraic Lethdeirg, 156
of Cenn Cuirrig, 74–5
of Tonn Chlidna, 25
díthir, 61
Do fallsigud Tána bó Cúalnge, 31
Dolb Scóinne, 134n.
Donegal, 28, 107
Donn, 101
Donn mac Áeda, 42n.
Donn mac Fionnlaoich, 135
Dooley, A., 9, 25–9, 35–6, 54, 62, 156
Downpatrick, Co. Down, 27
Drogheda, Co. Louth, 27
Druim Leithe (boar of), 93n.
Duanaire Ghearóid Iarla, 96
Dubdét, 132
Dubh mac Duinn, 136
Dubh ua Duibhne, 75–6
Dún Gáire, 136
Dún Iascaig: *see* Cathair Dúin Iascaig

Eargna, daughter of Áed Rinn mac Rónáin, 132–3
Échna, daughter of Muiredach mac Fínnachta, 36
Echtra Fergusa maic Léti, 79
Echtrae Chonnlai, 110
éclann, 61
ekphrasis, 138
Emain Macha, Co. Armagh, 111
Emer, 37, 68, 108, 114
Eógan (son of the king of Fir Maige), 36
Eógan mac Durthacht, 111
Eóganacht, 89n.
Érainn, 85–6, 93
Ercing, 148
éric, 133
Esnada tige Buchet, 72n.
Estonia, 46n.
Éuchtach, daughter of Diarmaid ua Duibhne, 104

'Father-and-son combat' (also known as 'Sohrab and Rustam'), 64–9
Feis tighe Chonáin, 19, 73, 77, 79, 141
Félire Óengusso, 142n.
Fenian lays, 19, 105, 130–9, 163
  'Abduction of Eargna, the' (beginning *Eól damh senchus Feine Finn*), 132
  'Bathing of Oisín's head, the' (beginning *A bhen dén folcadh mo chinn*), 133
  beginning *A chorr úd thall san léana*, 118
  beginning *Ceisd agam ort a Cháoilte*, 118
  beginning *Éuchtach inghen Díarmatta*, 111n., 142
  beginning *Sgríobh sin a Bhrógainn sgribhinn*, 122
  'Boyhood of Fionn, the', 141
  'Caoilte's mischief-making' (beginning *Maidhim in mhaidin fa ghlonn*), 134
  'Caoilte's sword' (beginning *Iss é súd colg in laoích láin*), 136
  'Caoilte's urn', 92n., 139
  'Chase of Slievenamon, the', 128n.
  'Crane bag, the', 139
  'Enchanted stag, the' (beginning *Fuaramar seilg iar samhain*), 135, 147
  'Fray at Loch Luig, the' (beginning *Fuar ar n-aghaidh a Loch Luig*), 133
  'Headless phantoms, the' (beginning *Aonach so a Moigh Eala in rí*), 131, 134
  'Household of Almha, the', 132n.
  in *Leabhar Ua Maine*, 132n., 139n.
  'Kinship of Fiamhain with Oisín, the', 132n.
  'Lament for the fiana', 127n.
  'Magic pig, the' (beginning *Domhnach lodmair tar Lúachair*), 138
  'Naming of Dún Gáire, the' (beginning *A Lorcáin mheic Luighdheach láin*), 92n., 124n., 136
  'Oisín and the crane', 118
  'Rise Up, Osgar' (beginning *Eirigh súas a Osgair*), 137
  'Rowan-tree of Clonfert, the', 132n.
  'Shield of Fionn, the' (beginning *Uchán a sgíeth mo ríogh réil*), 88, 132, 135
  'Sleep-song for Diarmaid, the' (beginning *Codail begán begán beg*), 135
  'Standing stones of Ireland, the' (beginning *A lía Thulcha Tuaithe shuas*), 78n., 136
  'Sword of Oscar, the', 139
  'Wild rush of the house of Morna, the' (beginning *Deargrúathar cloinne Morna*), 137
  'Womenfolk of the fían, the', 132n.
fénnid(i), 30–1, 37, 39, 41, 53–4, 57–61, 63, 78, 88, 113, 132–3, 135–8, 143–4, 147, 154
  attributes of, 63
  baptism of, 38
  death of, 49
  hounds of, 93n.
  lachrymose nature of, 35
  of Conn Cétchathach, 90
  of Lugaid Mac Con, 89
  overseas raiding of, 62
  stories of, 33
  wondrous nature of, 138
Fer Lí, 128
Fer Taí, 128
Ferchess, 89
Ferdowsi, 65
fergniae, 59, 61
Fergus Fairrce, 157
Fergus mac Róich, 102, 111
Fernmag, 111

Index 193

Fíacail mac Conchinn, 78
Fíacha mac Conga, 39, 78
fían, 19, 21–2, 28, 30–31, 35, 40–2, 49,
    53–5, 77, 80, 89–91, 99, 104, 110,
    122, 128, 133, 135–7, 147–8, 151,
    154, 158–9, 162–3
  proto-Christians, 32
  based at Almu, 85
  composition and historical background
      of, 60
  conversion of, 22n.
  etymology of, 57n.
  Finn attains leadership of, 39, 122, 146
  lachrymose aspect of, 40
  nature of, 57–63
  of Connacht, 154
  of Fothad Canainne, 157
  of Lugaid Mac Con, 88
  of Lúaigne (Temrach), 124
  of Munster, 154
  of Ulster, 142n.
  retrospective Christianization of, 43
fianas, 53, 60–1, 63
fiansruth, 20n.
fidchell, 72n.
fili(d), 34, 51, 55–6, 78, 81, 108, 142–4,
    151, 161
Findabair, 62
Findchú, Saint, 142n.
Finland, 45, 47
'Finn and Gráinne', 89, 92, 96–7
'Finn and the jester', 90–3, 143, 160
'Finn and the man in the tree', 74, 77, 79,
    91–2, 143
Finn Éices, 77, 140
Finn fili mac Rossa Rúaid, 84–5
Finn mac Cumaill, 19–21, 24, 40–2, 51,
    55, 60, 62, 74, 78, 80, 84–8, 91–3,
    102, 124, 132–7, 152, 154, 160,
    162–3
  ages of, 144
  and King Arthur, 146

  and the 'salmon of knowledge', 77,
      82n., 140
  and the wooing of Ailbe, 106–16
  as arbitrator, 144n.
  as *fili*, 142
  as *gilla*, 144n.
  as negotiator, 144n.
  as reflex of the divine hero, 39
  as shaman, 143n.
  attainment of 'thumb of knowledge', 79
  boyhood deeds of, 117–23
  called *rígfénnid*, 85n., 143, 156
  conflict with Oisín, 64–73
  connections with Gwynn ap Nudd,
      145
  connections with Lug, 149
  death of, 124–9
  his 'Jump', 122n., 125n., 126, 128,
      133
  his role in *Tóraigheacht Dhiarmada agus
      Ghráinne*, 95–105
  abilities of, 77, 85, 92, 126, 154, 162
  name derived from PIE *wind-*, 145
  naming of, 140
  portrayal of, 140–51
Finn mac Gleóir (alternate name for
    Finn), 142: *see* Fionn mac Gleóire
Finn mac Muirne (Finn's metronymic),
    142
Finn mac Regamain, 74
Finnish Hymnal Committee, 45n.
Finnish Literature Society, 46n.
Finnish rune poetry, 46n.
Finnsruth Fíthail, 124n.
Fintan mac Bóchra, 31n.
Fionn mac Gleóire, 142n.: *see* Finn mac
    Gleóir
Fir Bolg, 85n.
Fir Maige, 36
Fíthel the judge, 137
Flahive, J., 10, 118
Flann mac Maíl Máedóc, 155

folklore, 20, 39, 149, 157
  Arabic folk-epics, 69
  concerning Finn's death, 124, 128–9
  Finnish, 45n., 46
  folktale of the rabbit-herd, 98n.
  folktales concerning Diarmaid and
    Gráinne, 104–5
  motif of the external soul, 102
  motif of the magic helper, 98n.
  motif of the skilful companions, 98n.
  of Finn's youth, 122–3
  relating to King Arthur, 148
  Scottish Gaelic, 141
  versions of *Tóraigheacht Dhiarmada
    agus Ghráinne*, 111
Forgoll the poet, 86–7
Formáel, boar of, 128
Fotha catha Cnucha, 50, 86, 90, 117–18,
    123, 145
Fothad Airgtech, 86–7, 152
Fothad Cairptech, 152
Fothad Canainne, 30, 74–5, 87, 89, 93,
    150, 152–9, 161
  and *fíanaigecht*, 157
  as a Finn Cycle character, 157
  death of, 153
  later called Fatha Canann, 159
  spirit of, 157
Fothaid, na trí, 152, 157–8
Fuindche, daughter of Nár, 156n.
Fulda, abbey of, 66

Gabar (Gowra valley near Tara, Co.
    Meath)
  battle of, 91
Gabraige Succa, 85n.
Gáileóin, 85n.
Gaillinn, 135
Gallgoídel, 148n.
Garad mac Morna, 72n.
Garb Daire, 35
Gay, D., 45–6

Gearóid Iarla, third earl of Desmond, 95–6
geilt, 33, 64, 134
geis / gessa, 69n., 74, 147n.
Genelach Find meic hUmaill, 86, 142, 157
Germanic tribes, 66
giants, 34–5, 147, 162
gilla, 80, 91–2, 144, 151
  definition of, 92n.
Gilla Cóemáin, 125
Gilla in Choimded úa Cormaic, 50, 118
Giolla an Chuasáin (early name for Finn),
    141
Giolla na gCroiceann (alternate name for
    Finn), 141
Glasdic / Gla(i)s Díge (early name for
    Finn), 141
Gleór Lámderg, 142
Gnáthaltach, 157
God, Christian, 29, 32, 36, 38–9, 41, 135,
    138, 155
Goídil, 85n., 93
Goll mac Morna, 30n., 39–40, 122,
    126n., 149–50, 159
  original name, Áed, 118
Goths, 66
Grail 'Continuation', the, 80n.
Gráinne, daughter of Cormac mac Airt,
    95–105, 108–11, 135
Greece, 150
Greene, D., 72
Gúaire Dall, 134
Gwynn ap Nudd, 102n., 145–6, 149, 151
Gwythyr uab Greiddawl, 102n., 145,
    146n., 149

Hadubrand, 65, 68
Harmon, M., 9
Hatto, A.T., 67
hazelnuts and the attainment of
    knowledge, 81–2
Helgi, the Lay of, 153
Heptads, the, 59

Index

Herbert, M., 112
heroic biography, 123, 140
Hildebrand, 65, 68
Hildebrandslied, 65–6, 68
Historia Brittonum, 148
Hollo, K., 80
Honko, L., 47
Honorius Augustodunensis, 38
Howth, Hill of, 99
Hull, V., 81

Iliad, the, 23
Il'ya, 65, 68, 70
imbas forosnai, 80–82, 143
immanent epic, 47n.
Indo-European, 63, 68, 103
    heritage of Ireland, 40
    language(s), 62, 69
    motif, 70
    'Myth of the rival wooers', 102
    society, 62
Ipomédon, 70
Irish Folklore Commission, 104n.
Irish translations of adventure stories, 52
Irish translations of Classical texts, 52
Iseult, 103
Isle of Man, 19n.
Iuchna, daughter of Goll mac Morna, 126n., 128n.

Jackson, K., 24–5, 142
Jocelyn of Furness' Life of Patrick, 36

Kalevala, the, 44–8
    'New *Kalevala*, the', 45–6
    'Old *Kalevala*, the', 45
    versions, 45n.
Kanteletar, the, 45–6
Karelia, 44
Kaukonen, V., 45
Ker, W.P., 24
Kerry, 107n., 129, 138
Killamery, Co. Kilkenny, 142n.

Koch, J.T., 93
Kvetil Hvíte (Caittil Finn), 55

La Tène Celts, 62
láechsluinte lagen, 86
Láeg the charioteer, 114
Laigin, 51, 84–6, 93, 119
Lamraige, 142
Langobard, 66
laoithe fianaigheachta: see Fenian lays
Latteragh, Co. Tipperary, 80
Leinster, 85–6, 158
    early poetry of, 145
    sovereignty figure, 156n.
Lethderg, daughter of Conchobur mac Nessa, 156
Líath Lúachra, 117
Licat Amr, 148
Limerick, 38, 96
Llud Llaw Ereint, 102n., 145, 149
Lochán (son of the king of Fir Maige), 36
Lochlannaig (Norsemen), 19, 55, 133–4, 148
Lóegaire mac Néill, 43
Loígis, 86, 93
    genealogies of, 86n.
Lom Laine, 100
Lombardy, 66
Lomnae the jester, 90–1, 93
Longes mac nUislenn, 107–13, 115–16
longphort, 133
Lönnrot, E., 44–8
Lúachair, Co. Kerry, 127–8
Lúaigne (Temrach), 90, 93, 124–6, 128
Lug, 95n., 143, 149–51, 159
Lugaid Mac Con, 88–9, 156
Luigne (later name for Lúaigne), 91
Lydney Park, Gloucestershire, 145

Mac Airechtaig, Donn Óg, 26
Mac Cana, P., 50, 55, 58, 87, 129, 146, 150, 152, 158

McCone, K., 53, 57, 59–62, 87
Mac Domhnaill, S., 130
McGregor, D., 130
McGregor, J., 130
McLeod, N., 60
Mac Lughach, 136
MacNeill, E., 51, 55, 60, 94
Macpherson, J., 19–20, 83, 163
McQuillan, P., 62, 152
Macaire, 70
macc ailte, 61
macc beoathar, 61
macc té, 61
macc úar, 61
Macgnímrada Con Culainn, 117, 119–21, 123
Macgnímrada Finn, 19, 50, 52, 77–8, 85–6, 88, 90, 117–21, 123, 140, 142–3, 161
Máel Muru Othna, 142
Mag Life, 140
Mahābhārata, 65–6
Maher, M., 128n.
Maic Airechtaig, 26
Máillén mac Midhna: see Aillén mac Midna
Malinen, O., 45–6
Manannán mac Lir, 37, 135
Männerbund, 62, 119
Manuscripts
    Book of Ballymote (RIA MS 23 P 12), 25
    Book of Fermoy (RIA MS 23 E 29), 95
    Book of Lecan (RIA MS 23 P 2), 97
    Book of Leinster (TCD MS H.2.18 [1339]), 21n., 25, 34n., 78, 82n., 85, 100, 121, 125, 127, 131, 133n., 134, 137, 139, 161n.
    Book of Lismore (Chatsworth), 21n., 22n., 23
    Book of the Dean of Lismore (NLS Advocates MS 72.1.37), 19, 97, 130, 139

British Library Egerton MS 92, 126
British Library Egerton MS 1782, 125, 127
British Library Harleian MS 5280, 100
Duanaire Finn (UCD Archives, Franciscan MS A 20[b]), 19, 50, 56, 130–2, 137, 139
Leabhar Breac (RIA MS 23 P 16), 25, 72, 142n., 157
Leabhar Ua Maine (RIA MS D.ii.1), 89n., 132n., 139n.
Oxford, Bodleian Library Laud MS 610, 11, 22n., 23, 117, 126–7
Oxford, Bodleian Library Rawlinson MS B. 487, 22n., 23, 27
RIA MS 23 L 37, 100, 101
RIA MS 24 P 9, 95, 100, 101, 104
RIA MS D.iv.2, 74n.
TCD MS H.3.18 (1337), 79, 143
UCD Archives, Franciscan MS A 20(a), 22n., 23n.
UCD Archives, Franciscan MS A 4, 22n., 23, 46
Yellow Book of Lecan (TCD MS H.2.16 [1318]), 74
Manx song tradition, 19n.
Marbad Cúlduib, 72, 74, 77–8, 80, 92, 114, 119
Mark, 103
marriage
    first marriage performed by Saint Patrick, 29
    laws relating to, 37
    monogamy within, 36
Meath, 129
Medb, daughter of Eochaid Feidlech, 102
Medb Lethderg, 156n.
Meek, D., 25n., 105, 131–2
Mellifont, Co. Louth, 24, 27–8
Meyer, K., 9, 61, 66, 69–70, 80, 89, 154
Míach, 67
Middle English texts, 70

Index

Mide, 89, 91, 148
Miller, D., 65, 67
Miller, J., 69
Mittelirische Verslehren, 76
Moling, Saint, 33
Mongán mac Fíachnai, 86–8, 156
mucc slánga, 135, 138, 147
Muinter Roduib, 26, 29–30, 35
Muiredach mac Fínnachta, 26
Muirne, daughter of Tadg mac Núadat, 85–6, 125, 142, 145
Munster, 55, 87–8, 96
Murphy, G., 9, 25, 39, 50, 52, 80, 98, 121–3, 130–2, 138, 149–50
Mythological Cycle, 19

Nagy, J.F., 39, 43n., 78–9, 92, 102, 119–21, 154–5
Ness, 62
Ní Dhonnchadha, M., 63
Ní Mhaonaigh, M., 38
Ní Shéaghdha, N., 25, 95, 99, 103–4
Nōdons (Romano-British god), 145
Noísiu, 107–11, 113–15
Norman, F., 66
Norse-Icelandic, 65
North Channel, the, 105
Núadu Necht, 84, 145
Nuner, R., 25
Nutt, A., 9, 39, 146

Ó Briain, M., 9n., 35
Ó Cathasaigh, T., 89, 140, 150
Ó Coileáin, S., 24, 54, 60n.
O'Connell, J., 63n.
O'Curry, E., 100
O Daly, M., 100
Ó Duibhgeannáin, D., 95, 100–1
O'Grady, S.H., 23
Ó hAodha, D., 55
Ó hÓgáin, D., 9, 128
Ó hUiginn, R., 37

Ó Longáin, S., 21
Ó Máille, T., 24
O'Mulconry's glossary, 57
O'Rahilly, T.F., 39, 85, 90, 93, 159
Ó Riain, P., 89
oblaire, 71n.
oblirach, 71
óclachas, 92
Odyssey, the, 23
Óenach Téite (Nenagh, Co. Tipperary), 76
óenchiniud, 61
Óendía (alternate name for Fothad Airgtech), 152
ogam
    function of inscriptions, 87n.
    riddle, 91
Oidheadh Chloinne Tuireann, 150
Oinas, F., 47
Oircbél the poet, 78
Oisín mac Finn, 20–22, 31, 35, 41–2, 64, 75, 77, 133, 135–6, 138, 144, 158
    conflict with Finn, 64–73
    meaning of name, 21n.
    reputed Norse origins of name, 55
Old French, 65
Old Norse, 153
Ollarba (River Larne)
    battle of, 87–8
    killing of Fothad Airgtech at, 88
oral literature, 56
orality, 48, 56, 104
orc tréith, 147n.
Oscar mac Oisín, 133, 136–8, 144
    etymology of name, 133–4n.
    reputed Norse origins of name, 55
Ossetian, 65
Ostend, Belgium, 19, 130
Otherworld, 22, 32, 38–40, 42–3, 48–9, 55, 102, 135, 145, 149
    attacker, 117
    entrance, 143
    hostels, 138

Otherworld *(contd)*
   musician, 32, 34
   rival, 77–9, 119
   thief, 77, 93
   time in, 42
Padel, O., 103, 146, 148–9
Parsons, G., 43, 131, 154n.
Patrician churches, 36
Patrick, Saint, 21–2, 26–9, 31–9, 41–3, 49, 132, 133n., 136, 147
Persia, 66
Pictland, 148
poems
   beginning *A aencheard Bhérre*, 89
   beginning *A Mór Maigne Moigi Siúil*, 156
   beginning *A Rí Ríchid, réidig dam*, 50, 78, 118, 121, 123, 127, 140
   beginning *Almu Lagen, les na fian*, 161n.
   beginning *Annálad anall uile*, 125
   beginning *Áth Lïac Find, cid diatá*, 142
   beginning *Bec innocht lúth mo da lua*, 133n.
   beginning *Dám thrír táncatar ille*, 161
   beginning *Échta Lagen for Leth Cuind*, 78, 85
   beginning *Eól dam i ndairib dréchta*, 88, 155
   beginning *Éuchtach inghen Díarmatta*, 97, 104
   beginning *Fíanna bátar i nEmain*, 88, 90, 124, 127
   beginning *Fil duine*, 98, 100
   beginning *Find Taulcha*, 58, 62, 84
   beginning *Is maith do chuit, a Gráinne*, 99, 113
   beginning *Ligi Guill i mMaig Raigni*, 137
   beginning *Ochtur táncamar anuas*, 22n.
   beginning *Ro loiscit na lama sa*, 22n.
   beginning *Úar in lathe do Lum Laine*, 99n., 100
   beginning *Úathad mé a Temraig a-nocht*, 133n.
   Cétamon, 117n.
   'Finn and the phantoms' (beginning *Oenach indiu luid in rí*), 134, 161
   Kilpalaulanta ('The singing match'), 45
   'King and hermit', 113n.
Potter, M., 65

'Quarrel between Finn and Oisín, the', 64–73, 114, 161

Radner, J., 67
Rees, A. and B., 63
Reicne Fothaid Chanainne, 92–3, 153–4, 156, 161
Reinbrun, Gij sone of Warwicke, 70
Rennes dinnṡenchas, the, 75–6, 82
Rhonabwy, 147
rí túaithe, 107n.
Roe, H., 9, 54, 62, 156
roscad, 68, 79–81, 106
Roscommon, 26, 28
   Augustinian house of canons at, 30
Russia, 45
Russian Karelia, 46n.
Rustam, 64, 68

Saint Patrick's Purgatory, Co. Donegal, 36
Samain, 39, 78
Sanas Chormaic, 62n., 88, 90
Saxons, 148
Scáthach (Búanann), 37, 62, 92n.
Scél asa mberar combad hé Finn mac Cumaill Mongán, 31n., 62n., 86–7, 160
Scél Túáin meic Cairill, 31
Scéla Moṡauluim, 88–9, 92
Sceolang, 93n., 135
Schoepperle, G., 103
Scilti Scawntroet: *see* Caílte mac Rónáin

Scothníam, 36n.
Scotland, 19n., 101n., 104, 111, 123, 128, 130, 139, 163n.
  Highlands of, 106
Scott, R.D., 121
'Second vision of Adamnán, the', 101
Segais, 81
Senchán Torpéist, 84
senchas, 30, 45, 156, 161
Senchas már, the
  introduction to, 79
  Pseudo-historical prologue to, 31
Senchas na relec, 90, 124
Serc Caillige Bérre do Fothud Chanainne, 156
Sermo ad reges, 72n.
Shahnameh, 65, 71
Shannon, river, 82
Sharpe, R., 57
Síaburcharpat Con Culainn, 155
Síd Fer Femen, 77
Síd na mBan Finn, 128n.
Sigurd and Fáfnir, 77n.
Síl Muiredaig, 26, 28
Sir Degare, 70
Sir Eglamour of Artois, 70
Sir Triamour, 70
Sjoestedt, M.-L., 51, 61
Slíab Bladma, 86, 148
Slíab Fúait, 98n.
Sliabh Luachra, 96
Sligo, 28
Smirgat, daughter of Fothad Canainne, 126, 158n.
Smirnat, daughter of Fothad Canainne, 158n.
Sohrab, 64, 68
Sokol'nik, 65, 68, 70
Solomon, 72n.
Sommerfelt, A., 24
Stacey, R., 79
stichomythia, 107n.
Stokes, W., 23, 46

Sumner, N., 9
synthetic historians, 19, 51, 55, 148–9

Tadg mac Núadat, 85
Taillte (Teltown), Co. Meath
  fair of, 141n.
Táin bó Cúailnge, 23–5, 40, 102, 160
Tale-lists from medieval Ireland, 50, 54, 96, 99, 154, 156
Tara, Co. Meath, 37, 39, 43, 75, 78, 85, 89, 122, 149
  feast of, 106, 114
  king of, 151
  kingship of, 51
Tarbga, 86
Tech nDuinn, 87n.
Tecocsa Cormaic, 60n.
teinm laído, 91, 143
Téite, 74, 91, 93, 158
Temair Mairce, 86
Tesmolta Cormaic 7 aided Finn, 85, 126, 128, 161
Tethna, daughter of Cormac mac Airt, 100
themes in *fíanaigecht*
  cooking, 72, 77, 93, 135, 140, 162
  feasting, 72n., 138
  Finn's inability to form lasting relationships with women, 92
  gaining of inspiration, 92
  hunting, 72n., 93, 135, 138, 146–7, 162
  places where killing is allowed, 74–5
  severed heads, 74, 91, 93, 124, 126, 153–4, 157–8, 162
  spear slaying at *síd* entrance, 39, 77–9, 119
  treachery of women, 91, 162
  youth versus age, 72–3, 114, 144, 162
Timna Cathaír Máir, 90n.
tinnscra: see bride-price
Tírechán, 35, 88, 147

Tochmarc Ailbe, 19, 50, 52, 73, 96, 98, 106–16, 143–4, 161
Tochmarc Emire, 37, 69, 98
tochmarca, 107n.
Togail bruidne Da Derga, 58, 160
Togail Troí, 138
Tolkien, J.R.R., 72
tóraigheacht, 96n.
Tóraigheacht Dhiarmada agus Ghráinne, 19, 73, 92, 95–105, 107–16, 142, 144, 147, 149–50
  comparisons with earlier sources, 96
  later versions of the tale, 104
  mythological aspects of, 101
Torba, 86n.
Torrent of Portyngale, 70
Tréndía (alternate name for Fothad Cairptech), 152
tria genera animantium, 81
Triads, the, 143
trían tobaig, 60n.
Tristan, 103
Tromda mac Calatruim, 156
Tromdháimh Ghuaire, 101
Túán mac Cairill, 31n.
túath, 53, 58n., 59, 62
tuath-cuire, 58, 62
Túatha Dé Danann, 22, 32, 39, 49, 67, 102
Tuireann, sons of, 95n., 150
Tulach Thuaithe, 136
'Two brothers, the', 66n.
Twrch Trwyth, 147

Úa Conchobuir, Rúaidrí, 29n.
Úa Conchobuir, Toirdelbach, 29n.
Úa Conchobuir, Tomaltach, 27

Úaine, daughter of Fíal, 36
Uaithne, Cos Limerick/Tipperary, 152n.
Úath Beinne Étair, 99, 161
Úathach, 37
Uchtdelb, daughter of Aengus Finn, 37
Uí Chonchobuir, 26, 29
Uí Daigre, Co. Tipperary, 80
Uí Raduib, 26
Uí Thairsig (Úa Failge), 85, 93, 119
Uirgriu, 117
  sons of, 89, 124–6, 128
Uisliu, sons of, 107, 111
Ulaid, 67, 111–12
Ulster, 86–7, 111, 119
Ulster Cycle, 19, 51, 55, 67, 107, 110n., 121n.
Ulūpī, the serpent princess, 66n.
Uraicecht becc, 143

Velasco-López, H., 101n.
Vikings
  invasions of, 55
  role in medieval Gaelic literature, 148n.
Virgin Mary, the, 135, 138
Vita Cadoci, 149
Vita Tripartita, 35

Wales, 79, 103, 147
Wauchier de Denain, 80n.
Western European balladry, 131
Windele, J., 21n.

Yskithyrwyn Penn Beid, 148n.

Zecher, P., 110n.
Zimmer, H., 55, 89